Manufacturing the Bespoke

READER

Manufacturing the Bespoke

Making and Prototyping Architecture

Edited by Bob Sheil

WILEY

A John Wiley and Sons Ltd, Publication

For Caro and Ronan

The editor and the publisher gratefully acknowledge the people who gave their permission to reproduce material in this book. While every effort has been made to contact copyright holders for their permission to reprint material, the publishers would be grateful to hear from any copyright holder who is not acknowledged here and will undertake to rectify any errors or omissions in future editions.

This edition first published 2012
© 2012 John Wiley & Sons Ltd

Registered office
John Wiley & Sons Ltd, The Atrium, Southern Gate, Chichester, West Sussex, PO19 8SQ, United Kingdom

For details of our global editorial offices, for customer services and for information about how to apply for permission to reuse the copyright material in this book please see our website at www.wiley.com.

Wiley publishes in a variety of print and electronic formats and by print-on-demand. Some material included with standard print versions of this book may not be included in e-books or in print-on-demand. If this book refers to media such as a CD or DVD that is not included in the version you purchased, you may download this material at http://booksupport.wiley.com. For more information about Wiley products, visit www.wiley.com.

Designations used by companies to distinguish their products are often claimed as trademarks. All brand names and product names used in this book are trade names, service marks, trademarks or registered trademarks of their respective owners. The publisher is not associated with any product or vendor mentioned in this book. This publication is designed to provide accurate and authoritative information in regard to the subject matter covered. It is sold on the understanding that the publisher is not engaged in rendering professional services. If professional advice or other expert assistance is required, the services of a competent professional should be sought.

Executive Commissioning Editor: Helen Castle
Project Editor: Miriam Swift
Assistant Editor: Calver Lezama

ISBN 978-0-470-66583-1 (hb)
ISBN 978-0-470-66582-4 (pb)
ISBN 978-1-119-96911-2 (ebk)
ISBN 978-1-119-96912-9 (ebk)
ISBN 978-1-119-96913-6 (ebk)

Cover image © Kate Davies and Emmanuel Vercruysse/Liquidfactory
Design by Artmedia, London
Printed in Spain by Grafos

1006235943

Contents

Introduction

Bob Sheil

At the disposal of today's architect is an evolving array of interoperable tools and processes that allow the fabrication of design propositions to be increasingly complex, nonstandard and adaptive. As wet chemistry and nano-engineering laboratories generate an entirely new palette to explore, the scope of the designer has also entered the domain of specifying and manipulating the growth, structure and behaviour of materials. How are designers equipped to deal with such a growing breadth of new potential, and how are the underlying philosophies that underpin this potential being defined? *Manufacturing the Bespoke* attempts to address what is something of a contemporary dilemma in architectural production, as the constraints of industrial standardisation are relaxed. Have the roles of designers and makers changed in a way that we've not experienced before, and what else is conveyed in the work as a new approach to making architecture is emerging? As this collection of new essays conveys, the hybridisation of digital technologies in design representation and manufacture has shifted the scope and influence of design from a largely pre-emptive act into a creative and experimental process that occupies the full extent of architectural production, where particular, unique and tailored solutions are increasingly viable.

Conventional protocols of exchange on the key relationship between design and making have been thoroughly redefined by digital fabrication technology.[1] For centuries, the construction of prototypes, artefacts, buildings and structures has operated on a rolling tradition of visual and verbal communication between designers, consultants, makers, clients, users, regulatory bodies and contractors. In making buildings, roles were defined by where individuals and disciplines were located on a chain from concept to execution. All were reliant on its links being successfully forged, not only to achieve results, but also to underpin their status within their respective professions and trades. Guiding the entire process was *the design*, an assemblage of cross-referenced visualisations, specifications and quantities forming the templates and instructions to make. Given the numeracy of complex transfers from one step to the next, constructs in architecture have evolved as *negotiated translations*, and the most engaging are those that have recognised this in a creative and informed way from the very outset.

The redefinition of these historic protocols was initially led by the gradual adoption of computer-aided drawing in the early 1990s by practice and academia. As three-dimensional modelling and rendering became more available and sophisticated, a frenzy of liberated experimentation ensued. Speculative design looked to the weightless and scaleless domain of digital space as the new terrain for innovation and speculative discourse and as a means to compositionally define spatial and formal complexity.[2] The gap between the designer's vision and operations of the construction industry widened as fabrication processes remained largely analogue in how they were driven and delivered. A defining example of this challenge was Future Systems' Media Centre at Lord's cricket ground (competition winner 1995, opened 1999), in which the primary enclosure was entirely prefabricated by the Pendennis shipyard in Falmouth, Cornwall, as theirs was the only industry both familiar and experienced in extrapolating design information for the fabrication of such forms.

Concurrently though, new tools of computation, means to capture and analyse the performance of buildings, built environments and the behaviour of users, brought a fresh understanding of the complexity and density of dynamic contexts in architecture. Geometry was reignited as a great organiser, only now it was adaptable and smart, as developments in design software far outstripped those in the world of how such forms could easily be made, and more significantly the means to communicate from one realm to the other was restricted. In the first decade of the new millennium this restriction started to lift as CAD/CAM (computer-aided design and computer-aided manufacture) entered the mainstream. Subsequently, a vast expansion on the remit, scope and potential of the designer was released, allowing for his/her direct engagement and control of fabrication processes. Likewise, the capability of manufacturing and construction to fulfil design intent was expanded, and a creative dialogue between design and fabrication was converging once more.

Size Matters

The term bespoke is said to have originated over a thousand years ago from the old English 'bespeak', meaning 'to request', 'to order in advance' or 'to give order for it to be made'.[3] Tailors of London's Savile Row claim that the term was in common use on their street from the 17th century, when tailors kept their cloth on the premises and customers would 'bespeak' a particular length of fabric to be fitted as a suit or uniform. The first recorded use is thought to have been in 1755 in *A Narrative of the Life of Mrs Charlotte Charke*[4] on the life and experiences of an actress, cross-dresser and daughter of a famous playwright in 18th-century London.

Almost 275 years after suits and uniforms were first made there, the Savile Row Bespoke Association was founded in 2004, and within three years they trademarked the term 'Savile Row Bespoke' which defined a two-piece bespoke suit as 'crafted from a choice of at least 2,000 fabrics … made almost completely by hand, and requiring at least 50 hours of hand-stitching'. To qualify, Savile Row Bespoke suits must also be 'derived from a paper pattern, individually cut and produced by a master cutter, and subsequently undergo personal supervision by the master cutter in the course of production'. In June 2008,[5] the association lodged a complaint under the truthfulness rule at the UK's Advertising Standards Authority against international firm Sartoriani who had recently opened a nearby shop where machine-cut suits were promoted as bespoke. The ASA noted the complainant's argument that, 'the advertised suits were machine-cut abroad[6] to a standard pattern after initial measurements were taken and adjusted at the end of the process' and that the suits 'at best' should be described as 'made to measure'. Sartoriani claimed that the initial machine-cut fabric pattern was a 'working frame' that could be individually adjusted if the customer's measurements did not match a standard pattern size, and that this occurred in some cases.

The ASA concluded that following recent changes to the industry, the use of the word bespoke to describe the advertised suits was 'unlikely to mislead'. They went on to say, 'both bespoke and made-to-measure suits were "made to order", in that they were made to the customer's precise measurements and specifications, unlike off-the-peg suits'. The ASA did not rule on a fuzzy distinction between handmade or machine-made, nor the particular differences of approach either method adopts in making or fitting, nor even where the suit was made; they ruled on the rather neater and universal principle of measurement.[7] Whether the artefact is made to order, made on the premises, made to measure, made by hand, or manufactured by machine, our recent understanding of the centuries-old term bespoke has undoubtedly been altered.[8]

Designer as Maker
Today, the bespoke is referred to in the context of personalised stationery, customised software, pharmaceuticals, wines, cars, financial investments, even biscuits, suggesting it is increasingly common for everyday and mass-produced artefacts to be made to order. The bespoke is also a term associated with architecture, and in the first instance through the idea that most buildings are in some sense unique to their location, the time they were designed and built, who they were designed and built by, how they were built, and the circumstances that surround their occupation and use. More specifically, the architecturally bespoke has associations with craft, ornamentation, materiality, fit, uniqueness and the unrepeated. However, as with the core productions of Savile Row, and for many of the same reasons, the meaning of bespoke in architecture in recent years has shifted on methodological grounds. Key to this are two primary issues: first, radical changes in how architecture is designed and made; and second, a vast expansion in what might be regarded as materials for architectural specification – from the deployment of nanotechnologies to choreographing four-dimensional behaviour.

Unlike tailors, most architects do not make the things they design. They make design information; the equivalent of making the pattern, not the suit. Moreover, unlike tailors, architects make an immaterial substance, space, with this pattern, the equivalent of forming the host upon which the pattern is draped. A bespoke architectural design is therefore associated not only with the ability to establish rules for the artefact that is 'made to order', but also with generating a design that understands and anticipates the challenge and consequences of making that particular order. Thus, what is subsequently made reveals the manner in which design information prompted a skilled craftsman or specialist to respond, and how the overarching construct fits together. At its best, this collaborative dialogue has the capacity to transcend the drawing as a literal template and goad the maker and the material into new territories. Since the introduction of digital fabrication technologies, profound changes have been brought to bear on this relationship and the habitual protocols between design and making. Through the progressive elimination of craftsmen and skilled machine operatives, the expertise that designers relied upon to translate their work has diminished and in many respects transgressed into their own domain.

A further ingredient of the bespoke is how an intimate knowledge of materials and their performance in use informs design, and relates to its method. Cutting fabric on the bias and incorporating ease within a garment, each has its equivalent at architectural scales, such as the imprint of shuttering on cast concrete, or the deflection of steel under load. In tailoring a bespoke suit, drawing and making are synthesised from the outset where graphic and illustrative representation dissolves as the final artefact appears. Processes of measurement, pattern making, cutting, forming and joining components progress through three stages of fitting and fabrication known as the 'skeleton baste', the 'forward' and the 'finish bar finish'. Such intimacy between drawing and making is rare in the practice of architecture and the architectural drawing must therefore anticipate and understand the difference between the simulated and the actual and adapt accordingly. Clearly, the breadth of materials specified in architecture is substantially broader and more complex than that of tailoring, not least as it also incorporates strategies for immaterial qualities such as context, light, reflection, temperature, sound, culture, meaning, memory and emotion. In this regard, both the tools and the palette of the 21st-century architectural designer are rapidly expanding as they provide the ability to approach design as a strategic act with novel outcomes.

A Work in Progress
This book explores ideas on making architecture in this new paradigm. It contains new articles by makers, academics, practitioners, theorists and various interdisciplinary hybrids from an assembly of disciplines within architectural production. Contributors were invited to speculate, report and reflect on ways that architecture is being designed and made today. Each of the articles draws from the direct experience of the author, and in most cases is based on new works in progress. The articles expand on aspects of design and making that commonly evade formal documentation, aspects that are more accustomed to a part in the spoken dialogue of making things. By definition a reader is not a singular manifesto but a collation of many platforms and arguments. Among those presented here is an avenue into reading the digital as a stimulus for craft that is delivered with an unambiguous caveat on what has yet to be gained by this opportunity. Michael Stacey (pages 58–77) pays homage to architects of the pre-digital age for whom, he argues, the drawing and the building were more intellectually integrated. This tone of caution is echoed by two other contributors of distinction, first by Stephen Gage (pages 28–41), who asks if there are limits to the appropriateness or effectiveness of the bespoke, and how it is contextualised within the broader history of architectural practice and tradition. And second, by Mark Burry (pages 42–57), who suggests that digital fabrication has blurred definitions of the model and the prototype, and with it, a lack of clarity in the role

of the archetype has been initiated. These balanced and thoughtful critiques are essential parentheses, not only in leashing besotted enthusiasm that is often associated with new techniques and technologies, but also by acting as a grounded and informed check on attempts to prematurely formulate or construct an associated universal theory.

In their chapter entitled 'R-O-B: Towards a Bespoke Building Process' (pages 78–87), Tobias Bonwetsch, Fabio Gramazio and Matthias Kohler of the Institute for Technology in Architecture at the Faculty of Architecture at ETH Zurich, leapfrog the construction industry's hereditary lag in the use of programmable automation by approaching the technology as a tool awaiting a design instruction as a composed digital score. Through their choreographic guidance, the actions of commonly available robotic industrial arms are animated to perform experimental routines of sublime dexterity and meticulous craft. In establishing a lexicon of ornate and complex built structures and surfaces, their work offers an insight into experimental design as a time-based and malleable building process. They generously share their work in publications, lectures and online, as speculative demonstrators on the implicit potential of operating as a designer with programmable tools. As the engineer Hanif Kara has said elsewhere, it is this core generosity that singles Gramazio and Kohler out as a key influence in this field.[9]

Based at the University of Waterloo Toronto, Philip Beesley takes the idea of manipulating and exploring behaviour in another direction to challenge the status of building material itself (pages 102–19). In Hylozoic Ground, the latest in a sequence of projects he leads, what he calls naked hyperbolic meshworks are organised as a 'geotextile terrain', a fundament to the act of creating the earth itself. They are dressed with a primitive intelligence, layers of structure, muscle, wet chemistry, neurons, memory and an active circulation system. The resultant assembly offers the template for a responsive architectural system, a practical system that lives and breathes, that knows where it is and who is in proximity. Beesley asks if this could form the basis of a system that cares, architecture of hope and optimism? Beesley's chapter is embellished by a collaborator on the Hylozoic Ground project, Rachel Armstrong (pages 238–47). In 'Print to Protocell', qualified medical doctor, science fiction author, arts collaborator and architectural researcher Armstrong explores the possibility of growing building materials, and imagines buildings that will transfer from inert to living matter and become part of the biosphere.[10] Allied to the investigation of materials at a behavioural level is the work of Neri Oxman (pages 256–65), director of the Mediated Matter research group at MIT Media Lab. Oxman's essay presents the idea that examined and computationally manipulated at a structural and environmental level, material performance can lead to an entirely new way of approaching and developing form. These essays represent a collection that speculates on the processes of how future architecture may be built and what it may be built with, by exploiting automated, responsive and living systems.

Weaving through the book is another collection of essays dealing with a very different and more familiar palette, one that continues to extract the extraordinary from the ordinary. The collections are not posed against each other as counterarguments, as the book is a deliberately open and diverse collection of valid positions from esteemed contributors each of whom operates in socially, economically and culturally different circumstances, contexts and environments. In this set, we find the work of distinguished individuals such as Peter Salter (pages 120–31) and Mark West (pages 132–45), the unique organisation Rural Studio (pages 194–207), and the rising talent of Guan Lee (pages 182–93). Known for his deeply evocative drawings that seep with an intimate knowledge of materials and structure, Peter Salter reflects on his time as an assistant for the Smithsons. As he embarks on building three mews houses on Walmer Road, West London, he advocates a timeless approach for a design methodology that synthesises all scales of design, from overarching strategies of spatial organisation to those of detailed fabrication.

From the workbenches of his unique base, CAST (the Centre for Architectural Structures and Technology) at the University of Manitoba, Mark West is known internationally, more for how he has transformed the potential and understanding of concrete as a liquid material, than for his parallel explorations in drawing. In his essay entitled 'The Fore Cast', he retraces the evolution of his work from its earliest steps, and reviews as much as recounts how the site and practice of drawing is an integral act in the excavation and search for ideas. It is a typically generous invitation into his world, and one that provides further enlightenment on the strategies behind his world-class research. From over 2500 kilometres (1553 miles) south of CAST, regular visitor to the Rural Studio in Newbern, Alabama, architect Anderson Inge, reports on the outpost of Auburn University led by Andrew Freear, which has attained an almost mythical status in international architectural education. Here notions of the bespoke are at experienced first hand in the design and production of protoarchitectural constructs that challenge the very basic conventions of building materials and their collage. Going deeper, Inge presents the school as a chosen path requiring absolute commitment and an unambiguous attitude towards an ideology that relates to its immediate social, economic and legislative context.

This book is also populated with a number of case studies on a diverse set of new works in progress by innovative researchers in academia and practice. They represent authorship from individuals and collaborations, some at the beginning of their careers and from others who have an established body of work spanning recent decades of substantial change in practice. Among them, Xavier De Kestelier of Foster + Partners and Richard Buswell of Loughborough University (pages 248–55) illustrate an all too rare collaboration between cutting-edge research and practice. They share valuable insight into the evolution of deposition technologies upon design methods and strategies over the past two decades, and finish on the primary role that toolpaths play in shaping and forming large concrete elements without formwork. Their investigations remind us of the similarity and difference that continue to exist between architectural information and physical manufacture, and the essay is an urgent provocation for fruitful collaboration of this kind to become an everyday occurrence.

Echoing this cry, in his chapter entitled 'Microstructure, Macrostructure and the Steering of Material Proclivities' Phil Ayres (pages 220–37), from the Centre for Information Technology and Architecture at the Royal Danish Academy of Fine Arts Copenhagen, presents novel design strategies that exploit the potential of digital technologies applied to design, fabrication and use as a circular relationship through which intent is translated into artefact. In a detailed analysis of recent experiments in hydroforming, he provides vital insight into the development of new theories of design and representation. Within a similar vein, Nat Chard's chapter, 'Drawing Out an Indeterminate Duration' (pages 146–61) extends the discussion on fluid relationships between the drawn and the made, and the transition that exists between them. His fascinating and exquisitely crafted drawing instruments are both the construct of representation, and the means of constructing representation. These issues are further explored by architect, educator and researcher-in-residence Mary Vaughan Johnson in her scholarly diagnosis of Chareau's masterpiece of the bespoke, the Maison de Verre (pages 88–101).

Manufacturing the Bespoke is also populated with detailed accounts on the making of speculative and highly particular prototypes including the sequence of pavilions designed and built by AA Intermediate Unit 2 led by Charles Walker and Martin Self between 2006 and 2009 (pages 208–19), and for a more extreme context, Constance Adams documents her work for NASA on environments to house and sustain space travellers (pages 266–75). She illustrates how designing for the most extreme and uncertain of scenarios is considerably more than a technical task; by necessity it is a forecast on core human relationships with issues of survival, ability, skill and adaptation. In a very different manner, the idea of survival within an uncertain earthly future is speculated upon in a polemic chapter by the young experimental practice Liquidfactory, led by Kate Davies and Emmanuel Vercruysse (pages 162–73). As with all other included texts theirs is written exclusively for this publication, but Davies and Vercruysse go a step further and present an entirely new phase of an ongoing project as a response to the invitation. 'Incisions in the Haze' presents the power of the speculative project in constructing an apparently extreme speculative scenario through drawings, constructs and narratives. Their work exemplifies Stephen Gage's earlier message that 'The Bespoke is a Way of Working not a Style'.

In conclusion, I wish to thank each and every one of my contributors for their counsel and generosity in providing such stimulating and original material. Their diverse and varied insight has thoroughly enriched understanding and knowledge in this field, and their continued pursuit defining new frontiers in architecture is an inspiration. I owe a special thanks to Helen Castle, Calver Lezama and Miriam Swift of Wiley whose unrelenting support I have relied upon with considerable dependency. I also wish to thank my colleagues at The Bartlett UCL and in sixteen*(makers) for their support and fervent encouragement, in particular, Ruairi Glynn and Marilena Skavara with whom I was involved in organising an international conference at UCL while this book was in development. Finally, I wish to express my deepest gratitude to Caroline Rabourdin who endured the consequences of my imperfect project management. To her much is owed, and in recognition of my sincere appreciation for her graceful patience and persistent kindness, I dedicate this work.

Notes

1   B Sheil, 'Transgression from Drawing to Making', *arq* (*Architectural Research Quarterly*), 9.1, 2005, pp 20–32, 26.
2   Seminal publications of this period that explore these themes include a number of guest-edited issues of *Architectural Design* including Greg Lynn (ed), *Folding in Architecture*, *AD* Profile 102, Academy Group (London), 1993, and Neil Spiller (ed), *AD Architects in Cyberspace*, vol 68, John Wiley & Sons (London), 1998.
3   www.dictionary.com
4   C Charke, *A Narrative of the Life of Mrs Charlotte Charke, Youngest Daughter of Colley Cibber, Esq*, London, 1755.
5   http://www.asa.org.uk/ASA-action/Adjudications/2008/6/Sartoriani-London/TF_ADJ_44555.aspx
6   Germany at the time.
7   Recent developments in three-dimensional body scanning offer a route to broader and more perplexing questions on specific measurement (Treleaven 2004). Here, not only is the individual accurately measured in 3D, but the data may also be of assistance in monitoring their state of health, contributing to national welfare statistics and understanding their physical attractiveness to others (Swami, Tovée et al 2002, 2005).
8   Shortly afterwards Sartoriani went on to open a shop on Savile Row. However, at the time of writing the firm had ceased trading and existing orders had been taken over by online trader asuitthatfits.com
9   Hanif Kara interviews Matthias Kohler; R Glynn, B Sheil (eds), *FABRICATE*, Riverside Architectural Press, University of Waterloo School of Architecture (Cambridge, Ontario), 2011, pp 116–21.
10 See Neil Spiller and Rachel Armstrong (eds), *AD Protocell Architecture*, vol 81, no 2, John Wiley & Sons (London), 2011.

From Making the Bespoke to Manufacturing the Bespoke

Bob Sheil

Two co-authored design and make projects are examined here: a chair from 1995 and a small building from 2009. Both projects fit within the author's definition of protoarchitecture,[1] a genre of experimental design that challenges the methods and role of the designer particularly in relation to how and why the work is made. Secondly, and central to the arguments presented here, both projects identify a key transition in the definition of the bespoke that spans a period of significant change in design and fabrication methodologies and tooling. In analysing these projects together for the first time, it will be argued that many of the strategies in designing and making a bespoke piece of furniture that went beyond the realm of the conventional drawing, and were exclusively developed by hand, are now adoptable through digital design and fabrication technologies. It will also be suggested that these new facilities must be seen as essentially hybrid disciplines that are practised adjacent to the point of production. What is also being explored here is an underlying idea that integrated digital design and fabrication technologies have instigated a renewed relationship between the bespoke and the prototype, and that a pursuit to explore either presents opportunities for the other. What is new in this relationship is that these pursuits can be exercised mutually and synthetically, and for those who wish to take advantage of this potential, there are significant implications for the way they might practise and learn.[2]

At a glance these projects might appear considerably more than 14 years apart. Both were made by the same designers, both explored similar questions on the relationship between design and production, and both involved familiar materials. The former was handmade, and the latter was predominantly made using numeric controlled machinery fed by design data embedded within a three-dimensional digital file. Underlying the journey between both projects is the transformation of the purpose and property of the drawing as an instruction to make, and, inseparable from this idea, the role of the drawing maker. In the first example, without the preview or guidance of a scaled design drawing, the made artefact, in this case a chair, evolved as decisions on form, structure, dimension, materiality and technique were synchronised into the act of making. The artefact was at various stages a mock-up, a template and a completed construct. The need for the design drawing as an instruction for others to make was eliminated by the interdisciplinary authors, who acted as designers and makers, and who invested their tacit skills as drawing makers directly in the medium their drawings would have proposed. Likewise, the gap between the drawing and the artefact, always open to external error or internal naivety, was also erased, and the time that would have been expended on drawing was invested in the act of design through making.

Fourteen years later, through the mainstream adoption of CAD/CAM, the drawing as an instruction to make had undergone a significant evolution and this gap no longer existed. Stripped of the intermediary phase of interrogation and evaluation by appointed makers, digital design drawings were instructing digital fabrication machinery to make and the embedded instruction of the drawing, whether flawless or otherwise, was indeed made. The digital drawing became both the design and the making tool, and the skills of the designer as a maker were implicitly and irreversibly linked to the performance of the works they produced. In this regard the study of the second project, a small forest shelter, explores how the role and operations of the designer were relocated to the place of production, and the adaptive capacities of CAD/CAM as an interoperable set of representational and fabrication tools were deployed across a range of simultaneous frequencies, from virtual manufacture to preview of assembly. Fabrication drawings in this sense are not defined by boundaries of representation, and the scope for tactile experimentation that was sought in the freehand making of a bespoke chair was in many ways revisited on the shelter. As a result, this project represents one of the earliest examples of collaboration in digital fabrication and design in the UK.[3]

The chapter concludes by looking forward through the medium of lidar scanning, a process where high-resolution three-dimensional point cloud surveys may be extracted from built works providing an accurate record of the as-built design, and a 3D model from which it can be interrogated and perhaps at some future point, augmented. In this instance, and by virtue of the way the shelter was designed and made, these scans represent the final drawings of the project and could only exist because of its presence as a built artefact.[4] Visually and informatively fascinating as they are, they provide a powerful means to examine and understand a habitual consequence of making architecture that persists in the digital age, the difference between the design that is drawn and the design that is made. In summary, From Making the Bespoke to Manufacturing the Bespoke, identifies an alternative role for professional designers, one that utilises and transfers their highly developed and adaptable skills in the visual propositioning of space and form, and supplements these skills with the tacit experiences of making and assembly. This new role defines the designer as someone who is also a maker, and one that is directly engaged within the arena of production.

Making the Bespoke

The chair on page 17 was sixteen*(makers)'[5] first commission and was made for a management consultant in 1995 who noticed the collaborative's experimental approach to design and making on projects 'Plot 22' and 'Dartmoor'.[6] The practice was established while Callicott and Sheil were students at The Bartlett School of Architecture UCL. Both were midway through their undergraduate studies when Peter Cook was appointed as the school's Professor of Architecture in 1990, and under his charismatic stewardship the school became a vivacious and inventive forum of experimental ideas. Traffic through the school was highly notable and accelerated, with guest speakers including Enric Miralles as the Igualada

Cemetery was on site in Barcelona; Daniel Libeskind as the Jewish Museum (Berlin) was being designed; Coop Himmelb(l)au, as the Groninger Museum extension was under way; Brian Eno, as he started the Long Now Foundation; Bernard Tschumi when *The Manhattan Transcripts* had just been published; Lebbeus Woods on the publication of his articles on war and architecture in *A+U*; and the first appearance in London of young guns such as Greg Lynn and Neil Denari. The school's rapid transformation provoked a surge of ambition among students to challenge expected career norms and set about establishing the terms of their own practice before graduation. Somewhat against the grain, and cautious of becoming overly enthused by neo techno-narrative, the appellation sixteen*(makers) was chosen by the collaborative in order to become closer to the physical production of architecture, and thereby more actively involved as designers in its making. Deeply provoked by the quality of debate surrounding us, we were also critically influenced by the works, writings, drawings and methods of individuals such as Pye,[7] Potter,[8] Salter, Prouvé, Chareau and Pichler, under the watchful eye of our former first year tutor, the late Steven Groák.

The fee for the chair was a 50 per cent barter on our client's second-hand Macintosh PowerBook 100.[9] One handmade chair in part exchange for a laptop, it seemed the analogue and the digital were destined to be present in the history of our practice from the start. Our client was well travelled, an avid reader, a cinema-goer, a music collector, a squash player, rock climber, mountain biker and a keen chef. At the time of the commission he was practising the Alexander technique, a method of focusing and developing controlled body posture and balance habitually and intuitively. The commission was envisaged as a means to address this practice routinely, and to design an everyday point of support for reading, typing, dining and relaxing. Although widespread and particularly domestic public access to the Internet would remain two years away in the UK, operating a portable or desktop computer would be a prime occupation of the sitter. The particular movements and strains upon forearm, eye, head, neck and shoulders in relation to gizmos of the day, such as the centrally placed trackball, a mouse, a 23-centimetre (9-inch) 600 x 400 pixel resolution backlit LCD display with compact keyboard, were absorbed as essential but not every design criteria.

As a first commission for an experimental approach towards practice, workable terms and conditions were required to allow both client and designers room to explore, develop, reflect, revise and move forward. As students, sixteen*(makers) had developed a series of speculative constructs ('Plot 22' 1995 and 'Dartmoor' 1995) where few if any drawings were produced prior to fabrication and the works were developed on site and/or in the workshop through a process of trial and error as evolving physical representations. Decisions were made on the basis of verbal conversation between the designer/makers (two), iterative tests, challenges set by one another in a spiralling design combat, the feedback of the available material, and process being explored. In many ways the constructs were drawings, only drawings without paper.[10] Our purpose as fledglings was to operate on the other side of *the drawing as information to make*, and to become proficient in the tacit skills our tentative documents relied on. Subsequently, conversing design with our client would not rely on a flat visual forecast but would be based on its evolution and progression as a physical artefact through a series of staged 'fittings'.

left: Sixteen*(makers)' first commission, a bespoke chair made at Sunbury Workshops, Shoreditch, London EC1, 1995. Materials: oak, leather, 35 mm (1.38 in.) mild steel. Photograph: Bob Sheil. © sixteen*(makers).

below: Sixteen*(makers) first and second commissions, the bespoke chair seen against a large table both made at Sunbury Workshops, Shoreditch, London EC1, 1995. Photograph: Bob Sheil. © sixteen*(makers).

Somewhat in the traditions of Savile Row,[11] the client was surveyed, his frame and posture measured and noted, and other chairs and stools were commandeered as adaptable props. They were made higher, wider, more vertical, softer or cooler. Likes and dislikes of the function and form of chairs were identified and key objectives were agreed and marked on jigs, rulers, floors and walls. Issues of comfort and restraint were explored in relation to the chair's purpose and role, and environments where the chair would likely be located were noted for matters such as deflection and vibration. Materials from which to make the chair were also explored, not only for performance and visual preference, but also for their capacity to carry other narratives within the object. Lying about the studio in Shoreditch at the time were a number of speculative test pieces in mild steel, hardwood, acrylic, glass and rope, forming a haphazard library of experiments and assemblages in relatively simple techniques. Among these was an ongoing trait to customise materials, particularly steel, from their origin as extruded standard profiles, into ends, junctions, and limbs through abrasion and forging. Some of these traits had a highly graphic as well as tactile quality, portraying not dissimilar looks to those we once pursued in ink. However, it was their tangible properties, such as weight, surface quality, conductivity, resonance and reflectivity that were the predominant investigation and value.

From this catalogue of references, the design's first move was established in the form of a foot adapted from a short section of heavy rolled tee bar in mild steel. To the central web of the tee bar, a flat bar the same thickness and width as the central web was bevelled and arc welded. The joint was ground, filed and sanded until seamless and the shiny surface reheated with an oxyacetylene torch until black again. Overgrinding was always something to be mindful of, for as soon as the weld surface dipped below the adjoining sections the only course of recovery was to break the weld and start again. The inner and outer radii of the rolled tee bar, and the feathering of its tapered flanges, set a geometric tone for key positions where the chair's limbs would end or meet others. The length of this first element, about 1 metre (3.2 feet), far exceeded what was required, and so it remained as the key datum from which to strike the seat's horizontal axis until the remaining substructure of the chair's legs and spine was complete. Both front legs also stemmed from the same flat bar, but here they were jointed to a parallel square section of the same thickness. The heavier elements connected vertically to form the seat's substructure, while of the lighter, one swerved away on the left-hand side to receive a rigid arm, and the other tapered to finish short of a cantilevered right-hand arm with some give.

When our client returned for his 'skeleton-baste'[12] fitting, the chair's key dimensions and alignments were tested and adjusted. Movements and postures were simulated and marks were made on the chair's steel carcass in chalk. Rough boards were fashioned as jigs to form seats, and various blocks and wedges were positioned to judge the thickening of various elements such as arms and the spine. The torch was reignited and geometries of the frame adjusted before the client departed. As the chair passed through two more fittings, a small pile of reclaimed tongued and grooved oak strip flooring was rescued to form the seat and subsequently jointed to form two panels tied to the subframe with leather thong. The rigid left arm of the chair was filled out with a further section of jointed and reclaimed oak and the flexible right arm was wrapped in leather from a local upholstery merchant. Our studio was located at the western end of Sunbury Workshops in London's historical quarter of Shoreditch. In the two units beneath us were a shopfitter and an octogenarian wood turner. Next door below were silversmiths working above a frame gilder, and further along a prestigious upholsterer, and a team of glass-blowers. Although not formally organised, the range of skills being practised was highly influential and complementary to our aims as architectural graduates. We could witness at close proximity the vibrancy and vulnerability of an urban micro industry, and realise how little our education did to make us aware of how direct engagement with its potential could inform our design strategies.

Several months after completion, the chair was returned to the workshop as a visual and dimensional reference for the design and fabrication of a large adjoining table in steel and oak. The brief for the table was that it would be used as a working surface, a place to read and pile books, and in particular become a table to accompany this specific chair. The design language and materiality that evolved in the making of the chair would be referenced, and the table's height, width and length would be tied into the tailored dimensions of its predecessor, with the sitter present as mock-ups were assembled and measured. The top was made from six reclaimed oak French railway carriage planks, 50 millimetres (2 inches) thick, 2400 millimetres (94 inches) long, with an existing lap joint in good condition. Joints were cleaned and the six boards were clamped and glued together before only the top surface, which weighed over 80 kilogrammes (176 pounds), was sanded reasonably flat. The table's ends were treated with alternate edges, one as a rounded and tapered oak fin, which became the table's 'leading edge', and the other in squared black steel. Each referred to the different arms of the chair, and established the design rules for the table's two distinct trestles in steel. Like the chair, the table was designed and made without the production of any prior design drawings; key references were embedded in tailored fittings and a series of tacit negotiations between structure, materiality, behaviour and visual judgement. On the basis of acquired tacit knowledge, particularly in works of this scale, the time we would have spent in the past on the act of drawing was instead invested in acts of making. Materials were worked upon directly, in some senses as though they were drawing surfaces. As the project of a fledgling experimental design practice, these acts of meticulous production informed many of the foundations of our attitude to repositioning the designer as maker; however, it was clear that in terms of a critical place in our chosen industry they resembled more the world of the 19th-century artisan than the contemporary professional.

Bridging the Gap

Resolving the bridge to this divide would take us back to our exchange fee for the chair and the presence of a new realm for workshop tooling, that of the digital. As an indication of how fast changes in related technologies took hold in this time, Nick Callicott's *Computer-Aided Manufacture in Architecture: The Pursuit of Novelty* (Architectural Press) was published just five years and numerous operating system and hardware upgrades later. Sixteen*(makers)' subsequent portfolio increasingly addressed the evolving relationship between digital design and making through a series of speculative projects and publications including; 'Cut and Fold', 'STAC', and 'Blusher' (all 2000–01), *Design through Making* (2005)[13] and *Protoarchitecture* (2008).[14] In parallel, their work shifted further towards a directed stream of academic research into both digital and analogue practices, with Ayres and Leung embarking on related doctoral studies with particular focus on responsive systems, persistent modelling,[15] and environmental analyses. Greatly facilitating further opportunities for academic collaboration with industry, Callicott left UCL in 2005 to set up Stahlbogen GmbH in Blankenburg, Germany, with partner Kris Ehlert. At the time, sixteen*(makers) were establishing speculative proposals as architects in residence at Kielder Water and Forest Park Northumberland, on behalf of the Kielder Partnership. With an open brief, the appointment provided an extended period of speculative investigation on the difference between digital modelling (as the 'ideal') and physical installation (of the 'real'). On the basis of a series of built installations on remote sites, the work, which led to a solo exhibition at the Building Centre in 2007 entitled *Assembling Adaptations*, presented the potential for real-time monitoring of micro environmental change to drive the design of a bespoke dynamic architecture.[16] While this research remained ongoing and formed the core of both Ayres' and Leung's doctoral research, the practice was approached by the Forestry Commission to design a public shelter on a proposed perimeter walkway to the reservoir. The additional brief carried a set of performance requirements and budget that would restrict many of the immediate possibilities of the residency; however, it offered the first opportunity to collaborate with Stahlbogen GmbH from the outset of a new project, and a fresh set of investigations was embarked upon. The shelter, which was named 55/02, provides this chapter with the second of its reflections on the bespoke in our work.

Manufacturing the Bespoke

Completed in June 2009, the shelter is named after its coordinates: 55° 11.30 N, 02° 29.23 W, otherwise known as Cock Stoor, Lakeside Way, Kielder Water and Forest Park, Northumberland, UK. A general analysis, with background information on local context and project sequencing, is explored in an essay entitled 'A Manufactured Architecture in a Manufactured Landscape'.[17] Further additional essays by Ayres, Callicott, Sheil and Sharpe may be seen in a forthcoming project monograph.[18] Pertinent to the discussion here, the key issues that cross-refer in these papers include winning the commission on the basis of strategic information rather than an illustrated design visualisation, clearly positing an underlying intent to develop the built design on highly specific qualities of the final and 'real' site, and making it clear in the award of the commission that the built design would explicitly evolve in collaboration with Stahlbogen GmbH.

Qualities of the selected site that informed the primary aims of the work included the intersection of distant harvest lines, trenches, gouges and trails, and the atypical qualities of the site which overlooked the reservoir from a raised mound on the north shore. They also included orientation to prevailing weathers and sunlight, relationship to key views and

top: Pre-production design development. Early prototype of structural shell component for 55/02 in CNC-cut and CNC-folded plate steel, made at Stahlbogen's workshop at Blankenburg, Germany, 2009. This investigation had a seminal design influence on the project's final outcome. Photograph: Bob Sheil. © sixteen*(makers).

above: Production design development. Designer and maker Nick Callicott of sixteen*(makers) and Stahlbogen GmbH visually inspects 55/02 at near completion stage at Stahlbogen's workshop at Blankenburg, Germany, 2009. Despite the powerful array of tools available to the designer, there is nothing that can fully prepare the author for results at 1:1. Photograph: Bob Sheil. © sixteen*(makers).

The assembled
construct. 55/02 installed
on site at Cock Stoor,
Kielder Water, and seen
from above. The image
shows a detail of the
assembly of painted
roof components.
Photograph: Bob Sheil.
© sixteen*(makers).

distances from other resting points, and the particular spatial qualities of the surrounding plantation of preserved Scots pine and their array of geometric intersections through the loose grid of straight and bare tree trunks, each between 5 and 15 degrees off plumb. These, and the rich matrix of adjacent layers and nodes of orientation, generated a dynamic field of variable spatial depth and quality of light, sound, temperature and enclosure for the design to acknowledge. Collaboration with Stahlbogen GmbH was initiated from the very outset of the commission, with the manufacturers in attendance and taking part in the site analysis and selection visit. In this respect, access and manoeuvrability of plant and personnel was also considered, and it was thereby possible to renegotiate the proposed route of the Lakeside Way and determine the position of a planned temporary road spur for the supply of materials to build the new pathway. At the conclusion of the site visit it was agreed that the shelter should have no obvious boundary between its material edges and the rich constellation of its environment, and that in response to its exposed position it should offer substantial shelter to the north, with a greater degree of openness to the south.

In recognition of non-negotiable budget constraints, a key early decision was to ensure that the design took account of Stahlbogen's existing tooling and expertise. A further agreed constraint was to limit the number of materials to a minimum, and through reading the array of initial proposals, each of which commonly suggested an enclosure of folded linear structures and surfaces, it was also agreed to explore how successfully these could be met by stretching Stahlbogen's established knowledge in sheet steel fabrication, while retaining a close control on cost. On this basis, the design progressed through simultaneous speculative exercises in drawing and making which flowed between the factory in Blankenburg and studios in London and Copenhagen.[19] Flowing from one workstation to the next were images, drawings and comments on 1:1 physical prototypes produced by Stahlbogen, spliced with sketches, handmade models, 3D drawings and 3D prints emerging in London and Copenhagen. The 2009 paper goes on to examine in detail the evolution of the project's 'tank'-like walls, the idea for which was led by a series of 1:1 test pieces at Stahlbogen, which not only distinguished much of the project's formal character, but also informed the development of speculative design drawings and models, and established the unconventional order of exchanging design information between the drawing makers and the manufacturer. As it goes on to describe, once primary decisions on how to approach the fabrication and design of the enclosing walls were established, an entirely fresh CAD model was constructed through which every resulting form was assessed for potential conflict with the dimensions and limitations of the equipment and processes that would produce them.

Production design of 55/02 evolved by constant shuffling between fabrication, drawing, animation and assembly. Once production information for the tank walls was fully developed, they were cut, folded, capped, welded and connected as a structural unit in a few days. Assembled in the factory in the same configuration they would finally be placed in on site, they became for a period models upon which to judge and test propositions for overhead roof elements. Strategies for these elements were visually developed upon in the CAD file, and cross-referred to both 1:20 physical design models and the 1:1 partially built shelter of tank walls. In this sense, the design exercise became truly synthetic with making and the methodological strategies of the project's 1995 forerunner were resurfacing, albeit now equipped with considerably more adaptable and flexible design tools. Here, design decisions were being made and becoming available that would otherwise be excluded from the designer who might only have provided an initial set of drawings to be followed as instructions to make. In this instance, such information provided by the team was only being regarded as a prompt and a guide, and final decisions were formulated on how the design implied in those drawings might operate both visually and feasibly at 1:1 on the shop floor. Crucially, this critical analysis and subsequent decision was being taken by a designer with ownership over the design and advanced skills in production.

Subsequently, the design of each of the roof elements as built evolved substantially from initial design proposals as developed in model or CAD form. A number of factors played into this outcome including considerations of physical and visual weight, soffit qualities, complexity and physical geometry of surface in relation to vertical elements, and the feasibility of assembly, with very limited resources on site at Kielder.[20] In addition, and perhaps one of the most surprising points to make, is how the final iteration for the design of the roof elements was informed more by the visual language that was emerging from the preceding completed elements than that which was conveyed in initial drawings. This point can best be understood by comparing the somewhat stark quality of the project's production drawings and the more fluid quality of the built work's aesthetics. This is not to say that only through making was a fluid aesthetic found, but that the production drawings that were necessary to construct the work were not being judged in this way.

Such drawings were made as the necessary digital information to feed the digital manufacturing process. In a sense, they partially equate to traditional shop drawings where in the past makers would redraw the designer's drawings at 1:1, and through the act of drawing the makeability of the design was established. However, in this instance, with the maker inhabiting and continuing the role of the designer, production drawings were constructed in order to facilitate a desired outcome in making, and if in view or in print the subsequent drawings were deemed to be aesthetically odd or unappealing, this was ignored in the knowledge of the results they delivered. This aspect can be understood globally in plan and section, which is a form of information on the project typically requested by publishers. Through the conventions of reading such literal projections, these interrogations struggle to capture the central qualities of the built work. The graphics that are generated greatly overstate gentle folds as harsh creases, and the resultant complexity of overstated lines and geometries are all that the eye sees. Little of the subtlety that easily transmits from the formed and assembled materials is conveyed and it is very doubtful whether, were such drawings presented to the client in the first instance, the commission would have been awarded. By letting go of the design drawing as the primary instruction to make, and by reading such initial drawings solely as strategic intentions of spatial and material organisation, an otherwise unexplored architectural response is found in the place and process of production.

The post-production construct. Visualisation of 3D point cloud model constructed from a 3D terrestrial lidar scan carried out a year after the shelter was installed. The point cloud model can be mapped upon the original digital design file, revealing the difference between pre-production design information and the as-built construct. Scan by ScanLAB. Photograph: Bob Sheil. © sixteen*(makers).

A year to the month after 55/02 was assembled and installed on site, the building was captured as a 3D lidar scan using equipment on loan to UCL by the international instrument and measurement manufacturers FARO.[21] This technology has been developed for precision engineering and industrial applications over the last decade, but only in recent years, and coinciding with the evolution of point cloud modelling, has it entered the domain of the design and construction sector. With the potential to provide users with rapid and accurate feedback on existing structures in the form of exportable digital models, the capacity to exploit the resource of accurate and usable measured data is broad and deep. In this instance, it provided the authors of 55/02 with an asset from which to trace and record decisions that had not been developed through drawing. The scanned model may be overlaid on the CAD model and anomalies identified. In this instance such data would not be regarded as a fault but as a difference that was not documented. One can easily imagine, however, that a less positive conclusion might be drawn in other circumstances. As in a world of increasing regulation and accountability, design differences that are undocumented tend to be labelled as 'faults' or at the very least 'disputes'. Drawing, whether digital or analogue, is without doubt an essential process and tool in the production of architecture. Both the act and the product of drawing are also central in defining the role of the designer, but as I hope this exploration has conveyed, in an age when we are bypassing the translation of drawings by those with the tacit skills in how they are realised, we might wish to consider their bearing strength in this great task, and what we can do to ensure their best intentions are fulfilled.

Notes

1   See B Sheil, 'Protoarchitecture: Between the Analogue and the Digital', B Sheil (ed), *AD Protoarchitecture: Analogue and Digital Hybrids*, vol 78, no 4, John Wiley & Sons (London), 2008, pp 6–11.

2   See N Callicott, *Computer-Aided Manufacture in Architecture – The Pursuit of Novelty*, Architectural Press (Oxford), 2000.

3   See M Stacey, 'Folding into the Landscape', *Building Design*, 1880, 14 August 2009, pp 16–17. Illustrated article on the role of Stahlbogen in designing and building 55/02.

4   The scans and post-production imagery were carried out and prepared by ScanLAB Projects. To view an animation of the survey visit: http://scanlabprojects.squarespace.com/latest/sixteenmakers-5502.html

5   Sixteen*(makers) operate between practice and research, and between design and making. Established at The Bartlett School of Architecture in the mid-1990s, the group includes Phil Ayres, Nick Callicott, Chris Leung, Bob Sheil and Emmanuel Vercruysse. Throughout its life, members of the group have remained independently active in academia, practice and industry, as they have worked together on a project by project basis from respective bases in London, Paris, Copenhagen and Blankenburg. Callicott has since gone on to establish Stahlbogen GmbH, a subsidiary of Ehlert GmbH in the Harz region of Germany, while Ayres, Leung, Sheil and Vercruysse continue their ties with the Bartlett in design, research and teaching. The group now operates as an architectural consultancy at UCL. Further details may be found at www.sixteenmakers.com

6   S Groák, 'Board Games', a profile of sixteen*(makers) in N Spiller (ed), *AD Integrating Architecture*, vol 66, no 9/10, John Wiley & Sons (London), 1996, pp 48–51 and seven illustrations.

7   D Pye, *The Nature and Art and Workmanship*, Herbert (London), 1968, and *The Nature and Aesthetics of Design*, Herbert (London), 1978.

8   N Potter, *What is a Designer: Education and Practice*, Littlehampton Book Services (Littlehampton) 1969, and *Models and Constructs: Margin Notes to a Design Culture*, Hyphen (London), 1990.

9   The Macintosh PowerBook 100 was introduced on 21 October 1991.

10 See M Ramírez and T Papanikolas (eds), *Questioning the Line: Gego in Context*, The Museum of Fine Arts (Houston), 2003.

11 See B Sheil, Introduction to *Manufacturing the Bespoke*.

12 'Skeleton baste' is a term used in tailoring to describe the first and rough fitting of a bespoke suit. The second fitting is known as the 'forward', and the final as the 'finish bar finish'.

13 B Sheil (ed), *AD Design through Making*, vol 75, no 3, John Wiley & Sons (London), 2005.

14 B Sheil, 'Protoarchitecture: Between the Analogue and the Digital', *AD Protoarchitecture: Analogue and Digital Hybrids*.

15 See P Ayres (ed), *Persistent Modelling: Extending the Role of Architectural Representation*, Routledge (Oxford), due Spring 2012.

16 See B Sheil and C Leung, 'Kielder Probes – Bespoke Tools for an Indeterminate Design Process', in O Ataman (ed), *Smart Architecture*, ACADIA (Association for Computer Aided Design in Architecture), Savannah (Savannah College of Art and Design, Georgia, USA), pp 254–9.

17 R Sheil, 'A Manufactured Architecture in a Manufactured Landscape', in *arq* (*Architectural Research Quarterly*), vol 13, issues 3/4, 2009, pp 200–20, Cambridge University Press (Cambridge).

18 R Sheil (ed), *55/02, a sixteen*(makers) project monograph*, Riverside Architectural Press (Cambridge, Ontario), 2012.

19 From where Phil Ayres collaborated.

20 The site at Cock Stoor is four miles from the nearest car park and delivery point. It is accessible via an unstable forestry road or by boat and is without power supply. At the time of installation, it was also beyond the reach of a mobile phone signal.

21 The scan was carried out and post-processed by Matthew Shaw and William Trossell of ScanLAB Projects.

The Bespoke is a Way of Working, Not a Style

Stephen Gage

Have digital tools and methods provided us with too many choices and capabilities, and will they reduce the designer's practice to a selection process on what appears to be the most pleasing or beautiful form? Here, Stephen Gage, Professor of Innovative Technology at The Bartlett School of Architecture UCL, provides a steer through some questions that are in danger of being ignored as we become better equipped and arguably besotted with our new tools. Are there limits to the appropriateness or effectiveness of the bespoke? Does it have a new meaning, and how is it contextualised within the broader history of architectural practice and tradition?

Nick Callicott argues that the introduction of CAD/CAM technology frees architecture from the repetition that was derived from manufacturing processes in the 19th and 20th centuries and that this allows us to explore notions of the bespoke or specific in architecture.[1]

This chapter is an overview. In it I argue that the freedom offered by CAD/CAM can be deceptive, because architecture is aesthetically and socially constrained. I argue that there is a case for individual authorship of the bespoke and link this to concepts of craft, and discuss the implications of an architecture where individual pieces of work can coexist with each other and can be understood as a conversation. I also argue that the bespoke is more appropriate to the inside than the outside of buildings in urban and suburban settings, and that it is more appropriately considered as part of a system of spatial enclosure and decoration, or as furniture, in these cases.

Made to Measure

An essential distinction must be made between the specific in architecture as a result of parametric process and the specific in architecture as a result of bespoke design. Both are of value. The former can be thought of as a form of 'auto bespoke' architecture, perhaps more like a 'made to measure' rather than a 'bespoke' suit. A 'made to measure' suit is already fully predesigned and the auto bespoke in this context is a matter of fitting the suit to the individual wearer. This was done historically by ensuring that there was a sufficient variety of basic trousers and jackets at the shop and then locally adjusting them to individual customers. More recently the use of body scanning and digital cutting allows the suit manufacturer to make an auto-bespoke suit directly for

The art of 3D printing 1. Justin Goodyer, 'Adaptive Bloom', MArch (Architecture), Bartlett, 2009. This project is an exploration of interactive movement in architecture. The pieces that move are an array of 'flowers' that have been printed in nylon at the Bartlett Digital Manufacturing Centre. © Gavin Bambridge.

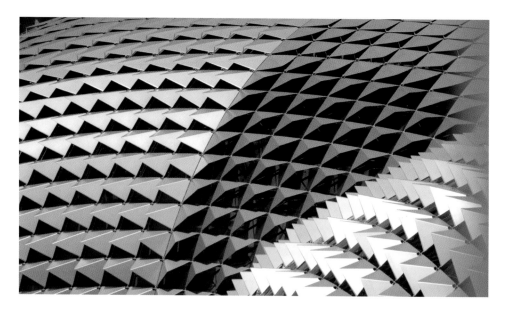

The technical auto bespoke. Michael Wilford & Partners architects, Atelier One structural engineers and Atelier 10 environmental engineers, Singapore Esplanade Theatre, 2003. The shade canopy contains apertures that are unique to their orientation and position within the canopy. © Bernard Tey.

an individual customer. Much recent 'parametric' design strikes this author as being like this; the same building is being tailored to fit different sites and uses. This is not necessarily a critique of the parametric process, which can produce excellent results if the original model is rich and of wide applicability.

The traditions that drive parametric design are very ancient. They can be traced back to the numerical ordering of architecture in ancient Greece. This approach gives a set of ratios between architectural elements (a system of proportions) that can be systematically varied to suit immediate needs. John Frazer, among others, has shown that the approach can be digitally parametricised. Frazer's work is inspired by the parametric understanding of growth and form first explored by D'Arcy Thompson at the beginning of the last century.[2] It is possible to represent many types of architecture in this way. For example, shape grammars have been identified in the work of many modern architects.[3] Mark Burry has digitised many aspects of Gaudí's architecture in his work on the Sagrada Família.[4]

More recently parametric transformation has been extensively used to auto-generate specific solutions for both formal and technical reasons. The father of this approach is Paul Coates.[5] Some of the most elegant technically derived forms include parametrically developed structural and solar shading designs, for example, the shade roof of the Singapore Esplanade theatre and concert hall by Michael Wilford & Partners. There is an inherent beauty in the technically driven auto bespoke. I have argued elsewhere that this lies in the mind of the observer, as the observer is driven to explore the relationships that are visible in the end result.[6] There are, however, other drivers behind auto bespoke production.

Both formal and technical parametric designs can be produced using physical models as well as computer models. The structural models by Gaudí and the soap bubble experiments by Frei Otto are well-known examples of the former. However, these physical models require interpretation before they can be developed as full-sized buildings. The goal of today's researchers in the technical and formal field is to be able to move directly from the model to fabrication. Auto-bespoke architecture, like auto-bespoke suit production, offers the possibility of reducing design-thinking time and therefore cost. If an idea can be mechanically tweaked to fit a particular brief, site or local condition then costs are correspondingly reduced. There is little difference in this to the use of 'pattern books' in 15th- to 19th-century Western architectural practice. Both details and whole buildings were 'lifted' in this way. The approach was often a combination of enlightened knowledge on the part of clients as a result of a 'Grand Tour' to Greece and Italy and reluctance to trust (or to pay) the local talent to design and make something new and unique. 'Signature' buildings, such as Palladio's Villa Rotonda were sometimes replicated as at Chiswick House in London. The 'pattern book' also offered a model for urban cohesion where the building blocks of cities could be built by different organisations at different times but still maintain a cohesive whole. A prime (in all senses of the word) example of this is the 'Georgian' extension of London produced as a result of the pattern-book types that were enshrined in the London Building Acts after the Great Fire of London in 1666.

The Romance of the Specific 1: Craft
The introduction of an auto-bespoke approach to architecture will inevitably diminish the role of individual designers and craftsmen, who will always seek to mould the world according to their own particular vision. This applies whether the procedure of replicating given forms is mechanical or whether it is done by hand. In the 15th to 19th centuries (and indeed for much of the 20th century), all the repeats and modifications of pre-existing ideas were drawn by hand by poorly paid draughtsmen and then either made by machine or by hand by poorly paid craftsmen.

The formulaic encoding of Palladian architecture in Britain in the 18th century was a conscious selection of a 16th-century model as a 'style' of architecture that was suitable for educated gentlemen. It set the scene for the sterile 'Battle of the Styles' in the 19th century. Styles could increasingly be mechanically produced, often in appalling conditions. There was little dignity in this type of labour before mechanisation and often even less afterwards:

> ... for it is not the material, but the abuse of human labour, which makes the thing worthless; and a piece of terra cotta, or plaster of Paris, which is wrought by the human hand is worth all the stone of Carrara, cut by machinery. It is indeed possible, and even usual, for men to sink into machines themselves, so that even hand work has all the characteristics of mechanism.[7]

John Ruskin was one of a number of prominent theoreticians and practitioners in the 19th century who instinctively objected to this trivialisation of human labour and creativity. It has often been argued that this objection came from a protosocialistic view of society, or from a romantic backward look at a society that had never been. I think that this misses a key point in Ruskin's argument. It is that work that is viscerally, rather than cynically produced can be viscerally enjoyed. The same is true today. Callicott's book explores the possibility of a direct link between design and making through digital representation linked to fabrication machinery. It is awe-inspiring to observe young designers working in programs such as Rhino, Inventor and SolidWorks where the discipline of direct fabrication is palpable. I am convinced that the designer/craftsman in the future will develop entirely new modes of working that will necessitate a substantial level of material understanding. The digital thumbprint of the designer will be observable in the work, if the architectural profession both desires and permits this.

We already produce many highly talented designers who work in the digital field, but how are they usefully employed? Kai Strehlke gave a disturbing but typical account at the ACADIA 09 conference. He works for Herzog & de Meuron where he is head of design technology. He is author, together with Russell Loveridge, of the paper 'The Redefinition of Ornament using Programming and CNC Manufacturing'.[8] In his presentation to ACADIA he described how he developed proposals for the facades of the 'City of Flamenco' project

in Jerez, Spain, through multiple elegant iterations.[9] One is struck by the fact that these are all very interesting, clever reworks of the same building element. Kai does not find it at all strange that these iterations should be presented to the practice partners so that they can 'make a choice'. It is, after all, common practice in architecture offices that have the luxury of time available to work in this way. This mode of working could be viewed as a huge waste of effort especially when the work goes well beyond a sketch to a point where the moment of fabrication is only a command away.

There must be a better way of making buildings that allows the individual designer/ maker to 'own' part of the work so that she, as in Ruskin's description, sacrifices her craft to the building. This must require a review of design procedures and we may need to develop new models by looking at the past and by drawing on metaphors from other disciplines. The aim would be to produce architectures that are aesthetically potent. Gordon Pask, the originator of conversation theory and an eminent second order cybernetician outlines this concept:

> With all this in view, it is worth considering the properties of aesthetically potent environments, that is, of environments designed to encourage or foster the type of interaction which is (by hypothesis) pleasurable. It is clear that an aesthetically potent environment should have the following attributes:

Plate from John Ruskin, *The Seven Lamps of Architecture*. Ruskin's book deserves to be read again today to set the scene for a resurgence of craft in architecture. It contains an impassioned plea for dignity and integrity in the process of the design and making of buildings. Reproduced from J Ruskin, *The Seven Lamps of Architecture*, George Allen (London), 1888 edition, pp 99–100.

a) It must have sufficient variety to provide the potentially controllable novelty required by a man (however, it must not swamp him with variety – if it did, the environment would merely be unintelligible).

b) It must contain forms that a man can interpret or learn to interpret at various levels of abstraction.

c) It must provide cues or tacitly stated instructions to guide the learning and abstractive process.

d) It may, in addition, respond to a man, engage him in conversation and adapt its characteristics to the prevailing mode of discourse.

If a group of designers are to work in this way they must look to create a common design 'language' that is sufficiently fluid to allow for the celebration of local differences, derived from differences in individual interpretation. This approach is likely to fulfil condition a). A common language that is intelligible to a group of designers is likely to fulfil conditions b) and c).

Pask goes on to suggest that:

Condition d) is satisfied implicitly and often in a complex fashion that depends upon the sense modality used in the work. Thus, a painting does not move. But our interaction with it is dynamic for we scan it with our eyes, we attend to it selectively and our perceptual processes build up images of parts of it. Further, consciously or not, the artist anticipated this dynamic interaction (if only because he looks at the picture himself). Of course, a painting does not respond to us either. So, once again, it seems deficient with respect to d). But our internal representation of the picture, our active perception of it, does respond and does engage in an internal 'conversation' with the part of our mind responsible for immediate awareness.[10]

If more than one designer/craftsman is responsible for the work as a whole then it is plausible that their conversations will be visible in the work, and enhance the internal 'conversation' to which Pask refers. This approach leads us to consider the twin ideas of 'themes' and 'seams', the themes being a common language and the seams being strategies of dealing with the boundaries between the works of the different designers who are working together. Are there traditions that might guide us? Like Ruskin and William Morris we may need to return to the medieval for our inspiration. But we could also look to the role that improvisation plays in music, specifically in the work of jazz and blues musicians. There is a vast array of literature dealing with this subject, much of which relates to the protocols of improvisation in time-based group work and the understanding of common languages. Less is known about group improvisation to give a compound result in three-dimensional spaces. We can speculate that in the medieval this was achieved through the use of a mode of hierarchical design where the seams and themes were defined spatially and individual craftsmen then worked within spatially defined areas within them. More dynamic conversations could be achieved using a continually transforming three-dimensional digital CAD model with CAM capability. A CAD model of this nature could be developed by individual designer craftsmen/women, each working in their own spatially distinct areas whose boundaries could shift. In theory, a BIM program could be developed to do this.

The Romance of the Specific 2: Place
We can trace the romance of the specific derived from craft from Ruskin to Morris and the Arts and Crafts movement, and from there to the 20th century where it appears in numerous guises. We must turn to the 18th century to find the origins of a romance about specific places in Western art, literature and design. The Picturesque taught the leisured classes to both frame and revere specific wild landscapes. It is a short step from this to delight in the idea of a totally site-specific building that is not 'adapted to' the landscape but 'grows out' of it. The most widely known building of this genre is Falling Water by Frank Lloyd Wright. Most landscapes owe as much to the hand of man as they do to 'nature'. Bob Sheil, Phil Ayres and Chris Leung have all made this point in various papers on the sixteen*(makers) Kielder projects. The inference is that even when the landscape is otherwise untouched by man, landscape and building can exist in a form of symbiosis.

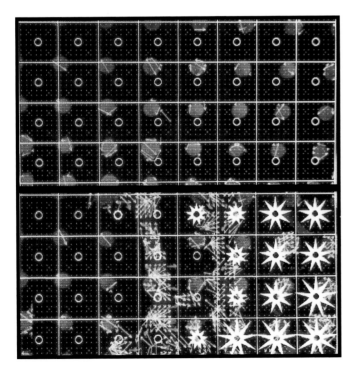

The art of 3D printing 2. Justin Goodyer, 'Adaptive Bloom', MArch (Architecture), Bartlett, 2009. Screen shot of the bespoke digital control panel, relaying real-time behaviour of the bloom array, thereby allowing adjustment on the reaction and integration of the array as a flock. © Justin Goodyer.

However, the majority of buildings are situated in the villages, suburbs, towns and cities that make up the megapolis in which most of us live. In these worlds the romance of place, the specific and the bespoke must be reframed to have a social dimension. Buildings in cities are subject to zoning restrictions, planning regulations and economic drivers, for example site, construction costs and market values. These are all social pressures that make the buildings that we see look very similar when they are built in a similar location at a similar time. Buildings are also the external manifestations of pressures on both owners and their architects to conform. In this context, extreme efforts to create difference often look tawdry after the initial 'wow' factor has worn off. Why is this? Some very effective arguments were put forward by Adolf Loos. In 'Ornament and Crime',[11] Loos contrasts the 'tattooed savage' who displays his ornamented body with the modern man who is discreet and wears his well-tailored clothes as a mask to his individuality so that he is part of a wider modern society. He is also scathing about the economic cost of a fashion in ornament; he observes:

> The form of the object should be bearable for as long as the object lasts physically. I would like to try to explain this: A suit will be changed more frequently than a valuable fur coat. A lady's evening dress, intended for one night only, will be changed more frequently than a writing desk. Woe betide the writing desk that has to be changed as frequently as an evening dress, just because the style has become unbearable. Then the money that has been spent on the writing desk will have been wasted.

This is a sustainability argument that carries considerable weight today, when buildings are being covered with scaleless fretwork screens that have no relevance to the spaces behind them or to the buildings that surround them. These buildings are designed to last for a minimum of 30 years. Loos would have concluded that their designers were degenerate criminals, likening the decoration to the graffiti in public lavatories. He had, one must assume, no experience of the level of today's graffiti and the extent to which personal tattoos are common currency in Western society. He would recognise that a search for individual expression leads to mass boredom. Of course his argument also traduces the naked savage when it suggests that the savage is striving for individual difference. All the anthropological evidence from studies of indigenous cultures suggests that the members of these societies are manipulating their signs and symbols collectively to create readings that reflect tribal rather than individual identities.[12] What does a bespoke exterior mean in this context? It does not lead one to think of rugged individualism or 'in your face' difference. It does, however, allow us to consider a building whose exterior is made by a group of designer/craftsmen who subtly differentiate its various parts and functions.

The bespoke in the city. The inside of the American Bar in Vienna by Adolf Loos. It is hard to convey the jewel-like quality of this interior. Loos was a master of internal elegance and craft. © ORCH Chemollo / RIBA Library Photographs Collection.

The bespoke in the country. Sixteen*(makers)' second project at Kielder is an exercise in site specificity. The building is a symbiosis of its material and its location, designed to relate to the incidental and the planned in this manmade forest. Photograph: Bob Sheil. © sixteen*(makers).

Interior Space and Time

One would anticipate from 'Ornament' that Loos's interiors would be white boxes. Anyone who has been to the American Bar in Vienna will know that they are often sybaritic and sumptuous. In *The Principle of Cladding*,[13] Loos defines cladding as the visible space-shaping surface, to be distinguished from the building structure that supports it. The argument is primarily about internal space and it outlines the necessity of an appropriate long term fit-out. In my paper 'Constructing the User',[14] I examine this proposition, taking the view that a rapid replacement fit-out cycle is potentially unsustainable for the reasons outlined above and that it may be possible to create settings for the rituals of everyday life that transcend their immediacy. These rituals are essentially performative, with performances that are closely related to time of day, day of week and season. They drift to a point where even if the overall function of a space is broadly the same, the way that it is manifested changes considerably over time. I argue that a sustainable long-term interior must be regarded as a landscape of possibility. The way that its observers might understand an a-functional environment is examined further in a chapter in *Persistent Modelling: Extending the Role of Architectural Representation* edited by Phil Ayres.[15] I think that it is in this context that a group of digital designers/craftsmen can create the kind of aesthetically potent environment that users will want to sustain rather than change, because it delights them. This argument also places a lot of weight on a further level of 'architectural furniture' design to facilitate immediate functionality. 'Architectural furniture' offers a further world of opportunity for the digital designer/craftsman. In this world an extreme design may be both possible and desirable.

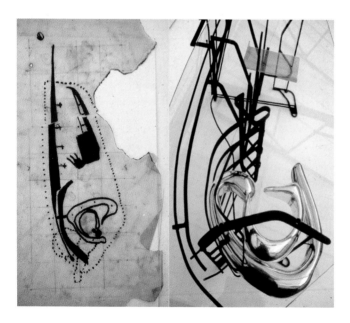

The bespoke as furniture. Neil Spiller and sixteen*(makers), Cyberdesk, 1995. To the left this image shows the only design drawing supplied by Neil Spiller to sixteen*(makers), an A4 sketch that was very nearly destroyed by fire. To the right is sixteen*(makers)' response, which was completed as an interpretation of the drawing and made 'freehand' without any further paper-based information. Spiller went on to develop a series of further 'post-production' drawings that explored the artefact's mythological status. Photograph: Bob Sheil. © sixteen*(makers).

The Bespoke is a Way of Working, Not a Style

The truly bespoke is the work of individual designers and craftsmen, working with sympathetic clients to create places and objects with high levels of specificity that relate directly to the materials from which they are made. I hope this chapter has offered some avenues for further exploration in digital design and digital design practice that might facilitate this in the 21st century. The practice of architecture is vulnerable to swings in fashion and it is my contention that the inappropriate use of the possibilities inherent in digital design and manufacture will mean that it is treated as a 'parametric style' to be applied wilfully and unthinkingly in every context, to the detriment of the city and to the detriment of both the designers and the users of external and internal urban space. When this happens, styles are ruthlessly abandoned. This chapter suggests an alternative view of the bespoke, where it can be both a spatial attribute and the attribute of an object or collection of objects within a space. It allows us to be optimistic about the future of architecture and design and the future of architects and designers because it gives room for the forces of individual creativity. It leaves one unanswered question, which is formal rather than technical. Both the Modern Movement and its more recent 'Parametric Style' offshoots aim at formal coherence in buildings and do not give many clues as to how individual designer/craftsmen might work together. I have suggested a 'themes and seams' approach; how this might be achieved in practice has to be left 'on the table' as a challenge for the 21st century.

Notes

1 N Callicott, *Computer-Aided Manufacture in Architecture: The Pursuit of Novelty*, Architectural Press (Oxford), 2001.

2 Thompson, D (JT Bonner, ed), *On Growth and Form*, Cambridge University Press (Cambridge), 1961, first published 1917.

3 G Stiny, *Shape: Talking about Seeing and Doing*, MIT Press (Boston), 2006.

4 M Burry, *Gaudí Unseen: Completing the Sagrada Família*, Jovis (Berlin), 2007.

5 P Coates, *Programming Architecture*, Routledge (Oxford), 2010.

6 S Gage, 'The Wonder of Trivial Machines' in *Systems Research and Behavioural Science*, John Wiley & Sons (London), 2006.

7 J Ruskin, *The Seven Lamps of Architecture*, George Allen (London), 1888 edition, pp 99–100.

8 K Strehlke, 'Computer Aided Architectural Design Futures 2005', conference, 2005, Part 7, 373-382.

9 K Strehlke, 'Digital Technologies, Methods, and Tools in Support of the Architectural Development at Herzog & de Meuron' in C Dittrich (ed), *Building a Better Tomorrow*, Proceedings of *29th Annual Conference of the Association for Computer Aided Design in Architecture (ACADIA)*, 2009, pp 26–9.

10 G Pask, 'A Comment, A Case History and A Plan', in J Reichardt, ed, *Cybernetics, Art and Ideas*, New York Graphic Society (Greenwich) and Studio Vista (London), 1971.

11 A Loos, *Ornament and Crime* (Vienna), 1908.

12 C Lévi-Strauss, *The Savage Mind*, Weidenfeld and Nicolson (London), 1966.

13 A Loos, 'Das Prinzip der Bekleidung', *Ins Leere Gesprochen*, 1898, p 140.

14 S Gage, 'Constructing the User' in *Systems Research and Behavioural Science*, John Wiley & Sons (London), 2007.

15 P Ayres, *Persistent Modelling: Extending the Role of Architectural Representation*, Routledge (Oxford), 2012.

Surviving photograph of Gaudí's original 1917 drawing of the Passion Facade portal, designed at least nine years before his death. The red rectangle indicates the three 1:1 prototypes developed 2001–04, and on display *in situ* up until 2009 [Sagrada Família Archive]. © Expiatory Temple of the Sagrada Família.

Models, Prototypes and Archetypes
Fresh Dilemmas Emerging from the 'File to Factory' Era

Mark Burry

'File to factory', an appropriation from the aeronautical design industry that is used to describe the direct transfer of CAD file data to CNC manufacturing plant, has been taken by many in architectural design to imply consistency and speed. Gone are the wasteful and vulnerable channels that pass through consultants, contractor, specialist contractor, maker and supplier. Executive Architect and Researcher to the Temple Sagrada Família in Barcelona and Professor of Innovation at RMIT Melbourne, as well as visiting professor and director at a host of international universities and design and technology institutes, Mark Burry challenges this popular claim. He argues, if anything, the opposite is about to be true. Here, he articulates through his extraordinary work on Antoni Gaudí's Sagrada Família spanning over 30 years, that digital fabrication has blurred definitions of the model and the prototype, and with it a lack of clarity about the role of the archetype has been initiated.

The timing of the international conference *FABRICATE* in April 2011 was perfect, coinciding with the moment when digital design and fabrication were finally recognised as extant within the building industry, if not necessarily core to mainstream design practice. Proof that this emergence from avant-garde techno-enthusiasm to affordable daily practice was the cover story run by *The Economist* just two months before *FABRICATE* was timed to take place. The one-page leader accompanied by a three-page in-depth article about 'additive manufacture' demonstrated real immersion in the subject, and not just a glossy 'wonders never cease' overview of '3D printing'.[1] The cover itself showed a reproduction Stradivarius violin made using this novel bespoke manufacturing technique, noting that it 'played perfectly'. It did not say that it played as perfectly as a Stradivarius original, and while that might not be the focus of *The Economist*'s agenda, it is a telling question that will ginger up this chapter's quest for a sense of the cultural ramifications of widespread take-up of manufacturing the unique and not necessarily crafting the exquisite. When we talk of 'digital fabrication' what exactly are we 'making' here – if we machine-print a design as a working object, do we need to redefine the role of 'model', 'prototype' and 'archetype' within practice in this context?

Evoking previous technologically driven seismic shifts in society:

Just as nobody could have predicted the impact of the steam engine in 1750 – or the printing press in 1450, or the transistor in 1950 – it is impossible to foresee the long-term impact of 3D printing.

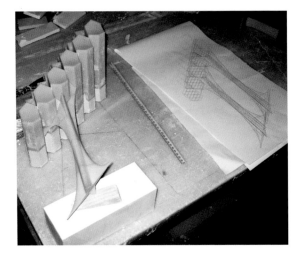

left: Design development for the Sagrada Família Church Passion Facade. 1:10 design model – 1:10 scale wax deposition rapid prototype combined with traditional gypsum plaster modelling. © Mark Burry.

opposite left: The challenges of stereotomy: 1:10 model of the north end of the narthex. © Model: Jane Burry.

opposite right: 1:1 prototypes *in situ* (2004). The prototypes remained in place for five years. © Mark Burry.

The Economist's cover, leader and three-page 'briefing' sought to raise awareness of the imminent shifts in manufacturing which, it conjectured, will be as profound as these: 'in the long run it will expand the realm of industry – and imagination'.

All very forward-looking, no doubt, but hardly critical at a cultural level. The purpose of my commentary here is therefore to call upon my 20 years of experience in digital fabrication, and ponder on the risks of 'reductive manufacture' becoming the sustainability pariah when contrasted to 'additive manufacture', principally when working with stone and timber. The irony is that timber, a sustainable material when resources are managed appropriately, and stone, effectively still an abundant naturally occurring material, are manifestly worked reductively – they are cut, carved, hewn and sculpted yet produce large volumes of waste in the process, although the waste can still find use as sawdust for wood pulp, for example, and road rubble. In the main, traditional architectural materials have come from raw materials that have been made ready by reduction, not accretion. Moulded (or drawn) materials such as concrete and steel have been part of the repertoire only since the dawn of the industrial age.

Here I intend to weave two issues together: on the one hand technology used to extend traditional practice and, on the other, a sideways glance at how this is obliging us to reconsider our representational paradigms including the model. I commence with a brief history of stonecutting for the continued construction of the Sagrada Família Church in Barcelona as a counterpoint to any unbridled enthusiasm for additive manufacture. The subtext is stonecutting made easier. While ultimately I might not be able to demonstrate 'stonecutting rendered much more economically viable', at least the rate of change will demonstrate how open this territory is for development and wider access. Research in this domain is rapidly moving from 'what is …' to 'how best to implement …'.

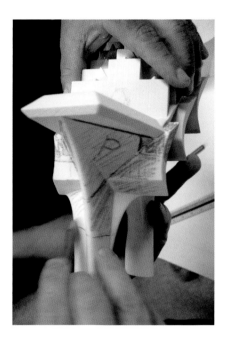 

A Brief History of Digitally Assisted Stone Preparation: Adventures 1 and 2

I have been deeply involved with all three adventures of digitally assisted stoneworking for making columns and masonry components for the continuing construction of Gaudí's Sagrada Família Church. These adventures, innovations in effect, span exactly two decades.

The first adventure was the production of the main columns at ground level for the nave, leading to innovation in semi-automated stonecutting. The columns range in diameter from 1.05 to 2.10 metres (3.44 to 6.89 feet) – there are four sizes altogether, and each size has a material selected by Gaudí for strength. In fact he conducted his own strength testing using a press that he kept on site. The materials range from local sandstone for the slimmest, through granite, basalt to porphyry for the four giants that form the crossing.

All four column types can be characterised by their curvilinear bases that morph to Doric flutings mid-height, morphing to almost perfect circles by the time they reach the 'knots' – the sculptured capitals that in turn are the points of bifurcation into the branches reaching up to the ceiling vaults that they support.

The columns each have a geometry in common: the base is a swirl of alternate concave and convex parabolas that intersect as cotangents to each other so furnishing a perfectly smoothed set of serrations. The columns are generated from initially two sets of profiles counter-rotating as the column ascends, the horizontal section of the column at any level being the intersection between the counter-rotated profiles at that level.[2]

The columns were the entry point for numerically controlled stonecutting for the project, pretty much at the beginning of take-up of this technology for construction anywhere. Gaudí's definition of each column by a single convex and concave parabola facilitated the introduction of a digitally controlled saw, for with the curve hard-coded within the machine, the simple instruction set simply took the machine to a point in space and steered it around the relevant section of parabola for that location.[3] The parabolas were drawn by hand 1:1 and then digitised into the numerical control unit on site using a drafting table with 2D crosshair measurement next to the robot saw. Each cut was 5.5 millimetres (0.21 inches) thick, which is why when the columns are examined closely from a distance of a metre or two (3 to 6 feet) there are faintly perceptible horizontal bands of this dimension rising up the column.

A decade later and a second set of innovations for sculpting stone came with the commission for the rose window (*rosassa* in Catalan) for the Passion Facade. Sitting between the two groups of two towers – the campaniles – the window design was a compositional extension of Gaudí's three 1:10 design developments undertaken during the decade before his death in 1926: the lower lateral nave window, followed by the upper lateral nave, and the culmination of his design thinking in this regard, the central nave clerestory. The rose window is approximately 25 metres (82 feet) in height and 8 metres (26 feet) in width.[4]

The sculptor Señor Manuel Mallo from Lugo, Galicia, in northwestern Spain was commissioned for the task despite his quarry and mason's yard being 1200 kilometres (746 miles) distant. We began in January 2000 with a six-week period on site with the design development proceeding in tandem with weekly visits from Señor Mallo. We had primary material, from former colleagues tackling the design as an extension to Gaudí's series of windows described above. The project was to be the first where the doubly ruled surfaces were to be sculpted from stone rather than moulded for making artificial stone components. We used parametric design software coupled with Excel™ spreadsheets (for the maths) because the cluster of four towers was a degree or two off axis and the two sets of towers had been designed as asymmetrical. Not only that, the rose window was to be built using a 'just in time' construction management approach: while the bottom quarter was being installed on site, the next was being carved at the mason's yard on the other side of Spain, and the third quarter was being templated in Australia. At the same time, the top quarter was still being designed in collaboration with colleagues at UPC (university) in Barcelona who were working on the ceiling with which it intersected.

Señor Mallo was perplexed by our fiddly little wax prototypes, the expensive output from the first echelon of 3D printer prototype makers available to architects. Ours were too small physically for his purposes – he preferred to make versions himself from polystyrene, at a more useful scale than our 3D prints and accurately carved by hand using a hot wire following our drawings. He also thought the act of making the prototype was an essential part of learning the geometrical intricacies for each piece, allowing him to engage deeply with the actual task of cutting the stone.

Another surprising innovation was his adaptation of the diamond-encrusted stonecutting wire that descended while slicing thin sheets of marble or granite for kitchen benches. Ordinarily the quarried stone piece being sculpted would be locked on the spot while the moving wire descended. Our 1:1 templates (a throwback to the 17th-century advances in stereotomy) were inscribed on to the pre-cut faces to the block being sculpted, and Señor Mallo had adapted his cutting machine by putting the raw stone block on to a turntable. As the wire steadily descended, an operative at each end of the block twisted it to ensure that the cutting wire followed the inscribed template at each

Señor Manuel Mallo with 1:10 scale prototype made by hand at a fraction of the cost of its rapidly prototyped equivalent. The masonry's warped surfaces have been cut close to finished size by a diamond-wire saw and are subsequently finished by hand. © Mark Burry.

side of the block. In such a way, the stone was rough-cut to within a centimetre (0.39 of an inch) of the finished ruled surface. The stonemason was freed from doing all the reduction by hand and instead could concentrate on the part of his trade that most relied on skill: finishing the stone surface to perfection.

The third innovation came from Jordi Barbany, descended from several generations of sculptors based in the granite region among the hills 40 kilometres (25 miles) north of Barcelona. He linked a five-axis robot stonecutter/router and a two-axis turntable giving him a remarkable seven degrees of freedom for working stone. This contribution to our collective repertoire is so sophisticated a leap I shall pause first to look at concomitant shifts in thinking about the role of the design model before continuing to outline our adventures in novel stonecutting for the Sagrada Família Church.

Homo Faber: Shifting Ground for the Design Model

In 2005, colleagues Michael Ostwald, Peter Downton, Andrea Mina, Alison Fairley and I commenced our Australian Research Council-funded investigation into the shifting role of the model, as part of the architect's design process: *Homo Faber*. We reviewed the world around us locating the *Homo Faber* project squarely within the complexities of representation and the vagaries of distinct architectural practice, as borne witness by

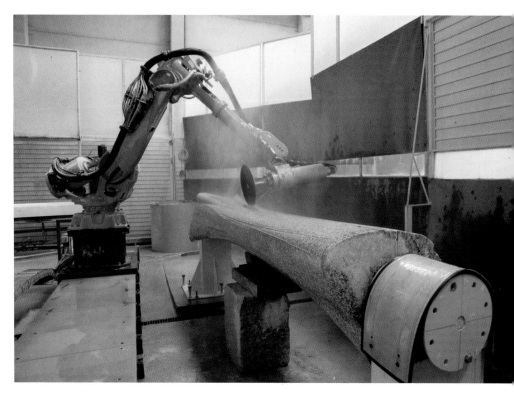

The first of the 18 narthex columns to be produced. In the life of the project, Jordi Barbany (stonemason) has succeeded in organising his seven-axis bespoke robot cutting and routing arrangement to allow us to produce the columns in 6-metre (19.68-foot) long single lengths, up from the original 3 metres (9.84 feet)(location: Granits Barbany, 2010). © Mark Burry.

specific practices in Australia. Peter Downton reminded us of the designer's investment of their essential self deeply embedded in the art of architecture, and the architectural speculation involved.[5] My contribution to the project sought to marry personal experience over (then) two and half decades at surely one of the most extreme architectural practices of all time to our broader enquiry. I refer to the ongoing challenge of completing the Sagrada Família Church beyond Gaudí's hands-on intervention, and subsequently through his surviving 'Technical Office'.

Why yet more lessons from the Sagrada Família Church? From 2001 we have been working on bringing Gaudí's design development of the Passion Facade to a conclusion, which is based principally on a painted-over drawing, crucial information that survives only as a high resolution photographic plate. In that time we have initiated and led the resolution of the design for the great space above the crossing where the six central towers join the adjacent nave and transepts. This research is based entirely on the *poché* of a single hatched-out section surviving only as a published etching. Just as our *Homo Faber* research project concluded, we began the labyrinthine journey into forming an understanding of Gaudí's unfinished design for the main front, the Glory Facade.

Our source material for the Glory Facade is two photographs of an unfinished large-scale model for the facade — each photograph varying from the other by a few degrees of difference in projection — and a small number of shattered model fragments that Gaudí was only partially through completing. There are no drawings at all for this facade. Possibly it would be convenient to assume that, as in many of the great Gothic cathedrals, the architect originating the project was several generations removed from the architect charged with completing that grand entry, separated in time only by force of circumstance. If Gaudí had generously assumed transference of authorship, how do we account for the half-completed model? An impossible question necessarily rhetorical in his absence; how fitting that our ongoing research into Gaudí's unfinished Sagrada Família Church project relies solely on the prototype model and not the drawing.

Looking at shifts in the model — its definition and use in the post-digital era — what does this bring to our *Homo Faber* project: closure or the additional complexity born from a wicked problem refusing to go quietly? I suspect the latter, because definitions have become muddied, and contexts sullied. Specifically, just as we begin to resolve the model's diverse role as part of the architect's design repertoire, we are confronted with new dilemmas: the model as model, as prototype and as archetype. Which is it, do we need to know, and does it matter? My brief responses to these provocations at this point are, respectively, 'not sure', 'yes', and 'most definitely'.

While only a short time in the history of the world, the past half-decade has been a long time in the history of architectural models, model making and prototyping. In this time we have seen laser cutters become mainstream tools even for the vastly expanded pools of undergraduate students. '3D prints' have become quite normal as prototypes at least and, at the time of writing, almost every school will be looking at the cost benefit equations of whether to purchase a multi-material 3D printer or not, if they have not already taken the plunge. During this time MoMA commissioned an exhibition called *Home Delivery: Fabricating the Modern Dwelling* from 20 July to 20 October 2008, much of it in a paved parking lot outside the museum. The exhibition (with its accompanying website www.moma.org/homedelivery) displayed:

> the process of architectural design and production in equal measure with the actual end result. Within the gallery, eighty-four architectural projects spanning 180 years are presented by means of film, architectural models, original drawings and blueprints, fragments, photographs, patents, games, sales materials and propaganda, toys, and partial reconstructions. This diverse collection of material illustrates how the prefabricated house has been, and continues to be, not only a reflection on the house as a replicable object of design but also a critical agent in the discourse of sustainability, architectural invention, and new material and formal research.

I shall remark on this exhibition of 1:1 scaled prototypes for near-future houses at the conclusion of this essay.

Completed column for the Sagrada Família Church Passion Facade. © Mark Burry.

The convergence of design disciplines and studio 'prototyping tools' grows apace, probably much faster than we have done as creative human beings. As has characterised the last 20 years, just when the digital divide looked like being resolved as no longer a relevant contest between 'CAD as media' and 'CAD as design adjunct', we are thrown deeper into the disciplinary dilemma around the boundaries of architecture and its practice. The arrival of machines that offer economical opportunities for industrial designers to prototype 'rubber' tyres on to rigid 'nylon' wheels in a single operation begs the question of architects as to how much use they might or should be making of this equipment. If this is now, what beckons in the not so distant future? It is possible that we have accidentally transcended from relatively straightforward design exploration, resolution, development and representation to a new state without really noticing.

When we were confined to the two-generation-old paradigm (Modernism) with its associated protocols, we accepted the role of the model as one of comfortable assistant, and of debatable value during the design process. But even during the relatively short period of our Australian Research Council-funded *Homo Faber* research into the contemporary design role of the architectural model, as a society we have become more comfortable in commissioning ever more complex building forms, sophisticated programmes and greatly improved environmental performance. 'File to factory' is no longer something that only a handful of cashed-up signature architects can be identified with as a distinguishing credential: an appropriation taken from the aeronautical design industry. Instead it is something even mainstream practice might now need to consider as part of their everyday repertoire. A design going straight from the designer's software to a complementary software controlling the machine making the object or component neatly leapfrogs all the many skill sets and associated professional interventions in one clean assault. What does this mean to the designer?

It is too easy to posit that this simplification of process eases the responsibilities of the designer: from my experience at the Sagrada Família Church the opposite might be about to confront us. It seems that we have a blurring of definition of the model and the prototype, and with it, a lack of clarity into the role of the archetype. While we did look on scale in the *Homo Faber* context in terms of the infinitesimally minute (with reference to human artifice) representing a view of the wider world, how deeply were we able to consider the opposite, that is the 1:1 prototype in the same enquiry?

I could easily slip into a semantic argument here in terms of interpretative differences of the concepts 'model' and 'prototype'. Depending on which dictionary is consulted, more than 20 definitions of model might emerge so I am going to stick with the following one: '*a representation, generally in miniature, to show the construction or appearance*

The first of the 18 narthex columns ranging in height from 7 to 10 metres (23 to 32.80 feet), each reduced to three elements only (from an originally projected five), tested for buildability at Granits Barbany. All 18 columns are unique – no mirror copies – which, without parametric design software assistance, would have required an order of magnitude of many hundreds of per cent extra labour. © Mark Burry.

of something'.[6] The prototype, in contrast, I am taking here as the *'original or model on which something is based or formed'.*[7] It could be that we may need the model to serve both purposes. We might want to make physical a representation of an idea in order to assist judgement and, at the same time, the representation might serve as a prototype. It is possible that our ability to make things more complicated if not more complex has, in turn, complicated the design process that is already complex. Raised client expectations can raise the design decision-making stakes in turn, and the model as an abstraction of an idea runs into opposition when it simultaneously acts as the prototype for a string of potential outcomes. An example of this is the model/prototype shown in my accompanying illustration of the 1:1 representation of our parametrically modelled design for the colonnade above the Sagrada Família Church Passion Facade narthex. Here is its short history – the process of idea into manufactured (as opposed to hand-carved) architectural component. Its relevance is as follows.

A Brief History of Digitally Assisted Stone Preparation: Adventure 3

Gaudí's design for the Passion Facade portal and narthex ended for him as a highly worked drawing that included a gouache treatment making it something between a drawing and a painting. The west-facing transept, which includes the Passion Facade, was far from being ready for construction at the time of his death in 1926. In fact, three of the four finials to the Nativity Facade bell towers on the other side of the building were still to be completed and the Passion Facade was not even a hole in the ground. His drawing/ painting is presumed to have been lost when his workshop was sacked during the Spanish Civil War occupation of the Sagrada Família Church, but a fine-grained photographic plate has survived and is the principal source of spatial information for the developed design of the narthex. The lower half of the facade was completed with the Passion Facade towers in 1978, but the top half is only in production now, although various interpretations of the upper-level colonnade columns have been attempted over the intervening decades.

Given the apprenticeship that the team succeeding Gaudí has undergone, and the intimate working knowledge of his geometrical system that he intended to be the guiding language for the building's completion using second order (doubly ruled) surfaces, whatever interpretation that could be made from this photograph still needs to conform to Gaudí's 'system'. The intervention of digital design within the broader working methodology encouraged us to consider using the second order geometrical surfaces in ways that Gaudí himself would not have been able to do in his time because of the attendant computational difficulties that contemporary digital design methods can otherwise attempt to resolve with a higher likelihood of success. In other words, we have striven to attain compositional simplicity in terms of idea (that is, defined geometry versus loose freeform), but in doing so we have added complexity to the design process because

Sagrada Família Church Passion Facade: 1:1 prototype prior to being placed *in situ* on the narthex. © Mark Burry.

we need to involve mathematicians and computer programmers with the parametric design software that we use for this purpose. In so doing, however, we are reductively making a 'prototype model' for the design of the columns. In more precise terms we are combining one hyperboloid of revolution with eight hyperbolic paraboloids. As a novel design strategy this required testing.

One of the conceptual issues about resolving Gaudí's sketch design for the construction of the narthex is the essential mix of sculpture and architectural detail: where does one stop and the other start? The column discussed here is a prime example of this interface issue, but nevertheless this part of the design has fallen to the architect and not the sculptor. This might be seen as an arbitrary or even a controversial outcome, because clearly from Gaudí's surviving material, we can see that these are not classical columns but a novel design highly integrated into the whole. We have seen them as skeletal in nature and have proceeded on that basis. Rapid prototyping technology was made available at exactly the same time as our early design development process for the narthex columns, and we were able to make good use of the emerging technology and at a scale that would have been extremely difficult to work to if we attempted to have models made by hand. But at 1:25 there was no real spatial sense that could be drawn from the scaled physical prototype, and full-size versions of columns 3, 4, and 5 from the nine that form each side of the narthex were produced in painted glass fibre-covered polystyrene, machine cut by a CNC robot more used to making boat hulls than ecclesiastical architectural components.

Once produced, the three columns were erected and remained in place for almost five years. In such a way the model became the prototype, and was used to test, first, our interpretation of Gaudí's design and, second, its constructability and proportions on a 1:1 basis. The constructability has seen further downstream innovation in the CNC stonecutting processes by which the columns are being made at the time of writing. In other words, the model (for testing the spatial qualities of the column) has become a prototype for a whole series of subsequent processes leading to its 'file to factory' production in granite. The accompanying series of images show the Passion Facade narthex design process with the main aspects of this 'file to factory' story.

The *model versus prototype* dilemma may not seem especially important in most cases. No doubt Sir Christopher Wren did not have to model his twinned columns physically for St Paul's Cathedral in London because he was working with an archetype, in this case a column based on the classical orders. In the case of the Sagrada Família Church Passion Facade narthex, we are seeing the emergence of the archetype through this process of architectural invention, and the intervention of the model as the test-bed. The prototype, once tested and accepted, becomes the archetype for subsequent decisions. The archetype here is taken as: 'the original pattern or model from which all things of the same kind are copied or on which they are based; a model or first form; prototype'.[8]

Is this just a case of the exceptional nature of the Sagrada Família Church, unrelated even loosely to other architectural projects and therefore not very relevant? I would contend the opposite by claiming that this example of a 1:1 model becoming first a prototype and subsequently the archetype may well be an example of an important emerging new paradigm. Evidence for my contention can be drawn from the *Home Delivery: Fabricating the Modern Dwelling* exhibition hosted at MoMA and referred to above. At least one of the five built projects, the 'Housing for New Orleans' (Dr L Sass and student colleagues from MIT) is a similar example. With rapidly evolving CNC technologies for both scaled and 1:1 prototyping as well as some essential materials becoming cost competitive, it seems that we are entering a new epoch. As the issue of *The Economist* cited at the beginning of this paper attests, we have arrived at a point where increasing the complexity of design in order to be more responsive to environmental factors potentially affords new manufacturing options and new roles for the model – that is, prototyping, and within this process we might be observing the emergence of entirely new archetypes for new architectural responses fitting for our time. I do not believe that I could have made this observation at the outset of our experiments in digitally assisted stone sculpting.

Notes

1 'Print me a Stradivarius', *The Economist*, 12–18 February 2011, vol 398, no 8720, cover, leader (p 43), and briefing (pp 75–8).
2 MC Burry, *The Expiatory Church of the Sagrada Família*, in 'City Icons' reprint of 1993 monograph Phaidon (London), 1999, p 60.
3 MC Burry, 'Building Techniques', *Architects' Journal*, vol 195, no 13, 1 April 1992.
4 MC Burry, JR Burry and J Faulí, *Sagrada Família Rosassa: Global Computer-Aided Dialogue between Designer and Craftsperson (Overcoming Differences in Age, Time and Distance)*, ACADIA 2001, University at Buffalo, State University of New York, Buffalo, New York, USA, 11–14 October 2001, and JR Burry, MC Burry, 'New Testament', *RIBA Journal* (London), June 2002.
5 P Downton, *Design Research*, RMIT Press (Melbourne), 2003.
6 Dictionary.com Unabridged, Random House, 19 December 2009: http://dictionary.reference.com/browse/model
7 Dictionary.com Unabridged, Random House, 19 December 2009: http://dictionary.reference.com/browse/prototype
8 Dictionary.com Unabridged, Random House, 19 December 2009: http://dictionary.reference.com/browse/archetype

Digital Craft in the Making of Architecture

Michael Stacey

'Can the digital design of architecture be considered a craft, even if there is no haptic element beyond the lowing of keys and the clicking of mice?' In an extended essay, Michael Stacey, Professor in Architecture at the University of Nottingham, profiles the relatively young tradition of digital design and builds a broad and highly constructive argument around what has yet to be gained and regained by its mainstream adoption. He pays homage to architects of the pre-digital age for whom the drawing and the building were more intellectually integrated and in deeper conversation with one another than many of their numeric descendants. He closes by asserting his belief in the importance of the integration of making into the design process.

This essay explores the role of sketches, drawings, models and prototypes in design with a particular focus on architecture that is assembled from prefabricated components, where prototyping has particular relevance. Underlying the essay is the argument that the making of architecture is dependent on ideas and the communication of ideas.

If we examine the etymology of 'prototype' we find that it addresses the very core of architecture as generated by typologies:

1. (n.) An original thing or person of which or whom copies or improved forms, etc are made.
2. (n.) A trial model or preliminary version of a vehicle, machine etc.
From the Greek *Prototypos*. *Protos* – first, original. *Typos* – impression, figure, type.[1]

Whereas if we look at 'innovation', an overused word of contemporary life, we find the etymology to be:

1. (v.) Bring in new methods, ideas, etc.
2. (v.) Make changes.
From the Latin *innovatus* 'altered'.[2]

Although this definition contains the notion of new ideas it is much more about transfer or borrowing. There is no need for the original and perhaps this is why governments find it easier to demand. In my view invention, to create by thought, is much more important.[3]

The potential elegance of architecture assembled from prefabricated components is generated by thinking through the architecture before it has been built. Vitally this requires investment in design time and early collaboration with the makers of the

Sverre Fehn sketching a timber column of the Aukrust Centre at 1 to 1.
© Sverre Fehn Archive/Guy Fehn.

components and systems. The overall gain is minimising the time on site combined with factory quality control. Prefabrication also has the benefit of minimising waste and facilitating closed loop recycling within factories. It offers, too, the potential to generate a sustainable process for all involved where individual skill is maximised and waste within the design process is minimised, by access to skill, experience and robust technologies. It is an excellent route for the production of performative architecture which has been prototyped and tested. Prefabrication, however, is not a panacea, designing architecture is not easy, it requires intellectual investment from the outset. Sverre Fehn observed, 'Architecture is not very complex, but the inspiration that creates good architecture is very complex, and constantly changing.'[4]

In contrast, the commercial development paradigm is to rush to build and muddle through on site. Some of the worst new buildings in Britain, often in our great industrial cities, have little or no intellectual investment. It is said that it is the cost that pressurises the time invested in design. However, a far-sighted developer could profit by using a carefully thought through prefabricated architecture as it shortens the site stage, which is clearly the most expensive part of the construction of new buildings. Why do more developers not invest in the initial stages, engaging with design that adds value? Often in contemporary construction, design and build contracts are cited for a loss of quality and

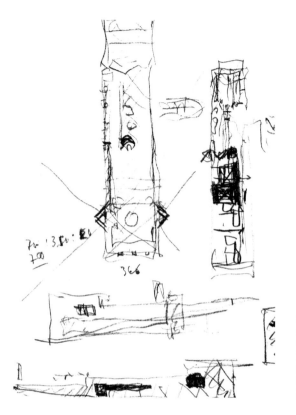

It is possible to see Sverre Fehn's thinking hand in his sketch plan and sections of the Busk House. © Sverre Fehn Archive.

I am concerned that some architects' offices are being deskilled by design and build as the vital engagement in detailed design is lost. I am also concerned that in contemporary practice architects are failing to engage with the full potential of the extensive material palette that is available in the 21st century. Sverre Fehn reflected, 'as an architect you scribe your tales into the sand of the earth and the language is the language of materials. In the beginning you meet materials as a challenge. You try with all your power. You force it. But the significant architects develop a dialog with materials.'[5]

However, the worst buildings recently constructed in Britain not only lack material integrity but also demonstrate an almost total absence of ideas. In too many of our cities, even in the context of high-quality architecture from earlier eras including great cathedrals, new buildings are little more than badly packaged containers. I have in mind student housing that is little more than a stack of 1000 bedspaces. Many bear responsibility for this poverty in the built environment including clients and particularly planners; nonetheless, collectively we should demand more. Britain has and can design and commission world-leading architecture. Good design need not be expensive – it requires investment in inventive processes and the development of skill and experience.

It is pertinent to observe that Renzo Piano's early projects have a long gestation period that is typically greater than the site time. The IBM Travelling Exhibition Pavilion designed with the inventive engineer Peter Rice has a simple extruded form that is built up from 12 semicircular arches of bespoke polycarbonate pyramids. These are tied together by

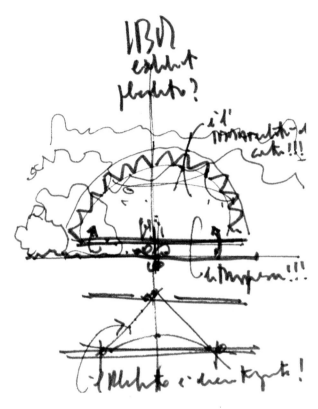

left: Renzo Piano Building Workshop, IBM Travelling Exhibition Pavilion, 1984–6. Renzo Piano's sketch of the pavilion exploring the special arrangement and the key detail of the polycarbonate and timber structure. © Renzo Piano Building Workshop.

below: Renzo Piano Building Workshop, IBM Travelling Exhibition Pavilion, 1984–6. The structure in the grounds of the ruins of St Mary's Abbey, York, UK. Photograph: Gianni Berengo Gardin. © Renzo Piano Building Workshop.

Foster + Partners' model of a node of the steel structure of Swiss Re Headquarters, 30 St Mary Axe, London, made by the architect's design team to understand the layers of construction and geometry of a node. © Foster + Partners.

shapely timber sections of laminated larch and jointed with cast aluminium nodes that are glued into the timber. It was explicitly detailed to be readily assembled and disassembled. The pavilion presented computers as a natural part of everyday life. Peter Rice observed that Renzo Piano had 'defined [the project] by making a romantic prototype which he photographed and showed to the client to demonstrate the central idea'.[6] He continues: 'Renzo had combined the timber with cast aluminium to emphasize the natural quality of the space. Polycarbonate as a material is light and robust but it is also not very strong: its load-carrying capacity and its stiffness are low.'[7]

The pavilion took about three weeks to assemble on each site, having been delivered by 18 articulated lorries. Peter Buchanan records the design period as 1982–4[8] and Piano considered the core design time to be 'nine months and what resulted was an artificial typology so perfect that it evoked the rhythmical structure of nature'.[9]

Between 1984 and 1986 the pavilion was erected in 20 cities in 14 European countries. At each location Buchanan observes 'a computer simulation was run of outside light and thermal conditions, taking account of the orientation of the pavilion, position of shading trees and so on. This determined the exact placing of opaque pyramidal elements, which were fixed within the transparent ones, and of the mesh screens. Together these controlled glare and heat loads.'[10] Piano's carefully crafted assembly of components of the IBM Travelling Exhibition forms a constructional system yet in each location a site-specific work of architecture was created.[11]

In many of his projects he demonstrates a desire to keep all components of a proposed architecture *live* in the design process. All components are variable and editable, leading to a holistic and highly integrated architecture. This is the opposite of conventional construction where packages are layered in independent zones, for say structure, services and building envelope. There are examples from this approach where the retrofitting of unconsidered fixings results in unnecessary and wasteful expenditure. Swiss Re Headquarters, 30 St Mary Axe, London, is a conventionally layered construction, from the planning envelope based on seven carefully chosen tangents just outside the building fabric to the diagrid structure. However Swiss Re, by Foster + Partners, is also an excellent example of investment in early and experimental design. The development of the parametric modelling benefited from the extended planning approval process on a 'controversial' site: the Baltic Exchange was the location of an IRA bomb.

Creating Architecture

Architecture is and always will be more than aesthetics, form or style, yet composition remains important. The discipline of plan and section remains the sheet music of architecture that cannot easily be skipped, however tempting the latest rendering technique may be.[12] Colin St John Wilson suggests, 'every building task has to be assessed in terms of its proportional composition of physical and metaphysical components, and therein lies its uniqueness'.[13] The ability to communicate by drawing is still key to the practice of design. Sketches and diagrams remain the rapid prototypes of communication, even in this digital age.

Juhani Pallasmaa observes: 'Drawings and models have the double purpose of facilitating the design process itself and mediating ideas to others.'[14] Whereas Peter Cook reflects on the struggle inherent in the creation of architecture: 'Herein lie thousands of moments of irritation and frustration on the part of (even) the motivated: when the concept – or maybe the image of a project is sitting inside one's brain, but the drawn version is but a poor thing: inhibited by technique, inhibited by clumsiness or inhibited because the imagined notion has no precedent in familiar imagery.'[15] I think that Cook is in danger of overemphasising concepts and imagery, qualities that have bedevilled architectural education since the rise of concept art in the 1970s. Cook admires 'the gentle power of the Norwegian architect Sverre Fehn's sketches. His buildings are characterised by a talent for placement that is both deft and subtle, anticipating the grasping and channelling of light. They are dependent upon the clarity of intention that is carried by the single-move drawing.'[16] Fjeld observes that 'each of Fehn's house projects is in some way a translation of social and lifestyle concerns into an architectural interpretation of the client. He also said that it took courage for clients to face the spatial picture of themselves, and those who hesitated seldom considered him as their architect.'[17] Architecture should be the translation of the social into a tectonic assembly. 'Fehn drew every house down to the smallest detail, and the work would not begin before the drawings – typically fifty to seventy per cent per project – were complete.'[18] Fjeld comments: 'His pre-computer-era drawings are beautiful and careful drawings in which the office took great pride.'[19] It is possible to fully capture the design intent, the imagined architecture, in the *parti* of a working drawing. Fjeld also notes in the construction of Fehn houses that 'the drawings were meticulously followed; there were no compromises in relation to materials of finishes; and no short cuts taken'.[20] This is a certainty in delivery that many architects only aspire to. Current paper-based drawings, and even two-dimensional CAD drawings, produced by architects too often appear to be little more that vague prayers and wishes. This has become institutionalised in contracts that call for the production of record drawings, a record of the builder's decisions on site.

The use of common digital data by a multidisciplinary design team in the form of a building information model [BIM] is a route to the regeneration of certainty in the delivery of architecture. There is a direct synergy between prefabrication and building information modelling. The computer-based three-dimensional model can contain almost all of the qualities of the completed project, in spatial and material terms as well as in cost and quantity. Gone is the wasteful and time-consuming process of scheduling. Best practice in generating a BIM is to use this virtual environment as a collaborative tool shared by all consultants and used by the fabricators to manufacture the component parts. Stephen Kieran and James Timberlake elegantly argued for the adoption of prefabrication in *Refabricating Architecture*, 2003, recommending that the construction industry can learn from the flexible prefabrication of major shipbuilding with its chunking of large often doubly curved elements to form the overall vessel, and from the tiered prefabrication of automotive construction.[21] This book ended with an essentially corporate vision of the prefabrication of houses, with an invitation 'to a worldwide assembler such as Boeing to engage with construction'.[22] In 2007, KieranTimberlake, Stephen's and James's practice, fulfilled the vision presented in *Refabricating Architecture* by assembling the Loblolly House. However, this is no longer a corporate vision, but one that delivered a bespoke site-specific and situated domestic architecture.

The Loblolly House is located on a barrier island off the coast of Maryland's Chesapeake Bay. This house seeks to deeply fuse the natural elements of its site to architectural form. Positioned between a dense grove of loblolly pines and a lush foreground of saltmeadow cordgrass and the bay, the architecture is formed about and within the elements of trees, tall grasses, the sea, the horizon, the sky and the western sun that define the place of the house. Timber foundations minimise the footprint and provide savannah-like views of the trees and the bay, and the staggered boards of the east facade evoke the solids and voids of the forest.

Stephen and James used off-the-shelf aluminium extrusions and designed custom connectors to extend its capability to form the internal frame structure; this also enabled for the rapid connection of factory fabricated components.[23] Loblolly House proposes a new, more efficient method of building through the use of a BIM and integrated component assemblies. The frame, comprised of Bosch Rexroth aluminium extrusions, is bolted together as opposed to welded, creating a structural system for the house, which can be disassembled without affecting the capacity of beam and column components to be reconnected. James and Stephen prototyped this extruded aluminium frame on the

The assembly of an explanatory prototype of the Loblolly House in the prototyping room at KieranTimberlake's office in Philadelphia. © KieranTimberlake.

The Loblolly House set on
the shore of Chesapeake Bay
among the loblolly pines,
from which it takes its name.
© Peter Aaron/Esto.

SmartWrap Pavilion in New York, 2004. The bolted scaffold of the Loblolly House serves as a frame into which off-site fabricated kitchen, bathroom and mechanical blocks, and floor and wall cartridges are inserted without the use of permanent fasteners or wet connections. Upon disassembly, cartridges and blocks are removed as whole units and column/beam scaffold sections are unbolted.

James and Stephen conceived the Loblolly House as assembled from elements not parts. This informed the making of the BIM: 'Each of these elements is first built virtually as an independent unit with parts integrated hierarchically. This manner of working allows the designers to move swiftly between individual elements, while categories for circumstantial information describe how different parts fit within the whole. At first, the modelling process focuses on specific qualities and appearances, then on joinery, and finally on integration into a full model.'[24] Through this design process the potential for fine craftsmanship re-emerges in architecture.

The Loblolly House gains its authenticity from the integration of space, structure and layered environmental systems. This house has been crafted from aluminium, timber, glass and polycarbonate. Yet it has a kinship with Arts and Crafts homes designed by Greene & Greene in its exposed structural elements and an acceptance of the material qualities by the architects. Loblolly House is not a slick superproduct of surface architecture and it is more interesting as a result. The architects are searching for substance and not a surface style in their architecture.[25] Meaningful architecture is the result of craft, care, skill and resourcefulness, in essence the intelligent and reflective practice of architecture. This is available to humankind today as much as in any era of civilisation.

The aluminium frame of the Loblolly House is expressed internally by KieranTimberlake. © Peter Aaron/Esto.

Digital Models and Prototypes

Although digital architecture has led to a return of interest in fabrication and making rather than just the virtual, the optimisation of designs and structures has become a rare quality. Rather than informing potential architecture by the tectonic means of production, some architects appear to believe if it can be digitally modelled it can and should be built. In my view, too many form-led projects are let down by the poor quality of the detailing. In some cases this is the unthinking pursuit of a rule-based architecture and in others joining of components has not been conceived as part of the architecture. In my experience, the prototype is the key feedback loop informing both the design outcomes and critically the quality of construction.

In making architecture it is of vital importance to fully engage with the spatial and tectonic potential of a project. Thus physical and digital modelling are central to the design process in my work as an architect. The first digital model of East Croydon Station was produced in 1989 to further our understanding of this 55-metre (180.5 foot) clear span structure, conceived as a sheltered public square that facilitates the interchange between different modes of transport. In the mid-1990s, when my practice committed to full digital production of all project information, we also emphasised physical modelling creating a flip-flop between the digital and physical. The physical models of Blains Fine Art Gallery are essentially the same as models produced in a studio of a school of architecture except that each option was costed for our client. Sverre Fehn is reported to have taken to drawing at 1:1 as a response to the use of computers in his practice. Fjeld suggests that after the introduction of drawing with computers 'some of the immediacy of his working method was perhaps modified, and to compensate he drew in a 1:1 scale on his old office blackboard'.[26] The tools selected to design with are key, the methods selected effect the outcome. I am concerned that many parametrically designed projects look the same. The

potential manipulation within the software is leading to a certain type of form rather than an inventive architecture. I think that it is the flip-flop from the digital to the physical that is key, the castings of Regional Rail, designed and developed by my practice, were rapid prototyped at 1 to 1 in the office simply with hand-cut foam core. Within the context of the carefully digitally modelled data of Ballingdon Bridge,[27] the bespoke bollards for this project were prototyped at 1 to 1 in paper and demonstrated to the client on site.

Digital Craft of Architecture

Can the digital design of architecture be considered a craft, even if there is no haptic element beyond the lowing of keys and the clicking of mice? Does the notion of craft depend on the thinking hand, to use Juhani Pallasmaa's eloquent term?[28] It is clear that the origin of craft is dependent on manual dexterity, but it is also generated by a desire to communicate cultural ideas.

Neil MacGregor, director of the British Museum, in *A History of the World in 100 Objects*, which he curated for BBC Radio 4, asked at the beginning of the series the compelling question about humankind some 50,000 years ago: 'Why does man the toolmaker everywhere turn into man the artist?'[29] The object under consideration is a sculpture of swimming reindeer carved from mammoth tusk, found at Montastruc, central France, and made around 13,000 years ago. It is the oldest piece of art in a British museum. MacGregor observes: 'In execution as well as in conception, this is a very complex work of art. And it seems to me that it has all the qualities of precise observation and interpretation that you'd look for in any great artist.'[30] The thinking hand is thus an ancient tradition. Professor Steven Mithen postulates, 'something, between say 100,000 and 50,000 years ago, happens in the human brain, that allows this fantastic creativity, imagination, artistic abilities, to emerge'.[31] Whereas Rowan Williams, Archbishop of Canterbury, observes of the two reindeer: 'You can feel that here's somebody making this, who was projecting themselves with huge imaginative generosity into the world around, and saw and felt in their bones that rhythm.'[32]

Clearly digital design is a much younger tradition. The development of computers has had a transforming effect on the architectural profession. In *Digital Fabricators*,[33] I observed 'the landscape of every architect's office has changed over the past 20 years, gone is the gentle squeak of Rotring pen on Mylar or tracing paper to be replaced by the hum of computers and the intense clicking of mice'. It is only possible in this chapter to sketch a brief history of the development of computing. However, it is interesting to note that at the Royal Observatory in Greenwich, London, in the 19th century, the young women who calculated the movement of the stars were described as computers.[34] The origins of modern computing probably lie in the Second World War code-breakers at Bletchley, England. ENIAC is considered to be one of the first reprogrammable electronic computers. Conceived and designed by John Presper Eckert and John William Mauchly, it was unveiled at the University of Pennsylvania, Philadelphia, on 14 February 1946. By the 1960s the mainframe computer was a familiar tool within the scientific community and, reviewing research being undertaken by MIT, Donald F Walker writing in the *New Scientist*, 12 November 1964, in an article entitled 'How the Computer Can Help the Designer' includes the reassuring comment: 'but the draughtsman's job is not in jeopardy yet.' It is pertinent to note that the introduction of AutoCAD in 1982 had a much swifter and more pervasive impact when compared to the introduction of the rapid-prototyping technique – stereolithography – in 1988. Nick Callicott in *Computer-Aided Manufacture in Architecture – The Pursuit of Novelty: Changing the Craft of Design* provides a history of the development of computer-aided manufacture: 'The 1950s was to see a period of concentrated development in the emerging field of computer controlled machine tools, predominantly within the United States.'[35] He observes that just like the development of interchangeable manufacturing in the mid-19th century for the production of rifles, 'the impetus and financial backing in the development of computer control once again came from the US military'.[36] The first decade of the 21st century has witnessed the dramatic uptake of digital manufacturing in contemporary architecture continuing the honourable tradition of beating swords into ploughshares.

In *The Craftsman*, Richard Sennett suggests that 'all craftsmanship is founded on skill developed to a high degree'.[37] He continues, 'by one commonly used measure, about ten thousand hours of experience are required to produce a master craftsman or musician'.[38] This definition of craft and craftsmanship has no explicit haptic component and he proposes that the open source development of Linux software should be considered 'a public craft'.[39] Thus Sennett appears to be clearly validating the notion of digital craft, a craft built of zeros and ones, the building blocks of all contemporary computer code.

However, Sennett specifically cites digital design as an example of the unthinking use of technology and the opposite of a craft tradition. His opening statement demonstrates how little he truly knows of contemporary architecture: 'CAD (computer-assisted design), the software program that allows engineers to design physical objects and architects to generate images of buildings on-screen.'[40] The suggested object and image separation between engineers and architects is at best a gross exaggeration of the worst of contemporary practice in the creation of the built environment. The best of contemporary architecture is a close collaboration between architects, engineers and industry often facilitated by a wide range of software.

Sennett suggests that, 'computer-assisted design poses particular dangers for thinking about buildings'.[41] However, his sole example of this dilemma is Georgia's Peachtree Center, a commercial development in Atlanta. His criticism of the poverty of much of contemporary commercial architecture may be valid; nonetheless this does not serve as a valid criticism of the use of digital design. It is as if one were to judge the literary output of the first decade of the 21st century on the basis of British red-topped tabloid newspapers. He also asserts that CAD provides 'instant modelling',[42] again a clear misunderstanding of the skill needed to use these tools wisely. I agree with his suggestion that 'computer-assisted design serves as an emblem of a large challenge faced by modern society: how to think like craftsmen in making good use of technology'.[43] The relationship between humankind and the technology we have invented is in my opinion more clearly addressed in Andrew Feenberg's book *Questioning Technology*.[44] He advocates the democratic rationalisation of technology, in part by the public participation in technical realms.

In *The Thinking Hand*, Juhani Pallasmaa laments the passing of the gentle craft of drawing by hand from architects' offices.

> While drawing, a mature designer and architect is not focused on the lines of the drawing, as he is envisioning the object itself, and in his mind holding the object in his hand or occupying the space being designed. During the design process, the architect occupies the very structure that the drawings represent. As a consequence of the mental transfer from the actuality of the drawing or the model to the reality of the project, the images with which the designer advances are not mere visual renderings; they constitute fully haptic and multi-sensory reality of imagination. The architect moves about freely in the imagined structure, however large and complex it may be, as if walking in a building and touching all its surfaces and sensing their materiality and texture. This is an intimacy that is surely difficult, if not impossible, to simulate through computer-aided means of modelling and simulation.[45]

At the University of Nottingham, Stephen Townsend's thesis project 'Digital Intimacy', addresses Pallasmaa's concern directly. However, this was not his primary intention. Rather, his design creates an interactive environment aimed at children with autism, providing sensory stimulation to assist with intervention methods and aid interaction with other children through shared kinesthetic experience. Throughout the development of this thesis, Townsend explored ideas of intimacy, interaction and multi-sensory experience. He conceptualised: 'Architecture as an interface and physical space has been fused with digital media in order to stimulate the imagination of inhabitants and foster a level of intimacy.'[46]

The key mechanical
components of Stephen
Townsend's prototype of
'Digital Intimacy', an immersive
learning environment for autistic
children. © Stephen Townsend/
University of Nottingham.

The space is formed by an interactive hypersurface, a hybrid system merging the physical surface with digital information and kinetic transformations. The set of standard components creates a diverse range of spatial conditions forming a part-to-whole relationship in which the individual elements collectively produce emergent phenomena far greater than the sum of the parts. Each component may be designed and evaluated individually but its effect can only be fully understood by experiencing the system as a whole, therefore a full-scale prototype was fabricated. Components including the tri-plates were digitally modelled and rapid-prototyped on a 3D printer and then countercast in silicone, as they need to move as the system responds to stimuli. Other elements were laser-cut from acrylic. The core of this dynamic system is an information bus that contains a linear actuator. Townsend's approach was to develop the thesis 'through a full-scale prototype that was constructed to enable the experience of the qualities of the surface, both visual and tactile, and the observation of its use, including people's responses'.[47] His thesis was commended in the 2009 RIBA President's Silver Medal.

In part inspired by Pallasmaa's earlier book *The Eyes of the Skin*,[48] Townsend ably integrates responsive technology, demonstrating a rigorous understanding of electronic and mechanical engineering, and creating a digital ecology which aims to stimulate communication. His integration of design, making and thinking shows that the handcraft of drawing is only one mode of intimate engagement within the exploration of architecture.

One of Sennett's other concerns with CAD is an overdetermination of the outcome, leading in his view inevitably to lifeless architecture and poor-quality cityscapes. I believe this is a misunderstanding of the remote fabricators of architecture. There is a strong parallel between jazz and prefabrication. In the former, typically a standard (tune) is selected, a known typology in Aldo Rossi's terms, a figure that the audience would recognise. Each player in the band has a role and has rehearsed or prefabricated their contribution in relation to the tune and each other. Jazz is like any language; it provides the pattern of speech to which the musician provides his or her own meaning.

This is delightfully demonstrated by sixteen*(makers) in their Shelter 55/02, Kielder, Northumberland. This project is well described elsewhere[49] or you can read my review of it in *Building Design*.[50] A key quality of this project is the evident enjoyment in its making by Bob Sheil, Nick Callicott and sixteen*(makers). It also demonstrates their long-term investment in new modes of practice that embrace research and industry. As I observed in *Building Design*, it is unusual to visit a factory that is run by two alumni of the Bartlett, Nick Callicott and Kristina Ehlert. Callicott is Technical Director of Stahlbogen GmbH and a partner in sixteen*(makers). He is also an author and academic, he taught at the Bartlett and has swapped this field of operation for a factory.

The three-dimensional BIM of the shelter appears to be the core of sixteen*(makers)' collaborative process. Nick Callicott also considers:

the 3D model is central to the assembly of the piece as it enables us to model each individual component and to specify and control the relationship from each component to the next. That is important to me when I have to make relatively complex pieces that then have to meet so they can be welded together within the workshop itself. But of course it is even more important when you then subsequently take those pieces to site in the hope that you will actually be able to bolt them together and walls will line up. Although it's theoretically possible, I think it's possible to say that nobody using traditional 3D drawing methods, even using a CAD package, would be able to prepare a set of drawings which would enable this to be constructed in a realistic time span. The 3D model is also important not just in providing information that enables us to program machines, the 3D model also enables us to produce the other production information which is necessary for people in the workshop to make the part. It's a point often missed, often by the older generation. Once you have actually modelled something in 3D using one of these modern manufacturing packages, your 2D drawings by which I mean the plan, the section and elevation, can be produced almost automatically.[51]

For my review in *Building Design*, Callicott had to generate plans and sections that reflected the dynamic process of the design and fabrication of the shelter as a record of the built project, 'two dimensional drawings were only really produced in order for architects and the trade press to actually begin to analyse the building'.[52]

The composition that is Shelter 55/02 was rehearsed in Stahlbogen's workshop. As Callicott reports:

The shelter was completely assembled in Germany in our workshops. Up to a point one could say that's a luxury; many fabricators who work on complex steel structures don't have the opportunity to assemble sculptures beforehand in the workshop. It takes time and often because of scale issues is not possible. But because of the nature of Kielder as a building site, because it is relatively hostile, and also we would have very little access to any kind of machinery, we felt that was absolutely necessary.[53]

Despite the digitally driven off-site fabrication, there was still room for improvisation – he continues: 'Some design decisions were left very much to the last minute. Where seats went was something that was discussed only once the shelter was constructed.'[54]

Subsequently, the shelter has been scanned in three dimensions, and a print of the scan was exhibited at the 2010 Royal Academy Summer Exhibition. In essence this is a recording of the performance that can be best enjoyed in Kielder. I think a key quality of this shelter is the delightful human scale of the components which remain readable in the final architecture; the means of production remain articulated in the completed architecture. This stands in contrast to many works of surface architecture where the aspiration appears only to be to realise the infinitely thin digital surface of a computer model, where it is almost impossible for tectonic details to exist and the architecture may be compromised in realisation.

The parallel between jazz and prefabrication also holds true in the work of Philip Beesley, particularly his installations. This may not be the wellspring of his inspiration, which includes landscape and humankind's relationship to the land, the interaction of people and the Earth.[55]

In *Orpheus Filter*, the organisational structure is a non-repeating Penrose tessellation. The figuration is flexible and rigid connectors create a language articulated through materials and prefabricated components, again all characteristics shared with jazz music. Skill, commitment and inventiveness are required to make great jazz. Within his installations Beesley demonstrates all of these qualities. It is his knowledge of materials and how they will perform in space that creates the improvisation, even before any active interactive technology is introduced. *Orpheus Filter*, unlike later works including *Orgone Reef* and *Hylozoic Soil*, was responsive to its environment only through its component parts.

The *Epithelium* installations by Beesley demonstrate a thread of improvisation in process and in detail. They underwent much variation in the hands of students exploring their own interpretations. He observes: 'Some of that resulted in quite homogeneous, rigid arrays, while at the same time certain inventions were enormously provocative and have opened up new ways of working.'[56] An example of this is a more highly tuned approach to proximity detection sensors, integrated within new generations of meshwork that use silicone joints, providing great resiliency and allowing for a lot of distortion. The silicone works in ways akin to cartilage, as an interface that is quite distinct from the rigidly polarised simulations of 'tension' and 'compression' in structural models. Elasticity in those joints and pads allows the components to alternate in their forces, carrying tension and compression depending on load-shedding patterns running within the meshwork. Arrays of proximity sensors fitted into that meshwork are configured to interpret the actions of occupants in varying ways, for example in convulsive rapid retreat, detecting fast approaches, or alternately in relaxed repose, detecting slow approaches. Philip suggests 'these "intelligent" patterns contribute to a general stance of "ambivalence" in the designed fabric'.[57]

Philip Beesley asks:

… can BIM tools accommodate ambivalence, or is that kind of quality still seen only as a negative one, implying indecision and inefficiency? I would like to pursue a next generation of BIM tools that readily accommodate ambiguity, as a virtue that yields great flexibility. I think deliberate support for ambivalence and ambiguity within software design simulation tools could permit full-blooded improvisation for designers, akin to jazz musicians. This could support potent innovation paths for designers.[58]

In this chapter the link between thinking and making has been explored, suggesting that a haptic past is essential and that drawing, sketching and making by hand should be an essential part of every architecture student's education. However, once learnt, issues such as scale can be explored completely digitally. Although a totally cerebral digital crafting of architecture is possible, in this process the prototype becomes an even more important tool. A flip-flop from the digital to the physical and back again stimulates thinking about design, the rigorous thinking through of architecture. In my view the externalisation of ideas, communicating with oneself and others in an architectural conversation, is more important than the means of drawing or making. This suggests that the integration of making into the design process is of key importance and more important than whether or not haptic means are used. We draw to make and make to draw.

Notes

1 *Oxford English Dictionary*, 1996 edition.
2 *Oxford English Dictionary*, 1996 edition.
3 In too many contemporary architectural texts innovation is used when invention is a more appropriate description.
4 Recorded in PO Fjeld, Sverre Fehn, *The Patterns of Thoughts*, Monacelli Press (New York), 2009, p 172.
5 S Fehn, in the foreword to *Knut Knutsen*, B Espen Knutsen and AS Tvedten (eds), trans. Kristian Bjerre, Gyldendal (Oslo), 1982.
6 Peter Rice, *An Engineer Imagines*, Artemis (London), 1994, p 107.
7 Ibid.
8 P Buchanan, *Renzo Piano Building Workshop: Complete Works*, vol 1, Phaidon (London), 1993, p 112.
9 Massimo Dini, *Renzo Piano Projects and Buildings 1964–1983*, Electra/Rizzoli (New York), 1984, p 74.
10 P. Buchanan, p 112.
11 Buchanan records that many contemporary critics observed that Renzo Piano's buildings 'were mere assemblies [of components] rather than real architecture'. Ibid, p 113.
12 The software SketchUp is the fast food of architectural design, with all the tasteless disappointments of fast food, and it seems to contain the same level of transfats: it leads to intellectual obesity. In my experience, the short cut of SketchUp takes longer than a more appropriate technique, be this a rigorous physical model or a digital one.
13 C St John Wilson, *The Other Tradition of Modern Architecture: The Uncompleted Project*, Black Dog (London), 2007, p 94.
14 J Pallasmaa, *The Thinking Hand*, John Wiley & Sons (Chichester), 2009, p 60.
15 P Cook, *Drawing: The Motive Force of Architecture*, John Wiley & Sons (Chichester), 2008, p 12.
16 Ibid.
17 PO Fjeld, Sverre Fehn, *The Patterns of Thoughts*, Monacelli Press (New York), 2009, p 99.
18 Ibid.
19 Ibid, p 104.
20 Ibid, p 99.
21 In the recent global economic crisis triggered by subprime mortgages, it seems pertinent to note that the failing North American car industry was not repurposed to manufacture affordable homes.
22 S Kieran and J Timberlake, *Refabricating Architecture*, McGraw-Hill (New York), 2003, p 173.
23 For more information on the Loblolly House and other architecture case studies prepared by the author see the website The Future Builds with Aluminium, http://greenbuilding.world-aluminium.org/
24 S Kieran, J Timberlake (eds), *Loblolly House: Elements of a New Architecture*, Princeton Architectural Press (New York), 2008, p 55.
25 M Stacey, 'Introduction, Loblolly House: A Situated Domestic Ecology', S Kieran, J Timberlake (eds), *Loblolly House: Elements of a New Architecture*, Princeton Architectural Press (New York), 2008, p 13.
26 Ibid, p 209.
27 See M Stacey, 'Searching For Excellence: Ballingdon Bridge', *arq*, vol 11, no 3/4, Cambridge University Press (Cambridge), 2007, pp 210–22.

28 J Pallasmaa, *The Thinking Hand*, John Wiley & Sons (Chichester), 2009.
29 www.bbc.co.uk/ahistoryoftheworld/about/transcripts/episode4/ accessed July 2010, now also available in book form, N MacGregor, *A History of the World in 100 Objects*, Penguin Books (London), 2010, pp 19–25.
30 Ibid.
31 Ibid.
32 Ibid.
33 M Stacey, *Digital Fabricators*, Waterloo University Press (Waterloo, Ontario), 2004.
34 R Harbison, 'Royal Observatory', *Architecture Today*, June 07, p 38.
35 N Callicott, *Computer-Aided Manufacture in Architecture – The Pursuit of Novelty: Changing the Craft of Design*, Butterworth (Oxford), 2001, p 46.
36 Ibid.
37 R Sennett, *The Craftsman*, Penguin Books (London), 2009, p 20.
38 Ibid.
39 Ibid, p 24.
40 Ibid, p 39.
41 Ibid, p 41.
42 Ibid, p 39.
43 Ibid, p 44.
44 A Feenberg, *Questioning Technology*, Routledge (London and New York), 1999.
45 Pallasmaa, *The Thinking Hand*, p 59.
46 S Townsend, 'Digital Intimacy', unpublished Special Emphasis study at the University of Nottingham, 2009.
47 S Townsend, 'Digital Intimacy' – Student's Statement RIBA President's Medal www.presidentsmedals.com/Project_Details.aspx?id=2424 accessed July 2010.
48 J Pallasmaa, *The Eyes of the Skin*, John Wiley & Sons (Chichester), 2005.
49 *55/02*, a sixteen*(makers)' project monograph, Riverside Architectural Press (Cambridge, Ontario), 2011.
50 M Stacey, 'Tectonics: Steel Folding into the Landscape', *Building Design*, August 2009, pp 19–20.
51 Transcript of Bob Sheil and Nick Callicott's lecture in the *Making Architecture* series, 30 March 2010, at the University of Nottingham.
52 Ibid.
53 Ibid.
54 Ibid.
55 M Stacey, 'From Flat Stock to Three-Dimensional Immersion', P Beesley (ed), *Hylozoic Soil: Monograph on the Work of Philip Beesley*, Riverside Architectural Press (Cambridge, Ontario), 2007.
56 Via email with author July 2010.
57 Ibid.
58 Ibid.

R-O-B
Towards a Bespoke Building Process

Tobias Bonwetsch, Fabio Gramazio and Matthias Kohler

The term robot has its origins in the Slavonic word *robota* and is associated with notions of work and servitude. It was coined in 1920 by Karel Capek in his play *RUR (Rossum's Universal Robots)*, which envisions a futuristic factory that assembles artificial people to carry out menial tasks. The subsequent association with repetitious, precise, nonspontaneous and nonvariant acts, became a defining image of automation in the 20th century. At the Institute for Technology in Architecture at the Faculty of Architecture at ETH Zurich, the work of architects and researchers Gramazio and Kohler dissolves this myth. There, programmable automation is approached as a composed digital score where the actions of commonly available robotic industrial arms are animated and choreographed to perform acts of sublime dexterity and meticulous craft.

Housed in a modified freight container, R-O-B is a robotic fabrication concept that enables the flexible production of architectural building elements. It combines the advantages of prefabrication – precision and consistent high quality – with the advantages of short transport routes and just-in-time production on the building site (Figure 1).

R-O-B also signifies a substantial shift for conventions of architectural design and architectural production. Although robots were conceived as highly flexible machines and have been around for half a century, they ordinarily perform precise repetitive tasks. This is especially true for industrial robots that are deployed to standardise and control complex production processes. However, by adopting robotic tooling as a means to facilitate nonstandard routines, this restriction is subverted and robotic assembly becomes a very different concept for the designer. Flexibility inherent in the machine is empowered through its programmability enabling the architect to manipulate and control the building process.

Moreover, R-O-B, and industrial robots in general, significantly expand the option for intervention in the fabrication process and thereby the scope of design. In contrast to common CNC machines specialised to perform a predefined task, R-O-B is a generic tool. It not only allows for the control of its movements, but also enables its user to define the material manipulation processes itself.

R-O-B allows the architect to control where to work, what material to apply and how to manipulate and assemble it. In consequence, the understanding of construction as an integral part of architectural design takes on greater significance. R-O-B thus continues and extends the tradition of constructive thinking in architecture.

Fig 1: The mobile fabrication unit R-O-B working from a flatbed truck trailer.
© Gramazio & Kohler, ETH Zurich.

1. Robotics in Architecture and Construction

Automating on-site building processes has been a field of research over the last 30 years. To date, over 200 different prototypes of robotic solutions have been developed especially for the construction industry and tested on building sites.[1] It is quite astonishing that despite this sustained effort, few of these developments have become established in the industry or passed prototypical stage.[2] Perhaps one reason for this is how the introduction of robots was largely channelled through manufacturing industries in order to substitute manual craft, raise the pace of standardisation and manage profit. Robots were predominantly regarded as advanced manufacturing and construction tools rather than programmable design tools, and thus their flexible potential was not focused at designers. Today, accompanied by changing technical and economic conditions, and a different conceptual approach, there are signs of this being overturned.

Although the concept of automation dates back to ancient Greece, the term 'robot' was first coined in 1922 by the science fiction author Karel Capek. Later, in the 1940s, another author of science fiction, Isaac Asimov, laid out the field of robotics in his writing. His view of the robot as a benevolent machine, put into the world to serve humankind and ease man's daily struggle, might be regarded as the inspiration for a scientific impetus for the field of robotics outside science fiction, for it became a popular goal to conceive of machines for specific tasks to replace in early robotic development manual labour, particularly labour that was hazardous, hard and exhausting.

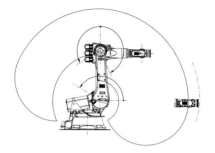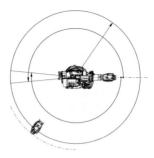

Fig 2: Diagram of a customary industrial robot. © Gramazio & Kohler, ETH Zurich.

Industrial robots are generally defined as automatically controlled, reprogrammable, multipurpose manipulators programmable in three or more axes.[3] It was George Devol who handed in a patent for a programmable manipulator in 1954. His company, Unimation, developed the first industrial robot that went to work for General Motors in 1961, extracting and separating parts of a die-casting machine. Soon after, Ford Motor Company applied the Unimate to spot welding, which became a primary application for robots as these jobs were particularly exhausting and hazardous for workers.[4]

In their limitation to perform only simple recurring operations, industrial robots of the 1950s and 1960s were nowhere near as sophisticated as the humanoid robots envisioned by Capek and Asimov. And, although future generations of industrial robots evolved their capability, mainly with regards to mechatronics, their assignments to perform repetitive recurring operations within industrial automation processes remained the same.

Following Victor Scheinman's so-called 'Stanford Arm' in 1969, the robotic arm as we know it today was substantially developed by industry in the 1970s (Figure 2). ASEA presented the IRB-6, a robotic arm with six degrees of freedom controlled by a standard computer, in 1973. This was the first microcomputer-controlled all-electric industrial robot that allowed continuous path motion. KUKA followed with their FAMULUS model in the same year[5] and by the mid-1980s such tools were a common industrial resource, flourishing under the economic boom of the Japanese automotive sector in the latter half of the decade.

This period also marks the beginning of primary developments on robotics and automation in the building industry[6] where research and development was also led by Japanese companies and universities. Here, focus was mainly directed on the development of new robotic systems as well as the automation of existing machinery. Robots were conceived to perform specialised tasks such as spraying, smoothing concrete, distributing materials, fitting equipment to ceilings, assembling formwork, installing facades, painting and many more.[7] In 1990, the Shimizu Construction Company prototyped and launched an automated high-rise construction site; in effect an automated on-site factory capable of building one floor after another in a vertical ascension. Kajima and Maeda among others followed and developed systems known as SMART, ABCS and AMURAD, largely concentrating on the automated assembly of premanufactured building elements.[8]

By inheriting many of its concepts on robotics and automation from manufacturing, the construction industry ignored its own unique structure and initially developed specialised machines engineered to fulfil one specific task or to automate the building process as a whole. Contrary to the industrial production of a high-performance mass-produced object such as the automobile, the construction industry is a project-based endeavour where every building is one of a kind, designed for a special purpose on a particular site, with a unique team who are charged with meeting a client's special demands.[9, 10] In addition, the construction industry, as it has evolved over many centuries, is mainly comprised of small to medium enterprises (SMEs) rather than large capital investment firms.[11]

Thus, applying robotics in construction largely concentrated on efficiency and focused on monetary gains through the use of machines to save labour, reduce costs and obtain a quality control in production. In addition, the introduction of highly specialised robotic systems was also limited by their unaffordability for many SMEs. Their inherent flexibility to adapt to different design situations or challenge designers was a capability beyond the scope of the industry to exploit.[12]

In addition, as Gassel and Maas argue, research and development on early construction industry robotics was primarily executed and led by process engineers. Architects and professional builders were not included at the development stage yet process engineers did not possess the specialist building knowledge required in construction and its direct relation to the architectural design process. Architecture is a highly complex practice and a good understanding of the work processes is essential for the successful construction of buildings. The implicit knowledge required by the architect and the builder on the sequence, assembly and connection of elements is a vital ingredient.[13]

It is a paradox that as robots were initially conceived to replace human labour and in particular the dexterity of the human arm[14] – with its inherent flexibility and usefulness to control a multitude of different tools – such potent machines were constrained to perform repetitive single tasks. Sadly, one reason might be that extensive deskilling of the labour force had already been in place by the time of their arrival, where mainly unskilled workers performed only a limited number of simple tasks. Hence, the skill set demanded of the robot was limited to the same operations and the flexibility and potential of both machine and the worker, who in the past would have been more variously skilled, was neglected.

2. Conceptual Turn

For robots to successfully prevail in the building industry and thus become relevant to architectural design, a new conceptual approach is urgently required that differs from the endeavours of the past and unleashes systematic flexibility.[15] In this approach, the robot is no longer merely a mechanical subworker, aiming to make construction faster and cheaper, but an agent that opens completely new potential within architectural design, realising structures and building elements that would not be possible to conceive otherwise.

In contrast to the use of robotics in construction during the 1990s, this conceptual approach is framed by changing surrounding circumstances. Firstly, performance-to-cost ratio of computer components has improved drastically, and robot manufacturers

today integrate off-the-shelf personal computer technology in their controllers as well as in programming and control software. Information technology has also entered the everyday domain of architects, where practice in computer-aided architectural design and computer-aided manufacturing have become mainstream skills, and thus allow for a seamless connection between design data and fabrication data. This enables the direct control of the production machines, allowing for differentiated designs in an automated process. Furthermore, as worldwide installation of industrial robots has doubled and prices have decreased by more than half, the SMEs that constitute the majority of the building industry can now afford to invest. In other words, industrial robots and the means to control them are on the verge of becoming a public domain.

Potential for architectural design offered by such technology is determined by two main factors. On the one hand, control software plays a crucial role. As with other computer numerically controlled (CNC) machines, robots enable the manufacture of objects directly from their digital description, and therefore allow the designer an in-depth engagement with the manufacturing process and a high differentiation or nonstandard project-specific fabrication can easily be realised. Due to the enormous computational power available to us today, these objects can be permeated with information.[16] Material is combined with data, creating a richness of detail, which in its logic expresses the possibilities of the computer. This digital materiality is a direct consequence of the changing production conditions of architecture.[17]

On the other hand, in addition to digital control, industrial robots substantially expand the option for a physical intervention in the fabrication process and thereby the scope of design. Unlike common CNC machines that are specialised on a single manufacturing operation (for example, milling, laser cutting), the action and actual processing of material performed by an industrial robot is not predefined. In essence, it offers a generic arm that can reach any position in space in accordance to its kinematic range. The arm can be

opposite: Fig 3: Transportation of R-O-B to the grounds of the Venice Biennale. © Gramazio & Kohler, ETH Zurich.

left: Fig 4: R-O-B prefabricating brick wall elements on site in front of the Swiss Pavilion. © Gramazio & Kohler, ETH Zurich.

combined with any given end effector, which defines the physical material manipulation. The definition of these end effectors can be highly specific and unique for a particular project and thereby become part of the overall design process.

Due to this flexibility in programming, and in defining the actual fabrication process, specific constructive systems can be realised, applying a multitude of different materials. The integration of material processes and digital control techniques revives and extends the tradition of constructive thinking in architecture and gives evidence to a new culture of craft that combines the physical and the digital. Thereby, architectural design evolves into the interplay between conceptual intentions and the engineering of a fabrication process with its possibilities as well as its constraints.

3. R-O-B

The mobile fabrication unit R-O-B picks up on this conceptual approach. It respects the uniqueness of the building industry, while still benefiting from the advantages of automation that were driving forces and already present in earlier robotic developments for construction.

The generic set-up of R-O-B allows it to be applied to building processes at an architectural scale using various materials. In addition to the freedom given by its programmability and the freedom in choosing a specific fabrication process, R-O-B is liberated from a fixed production location. The unit consists of a customary industrial robot mounted on a linear axis and housed in a specially adapted freight container of standard size. As such R-O-B can cover a workspace big enough for architectural elements and can easily be transported directly on to the building site, where it can prefabricate highly precise elements on site or build directly *in situ* (Figures 3, 4, 5). This brings about both economic and ecological plus factors. Instead of complete building elements, only the raw material has to be brought on site, hence drastically reducing transport needs.

Fig 5: View of the completed installation 'Structural Oscillation' in the Swiss Pavilion at the Venice Biennale 2008. © Gramazio & Kohler, ETH Zurich.

Consequently, accommodating the regional nature of the building industry, local materials may be applied. Also, fabrication processes can be planned, implemented and tested off site and then be distributed on compatible robot units worldwide that produce with the same accuracy and quality. The production of building parts is synchronised to the progress of the building. Design and fabrication can therefore easily be adapted to unforeseen changes in the course of the construction process. Probably the most significant aspect of applying R-O-B is the ability to exploit the flexibility of the industrial robot in making use of its programmability. For once, there is a way for designers and builders to react to strategic changes while the fabrication process is already running, or even go as far as to change materials that may differ in dimensions and tolerances.

Furthermore, as the digital control of the machine allows the architect direct engagement with the fabrication process, automation is combined with an architectural culture in which design and construction are intrinsically tied to one another. Conceptual design and practical realisation are no longer sequential phases, as the data set that describes a formal shape is identical to the code of its making. The inherent knowledge of the architect to assemble and join discrete elements and material in order to accomplish a specific design intention is transformed into explicit commands for the robot. Programming the construction steps for an architectural element, design is now the explicit description of its making (Figure 6). Due to the ability of computers to manage and process a large volume of data, a 'digital description' can be highly specific and consist of a myriad different instructions that the robot can transform into precise physical actions. Additionally, by digitally formulating the description, the designer has the possibility to intervene in and possibly alter and tweak the fabrication process at each operational step.

Thereby, existing traditional construction methods can be converted into digital processes. In making them explicit and combining them with the computational power available to us today, as well as applying a robot that can perform an arbitrary number of highly precise movements and material manipulations, these processes can be

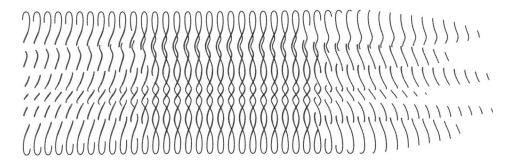

top: Fig 6: Explicit description of the 'Pike Loop' project, defining the position and orientation of each brick. © Gramazio & Kohler, ETH Zurich.

above: Fig 7: Student project 'The Sequential Wall'. Stacked wooden battens form a constructive system that merges functional properties (load-bearing, weatherproofing, isolation) with an ornamental expression. © Gramazio & Kohler, ETH Zurich.

Fig 8: R-O-B constructing the installation 'Pike Loop' directly *in situ*, New York, 2009.
© Gramazio & Kohler, ETH Zurich.

transformed and reimagined. Manual operations are not simply imitated and automated, but are enhanced by the logic and the specific characteristics of the machine. Explicitly controlling the construction process, functional aspects can be synthetically integrated into a building element, while at the same time the boundaries between structural order and ornamental expression are blurred (see Figure 7). Contrary to former engineering solutions for robotics in construction, the concept of R-O-B does not limit but expands the architectural possibilities. Its artefacts are the creative amalgam of robotic processes, material manipulation and control software.

4. Conclusion

R-O-B demonstrates a radically different approach to robotics than that applied in industrial manufacturing. By using the robot not only as a means for automation but as a design tool, the goal is to engineer not a perfect and widely applicable fabrication process but a unique one. The process of making remains a combination of several factors each specific in itself: a chosen material, the tool manipulating it and the design data controlling the tool and thus the process as a whole. Their combination is unique to a specific project and even more to the author of the process defining each factor. In the synthesis of these factors, an architectural design solution emerges which embraces architectural diversity. Thus buildings may remain singularities, prototypes designed for a specific context, each having a specific site, client and programme. There is a great diversity of architectural solutions and crafts involved, where robotic solutions may enable adaptive building processes and enrich the spectrum of constructive and architectural solutions (Figure 8). Thus it can be said that through flexible and adaptive robotics, construction processes and material manipulation not geometry, are the drivers of design. In this manner, innovative architecture may be developed as an interplay of the custom engineering and controlling of fabrication processes and, more importantly, specific design intentions.

Notes

1 This number includes various mechatronic devices from completely autonomously working machines to teleoperated apparatus. Also, not all perform tasks that are stringently necessary for construction, as for instance painting (Bock 2008; Howe 2000).

2 C Balaguer and M Abderrahim (eds), *Robotics and Automation in Construction*, In-Teh (Vienna), 2008.

3 ISO Standard 8373, *Manipulating Industrial Robots – Vocabulary*, 1994.

4 JF Engelberger, 'Historical Perspective and Role in Automation', in Shimon Y Nof, *Handbook of Industrial Robotics*, John Wiley & Sons, Inc (New York), 2nd edition, 2007, pp 3–10.

5 M Hägele, K Nilsson et al, 'Industrial Robotics', in B Siciliano and O Khatib (eds), *Springer Handbook of Robotics*, Springer Verlag (Berlin and Heidelberg), 2008, pp 963–86.

6 A Warszawski and R Navon, 'Implementation of Robotics in Building: Current Status and Future Prospects', *Journal of Construction Engineering and Management*, 1998, 124(1), pp 31–41.

7 T Bock, 'Construction Automation and Robotics', in C Balaguer and M Abderrahim (eds), *Robotics and Automation in Construction*, pp 21–42.

8 AS Howe, 'Designing for Automated Construction', *Automation in Construction*, 2000, 9(3), pp 259–76.

9 S Groák, *The Idea of Building: Thought and Action in the Design and Production of Buildings*, E & FN Spon (London), 1992.

10 R Harris and M Buzzelli, 'House Building in the Machine Age, 1920s–1970s: Realities and Perceptions of Modernisation in North America and Australia', *Business History*, 2005, 47(1), pp 59–85.

11 J Barlow and R Ozaki, 'Achieving "Customer Focus" in Private Housebuilding: Current Practice and Lessons from Other Industries', *Housing Studies*, 18, 2003, pp 87–101.

12 S Obayashi, *Current Status of Automation and Robotics in Construction in Japan*, 9th International Symposium, Automation and Robotics in Construction, Tokyo, 1992.

13 Fv Gassel and G Maas, 'Mechanising, Robotising and Automating Construction Processes', in C Balaguer and M Abderrahim (eds), *Robotics and Automation in Construction*, In-Teh (Vienna), 2008, pp 43–52.

14 From the beginning, the human arm with a weight-to-load ratio of 1:1 was considered the ultimate benchmark in a primary research target to reduce the mass and inertia of robot structures. This goal was met in 2006 with the lightweight robot from the company KUKA (Hägele, Nilsson et al 2008).

15 Applying robots for nonstandard manufacturing remains surprisingly unusual, even in industries outside construction. But for the building industry, with its unique structure as outlined above, this is a necessity in order to be able to establish robotic processes at all.

16 A Picon, 'Architecture and the Virtual : Towards a New Materiality?', *Praxis: Journal of Writing + Building*, 6, 2004, pp 114–21.

17 F Gramazio and M Kohler, *Digital Materiality in Architecture*, Lars Müller Publishers (Baden), 2008.

The Matter of *Pochoir* and the Imaging of the Maison de Verre

Mary Vaughan Johnson (Association de la Maison de Verre, Paris, France)

The originality of 31 rue Saint-Guillaume, Paris 75007, and the portfolios of its designers, continue to provide a fertile resource for enquiry into cultural, historical and disciplinary practices. As a collaboration, the Maison de Verre (1928–32) by Pierre Chareau, Bernard Bijvoet and Louis Dalbet is not only a physical prototype, but an experiment in the relationship between design and making, the designer and the maker. Here, resident scholar Mary Vaughan Johnson argues for a reinterpretation of Chareau's contribution to the building's extraordinary interior, by examining his work as an architectural collage of representational and physical design.

In this chapter I propose an examination of *pochoir*, a technique of representing architectural interiors that originated in traditional Japanese stencil art and was adopted by French *artistes décorateurs*, or *ensembliers* during the Art Deco movement in the 1920s. I will argue that there are underlying phenomenological similarities between the technique of *pochoir* – with its inherent quality resulting from a labour-intensive process that occupied an ambiguous place, being neither entirely the result of mechanical reproduction nor entirely a handmade product, but a combination of both – and the making of the Maison de Verre (1928–32) designed by Pierre Chareau (1883–1950). Chareau, trained as an *ensemblier*, frequently participated in the *Salon des Artistes Décorateurs* and was an active member of the Société des Artistes Décorateurs. It is my contention that Pierre Chareau's experience in the making of the *pochoir* embodied a particular *habitus* that makes itself visible in the Maison de Verre.

Introduction to the History and Technique of *Pochoir*

The term *pochoir* is a French word meaning, stencil. Although tradition in stencilled, or *pochoir* prints had long existed in the West since the 14th century, its adaptation in the 1920s by French *artistes décorateurs*, or *ensembliers* was nurtured by the Japanese stencilling tradition known as *katagami* used on silk textile.[1] Its simple colourful motifs from nature had a particular appeal to the Art Nouveau and the later Art Deco movements that emerged out of a desire by *artistes décorateurs* to re-establish themselves during the latter half of the 19th century when the French decorative arts had settled into a period of pastiche and imitation of historical styles mass-produced by new industrial technologies, which had led to a decline of quality standards that had, in previous centuries, established France's leadership in luxury goods.[2]

Notch in the sliding wall allowing it to pass the handrail at the top of the grand stair into the main living room of the Maison de Verre. © Mark E Lyon.

PLANCHE XV

Premier état. — Démonstration du dé-
gradé.
(Voir pages 63 et 64.)

Illustrations showing
technique of *pochoir*
from Jean Saudé's
*Traité d'enluminure
d'art au pochoir*
(L'Ibis, Paris, 1925).
© Mark E Lyon.

Art Nouveau, a late 19th-century movement built upon applied Japanese art, is a term coined by one of its great pioneers in Paris, Siegfried 'Samuel' Bing. Bing was an established art dealer in Japanese art objects and promoter of Japonisme, a movement that came to its culmination with his publication of *Le Japon Artistique*, a monthly periodical lasting from mid-1888 until 1891 that was written in three languages, French, German and English, with the intention of educating the European and American public on the art and culture of Japan.[3] According to Bing, in its search for originality Art Nouveau, which focused on the decorative arts, was conceived not in order to sever all associations with the past but rather to resurrect the spirit that had inspired authors of former great art, thereby condemning their immediate predecessors for 'servilely' copying its forms.[4] In support of those 'young spirits anxious to manifest their modern tendencies', Bing, while insisting that no definite style be prescribed, had two guiding rules for the selection of work he sponsored, 'Each article to be strictly adapted to its proper purpose; harmonies to be sought for in lines and colors.'[5]

As Nancy Troy points out, it was the threat of competition from the German designs coming out of the Werkbund, which by 1907 had succeeded in bringing together design teams of artists and manufacturers to collaborate and create complete 'ensembles',

ANDRÉ-MORISSET.

wherein each part was in harmony with the whole, that was the driving force behind the development of the decorative arts in France, culminating with the ensembles displayed at the *Exposition Internationale des Arts Décoratifs et Industriel Modernes* in 1925.[6]

The Art Deco movement, a name given to the 'modern' style that came to prominence in the interwar years, while using the same underlying principle as that of Art Nouveau in its desire to be both decorative and functional, felt that the excessive ornamentation of the organic Art Nouveau was threatening this very principle and was, at the same time, not conducive to the new technologies of production being introduced by the industrial revolution. The elements borrowed by Art Deco from the Japanese applied art were therefore used with the intent to reconcile tradition and modernity so that rather than being limited to direct borrowings such as the familiar materials, techniques, forms and motifs prevalent in Art Nouveau, there were also 'indirect borrowings' related to its concepts and principles such as those found in the technique of *pochoir*.[7]

The appeal of *pochoir* for the *artiste décorateur* was therefore not only its simplicity in form and its ability to faithfully reproduce the selected colours of the interior's ensemble, but also its tactile and opulent quality placed by the individual hands of the artisan, using a special ferrule and pompom-like brush for each colour, on to the carefully positioned

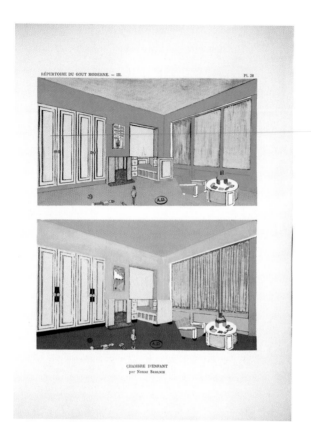

left: Typical *pochoir* from the *Répertoire du goût moderne* (A Lévy, Paris, 1928). © Mark E Lyon.

opposite: *Pochoir* by Pierre Chareau in Jean Badovici and Émile Ruhlmann's *'Harmonies': Intérieurs de Ruhlmann* (A Morancé, Paris, 1924). © Mark E Lyon.

and high crafted zinc stencil in layers that evoked an almost tangible depth, giving each print its uniqueness albeit produced in multiples. While the flatness of the colour appealed to the prevailing concept of abstraction, the line drawing enhanced by the technique of *pochoir* revealed its constructive qualities and therefore played a part in creating harmonies between line and volume. In 1925, with the publication of Jean Saudé's *Traité d'enluminure d'art au pochoir* (Treatise on the art of illumination using stencil), the *pochoir* technique was raised to an art form, advocating a return to the apprenticeship system in order to properly educate artisans.[8] Despite its emergence in the midst of a world where mass-produced paper and chemical inks, machine binding and mechanised lithograph processes were becoming commonplace, the labour-intensive technique of *pochoir* flourished as it seemed to provide the desired link between traditional artisanship and modern industry so essential to the *artistes décorateurs*, or *ensembliers*.

Pierre Chareau (1883–1950) as an *Ensemblier*

Not much is known of Pierre Chareau's education except for the little we know from his wife, Louise 'Dollie' Dyte, who met her husband when he was just 16 years old (she was 19); they were married five years later. Chareau was born in Bordeaux and moved to Paris when his father, a wine merchant, lost his business and went to Paris to work on the railway. As was typical of this time, Chareau learnt his *métier* on the job. His apprenticeship began

INTÉRIEURS FRANÇAIS
PIERRE CHAREAU
SALLE A MANGER

Éditions Albert Morancé
Copyright 1924

in 1908 and ended 1914; he worked as a draughtsman for the decoration department in the Paris branch of a well-known English furniture and interior design firm, Waring and Gillow, which had a reputation for outfitting the interiors of luxury yachts and liners. On his return from the First World War, in 1919 Chareau was commissioned by the Dalsace-Bernheim family to renovate the interiors of their apartment at 195, Boulevard Saint-Germain, the design for which he presented at the *Salon d'Automne* the same year.[9] As was true for his contemporaries, it was exhibitions such as the *Salon d'Automne* and the *Salon des Artistes Décorateurs* that brought him into the public eye and he quickly gained notoriety not only for his furniture designs but also for his ensembles.[10] By 1925 Pierre Chareau was an established *ensemblier* and a respected member of the Société des Artistes Décorateurs. Along with other members, Chareau's work appeared in limited editions of loose-leafed portfolios using the *pochoir* technique, such as, *Intérieurs français*, 1925, and *Répertoire du goût moderne* published in five volumes between 1928 and 1929.[11]

Among Pierre Chareau's ensembles was a collaboration with Robert Mallet-Stevens, Gabriel Guévrékian, André Lurçat and Jacques Lipchitz for the 'Study-Library of a French Embassy' that was sponsored by the Société des Artistes Décorateurs for the *Exposition Internationale des Arts Décoratifs et Industriels Modernes* in 1925.[12] In this exhibit a significant change was observed in the role of the *ensembliers*, a term first introduced to France at the 1910 *Salon d'Automne*, a joint exhibition with the Munich decorative arts association. Whereas the ensemble had then consisted of a group of objects contributing to a single effect, it had now evolved into architecture being subordinated into its totality, so that rather than being a showpiece the ensemble now took on 'an overwhelming impression of permanence'. The builder was no longer in charge but rather 'the organizer of the ensemble in which the architectural plans, the interior decoration, lighting, hangings, and furniture (were) all equally important' and in this respect Pierre Chareau was considered the most faithful to its rational principles, earning himself the name *ingénieur constructeur*, a term used in opposition to the *coloristes décorateurs*, the group of *ensembliers* that emerged in the wake of the 1910 *Salon d'Automne*.[13]

The Maison de Verre and the Question of *Habitus*

Recognised as a modern masterpiece, the Maison de Verre at 31, rue Saint-Guillaume in Paris, a house commissioned by the Dalsace-Bernheim family and built between 1928 and 1932, is Chareau's only architectural testimony still standing today. While it has been the inspiration for High Tech architects such as Richard Rogers and is considered to have been ahead of its time, it was in fact a true modern construct caught in its own time and place.[14] The story of its construction perhaps says the most about its modern disposition. The original intention to demolish an existing three-storey 18th-century *hôtel particulier* enclosed within a courtyard and replace it with a single modern villa was prevented by an existing tenant on the top floor who, being protected by law, refused to move. Rather than give up on the project, it was decided to hold up the apartment above using composite steel columns and beams typical of bridge construction at the time, and insert the new villa underneath. To imagine such a solution reflects precisely the work of an *ensemblier*, or *ingénieur constructeur* like Chareau, perfecting his *habitus* by inserting a space within a space like a piece of furniture, or an ensemble.

In elaborating on the concept of *habitus*, Pierre Bourdieu, whose work is built upon that of Wittgenstein, Merleau-Ponty, Husserl, Bachelard and others, extends the theories of Marcel Mauss on the notion of body techniques to the concept of creativity and innovation. He argues that, 'to contrast individuality with community so as to better safeguard the rights of creative individuality and the mystery of individual creation is to forgo discovering community at the heart of individuality in the form of culture … or, *habitus* … through which the creator partakes of his community and time, and that guides and directs, unbeknownst to him, his apparently most unique creative acts.'[15] What Bourdieu then suggests is that, 'the ultimate truth of a style is not contained in embryo in an original inspiration but is continuously defined and redefined as a constantly evolving meaning, which constructs itself in accordance to itself and in reaction to itself', so that what may appear as inventive and creative acts of certain individuals could only have come about by a mind well-equipped with a certain customary way of questioning reality … a particular *habitus*.[16]

Whereas the architecture of Mallet-Stevens on Rue Mallet-Stevens is more easily identifiable as embodying an Art Deco sensibility, it is much more difficult to classify Pierre Chareau's Maison de Verre in the same way; yet, the basic principles of Art Deco

Alignment of the
transparent bookshelves.
View from the bedroom
floor of the Maison de
Verre looking towards the
glass-block front facade.
© Mark E Lyon.

are visible everywhere, particularly when seen through the *habitus* of the *pochoir*.[17] In preparing for the *pochoir*, the *ensemblier* searched for harmony between the lines that he drew and the volume created by the different layers of colour planes added by each stencil. This technique of establishing complete harmony between line and volume is perfected by Chareau in the Maison de Verre from the smallest detail, such as the line in the tile joints of the bathroom wall aligning with the seam lines of the removable chrome flooring designed to allow access to the plumbing underneath, to the larger detail, such as the dimension of the glass block panels on the exterior of the house which becomes the measure for the rest of the interior so that the lines of their frames align not only with the lines dividing bookshelves but also the lines defining the edges of doorways across the volume of the living room and into the family bedrooms.

Just as the *pochoir* in representing an interior ensemble tended to blur the boundary between architecture and furniture, so it is in the Maison de Verre where, for instance, a mirror attached to a column is hung in such a way that the mirror becomes part of the column, the column part of the mirror; a credenza in the doctor's office becomes part of the wall, the wall part of the credenza, as well as the wardrobes on the bedroom floor that are also the walls separating the passageway from the bedrooms.

Most significant, however, is the inherent quality embodied in the *pochoir* print, the result of a labour-intensive process that occupied an ambiguous place being neither entirely the result of mechanical reproduction nor entirely a handmade product, but a combination of both. This is also reflected in Chareau's approach to the making of the Maison de Verre. Here, the use of industrially produced parts, like the stair between the master bedroom and Madame Dalsace's *petit salon* which was manufactured for a ship, as well as the exterior wall of the *petit salon* manufactured for a train, were assembled to create what was conceived as a kind of prototype, but is in fact a labour-intensive work embodying an aura belonging to its own time and place, so that, like the *pochoir* print, it is not reproducible. The care given to every detail, not only in its execution, but also in its practicality, is evident from the smallest detail – such as the door knob at the entrance to the receptionist's office from the doctor's office, which reflects not only an ergonomic relationship between the body and architecture, but also Dalsace's habits and concern for manners – to the design of the stairs: all five stairs in the house are completely different in character, using different materials and each responds to its particular purpose and circumstance.

None of these could exist without the hand of the craftsman, most visible in the notch of the moving wall made to enable the wall to move past the metal tube railing at the top of the main stair into the *grand salon*, as well as in the mason's signature left underneath the terrazzo countertop in what may have been the gardener's washroom and is today the laundry room.[18]

Mirror on one of the original columns in the Maison de Verre designed to hold the 18th-century *hôtel particulier* above it. © Mark E Lyon.

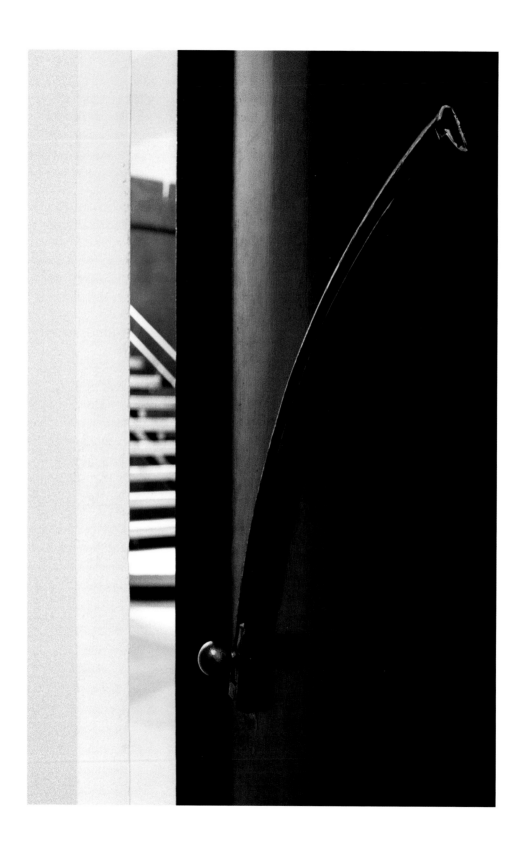

Conclusion

In referring to the theoretical basis for Chareau's work, critics during the Art Deco period confined themselves to the term rationalism, which suggests an intellectual quality closely related to the practical, or common sense.[19] According to Francis Jourdain, Pierre Chareau 'enjoyed discovering beauty in the commonplace' and it was his ability to reveal and 'to captivate us with the charm or to move us with the grandeur of all that we look at day after day and do not actually see' that made him the poet that he was, an inventor who 'had something of the rebel in him ... a nonconformist in the fullest sense'.[20] Bourdieu concludes his Postface to Erwin Panofsky, *Gothic Architecture and Scholasticism*, by quoting Panofsky in *Studies in Iconology* (1939) when he declares that, 'the art historian differs from the naïve spectator in that he is conscious of what he does', suggesting that he can do what he does only on condition that at any given time he must know what he does and what it takes to do it. Chareau understood that this kind of distancing was required in his *modus operandi*, or *habitus*, distancing that Bourdieu has argued is worth the full value of the theoretical conscience that accompanies it. Chareau believed that most people when confronted with a creation of the human mind were unaware of all the stages in the process between its original conception and its realisation.[21] It is possible that Chareau also saw in the *pochoir* a kind of collage, or assemblage, thereby liberating himself as a true modern craftsman by assembling cogwheels for operating ventilation mechanisms in the house, along with stairs from ships and sliding windows from trains.

Notes

1 A recent exhibition at the Maison de la Culture du Japon in Paris from October 2006 to January 2007 entitled *Katagami: Paper Stencils and Japonisme* paid homage to this age-old tradition and its influence on the French Art Nouveau and Art Deco movements.

2 For an elaboration on this period see Nancy Troy, *Modernism and the Decorative Arts in France*, Yale University Press (New Haven), 1991, and Debora Silverman, *Art Nouveau in Fin-de-Siècle France: Politics, Psychology, and Style*, University of California Press (Berkeley), 1989. Both argue that nationalism and economic considerations, particularly the need at the end of the 19th century for France to compensate for its weakness in heavy industry, relative to other nations, were significant contributing factors to the emphasis on luxurious craft objects.

3 In 1895 Siegfried Bing, originally from Hamburg, opened a shop specialising in the modern tendencies of the decorative arts, which he named *L'Art Nouveau*, and at the *Exposition Universelle* in Paris in 1900 he named his exhibition pavilion Art-Nouveau Bing. For more information on his periodical see article by Gabriel P Weisberg, 'On Understanding Artistic Japan', *The Journal of Decorative and Propaganda Arts*, vol 1 (Spring 1986), pp 6–19. Samuel Bing's Art Nouveau pavilion at the 1900 exhibition was praised by many critics as representing a true embodiment of the national self-image of aristocratic refinement and good taste.

4 S Bing, 'L'Art Nouveau', *Architectural Record*, vol 12 , August 1902, pp 279–85. While the scope of the paper is limited to the influence of Japanese applied art as it pertains to the *pochoir*, this is not to diminish influential theories like those of Viollet-le-Duc which were partially responsible for Art Nouveau's turn to nature and the organic. For a phenomenological reading on Art Nouveau *see* Joseph Rykwert, 'Organic and Mechanical', *RES*, 22, Autumn 1992, pp 11–18.

5 Jean Badovici in 'Harmonies': *Intérieurs de Ruhlmann*, A Morancé (Paris), 1924, presents Ruhlmann's Art Deco designs in *pochoir*, describing Ruhlmann's work as 'true symphonies ... always using color to harmonize the play of volumes and lines'. Furthermore, according to Nathalie Dombre,

Doorknob used by Dr Dalsace to enter the receptionist's office. © Mark E Lyon.

wife of André de Herring who worked as a journeyman draughtsman for Pierre Chareau and became his pupil and spiritual son, 'harmony' was Chareau's favourite word. She writes this in a letter published in Marc Vellay's book *Pierre Chareau*, Rizzoli (New York), 1985, p 22.

6   Nancy Troy, 'Le Corbusier, Nationalism, and the Decorative Arts in France, 1900–1918', in Richard Etlin (ed), *Nationalism in the Visual Arts*, National Gallery of Art (Washington), 1991, pp 65–87. See also Simon Dell, 'The Consumer and the Making of the "Exposition Internationale des Arts Decoratifs et Industriels Modernes", 1907–1925', *Journal of Design History*, vol 12, no 4 (1999), pp 311–25 for a discussion of the ensemble as a fashioning of the needs of the consumer, in this case the French bourgeoisie. It was from this exhibition that the term Art Deco was derived.

7   The article by S Bing, 'L'Art Nouveau', which he wrote in defence of these very criticisms, is testimonial. For the argument on the elements borrowed from Japan by Art Deco, and its intentions, see Jennifer Maatta, 'Japanese and Chinese Influences on Art Deco', *Athanor*, vol 18, 2000, pp 63–9.

8   At *pochoir*'s height of popularity in the 1920s it is thought that there were as many as 30 ateliers in France, each employing up to 600 workers, and while it has practically disappeared today there are still one or two remaining ateliers such as the Editions de l'Ibis/Atelier du Lys, which has been in existence since 1868 and was established by Jean Saudé himself. See Christophe Comentale, '*Le pochoir: entre unique et multiple*' (The stencil: between unique and multiple), *Art et Metiers du livre*, no 220, 2000, pp 46–9. For more information on the significance of the stencil technique in the 1920s see Sarah Schleuning, *MODERNE: Fashioning the French Interior*, Princeton Architectural Press (New York), 2008, published as part of a recent exhibition at the Wolfsonian-Florida International University in Miami Beach, Florida.

9   Dr Dalsace and his wife Annie, daughter of Edmond Bernheim, were to become not only Chareau's staunchest supporters, but also his very close friends, a relationship that goes back to Chareau's wife, Dollie, who was Annie's former dance teacher and English tutor.

10   For a chronology of Chareau's participation in exhibitions from 1919 to 1939, the year before he left France for the United States to escape the Second World War, see Vellay, *Pierre Chareau,* pp 201–06, 344.

11   The Galerie Doria in Paris has published a collection of drawings and *pochoirs* by Pierre Chareau entitled *Pierre Chareau, dessins*, Galerie Doria (Paris), 2001.

12   The 1925 *Exposition Internationale des Arts Décoratifs et Industriels Modernes* is where Le Corbusier presented his Pavillon d'Esprit Nouveau and where Chareau met the Dutch architect Bernard Bijvoet, who was to collaborate with him on the Maison de Verre.

13   Vellay, *Pierre Chareau*, pp 61–2. In 1929, Chareau moved away from the Société des Artistes Décorateurs to join the Union des Artistes Modernes, whose aims were to focus on the alliance of the beautiful and the useful with a desire to use modern mass-production methods to create a pure art that would be accessible to all. According to Vellay, however, it was because of Pierre Chareau's marginal position as the oldest of the moderns in 1930 and the youngest of its forerunners in 1913 that he never knew the world of true industrial art, and continued to work with craftsmen rather than the factory. See Vellay, *Pierre Chareau*, p 147.

14   The term modern in this case refers not to style but to the concept of time. In other words, to be modern is to be in the present.

15   Bourdieu, trans. Laurence Petit in Appendix II, Bruce Holsinger, *The Premodern Condition: Medievalism and the Making of Theory*, University of Chicago Press (Chicago), 2005, p 226. Marcel Mauss, 'The Notions of Body Techniques', *Sociology and Psychology: Essays by Marcel Mauss*, Routledge & Kegan Paul (London), 1979.

16   Bourdieu, *The Premodern Condition*, p 238.

17   In reference to identifying the Art Deco sensibilities in Mallet-Stevens' project, see Tim Benton, *Art Deco 1910–1939*, V&A Publications (London), 2003, p 248.

18   Chareau's commitment to craftsmen is confirmed by Marc Vellay, who writes, '[w]ithout craftsmen, he [Chareau] would have been like a conductor without an orchestra'. Vellay, *Pierre Chareau*, p 143. Louis Dalbet, whose name is noted on the facade of the Maison de Verre as an iron craftsman, set up his atelier on site during the three to four years of the building's construction and Chareau is known to have spent some nights at the Maison de Verre during this time.

19   Vellay, *Pierre Chareau*, p 62.

20   Ibid, p 29.

21   Translation of Pierre Chareau's article for *L'Architecture d'Aujourd'hui*, September 1935 in Vellay, *Pierre Chareau*, p 197.

References

- Badovici, Jean and Émile-Jacques Ruhlmann, *'Harmonies': Intérieurs de Ruhlmann*, A Morancé (Paris), 1924
- Benton, Tim, *Art Deco 1910–1939*, V&A Publications (London), 2003
- Bing, S, 'L'Art Nouveau', *The Architectural Record*, vol 12, August 1902, pp 279–85
- Bourdieu, Pierre, trans. Laurence Petit, Appendix II, Bruce Holsinger, *The Premodern Condition: Medievalism and the Making of Theory*, University of Chicago Press (Chicago), 2005, pp 221–42
- Comentale, Christophe, *'Le pochoir: entre unique et multiple'* (The stencil: between unique and multiple), *Art et Metiers du livre*, no 220, 2000, pp 46–9
- Maatta, Jennifer, 'Japanese and Chinese influences on Art Deco', *Athanor*, vol 18, 2000, pp 63–9
- Mauss, Marcel, 'The Notions of Body Techniques', *Sociology and Psychology: Essays by Marcel Mauss*, Routledge & Kegan Paul (London), 1979
- Rykwert, Joseph, 'Organic and Mechanical', *RES, 22*, Autumn 1992, pp 11–18
- Schleuning, Sarah, *MODERNE: Fashioning the French Interior*, Princeton Architectural Press (New York), 2008
- Silverman, Debora, *Art Nouveau in Fin-de-Siècle France: Politics, Psychology, and Style*, University of California Press (Berkeley), 1989
- Troy, Nancy, 'Le Corbusier, Nationalism, and the Decorative Arts in France, 1900–1918', in Richard Etlin (ed), *Nationalism in the Visual Arts*, National Gallery of Art (Washington), 1991, pp 65–87
- Troy, Nancy, *Modernism and the Decorative Arts in France*, Yale University Press (New Haven), 1991
- Vellay, Marc, *Pierre Chareau*, Rizzoli (New York), 1985
- Weisberg, Gabriel P, 'On Understanding Artistic Japan', *The Journal of Decorative and Propaganda Arts*, vol 1, Spring 1986, pp 6–19

Soil and Protoplasm
Designing the Hylozoic Ground Component System

Philip Beesley

The concept of hylozoism has its origins in ancient Greece, and refers to the belief that all materials possess life. Hylozoic Ground, the latest in a sequence of projects led by Philip Beesley, examines this idea in relation to a palette of subtle and synthetic materials that weave together dynamic interactions that at first simulate a primitive form of life. Naked hyperbolic meshworks are organised as a 'geotextile terrain'; a fundament to the act of creating the earth itself, the meshworks are dressed with a primitive intelligence, layers of structure, muscle, wet chemistry, neurons, memory and an active circulation system. The resultant assembly offers the template for a responsive architectural system, a practical system that lives and breathes, that knows where it is and who is in proximity. Could this form the basis of a system that cares, and architecture of hope and optimism?

The Hylozoic Ground project is a collaboration between architects and engineers in Canada, Britain and Denmark, which is developing new layers of synthetic soil as a primary architectural building system. Organised as a textile matrix, Hylozoic Ground[1] is a manufactured environment supporting responsive actions and 'living' technologies. It is conceived as the first stages of self-renewing functions that might take root within a future architecture. It can be described as a suspended geotextile,[2] gradually thickening and offering a fertile matrix as it draws materials from its surroundings. It consists of an array of articulated meshwork filters and protocell circulation systems programmed to pursue methods for building synthetic earth. Dense groves of frond-like 'breathing' pores, tongues and thickets of twitching whiskers are organised in spiralling rows that curl in and around a complex assembly. A distributed array of proximity sensors activates these primitive responsive devices, stirring the air in thickened areas of the matrix. Akin to the functions of a living system, this embedded machine intelligence allows human interaction to trigger breathing, caressing and swallowing motions, and hybrid metabolic exchanges within this material. These empathic motions ripple out from hives of kinetic valves and pores in peristaltic waves, creating a diffuse pumping that pulls air, moisture and stray organic matter through the filtering membranes within the system. This paper examines the cultivation of the Hylozoic Ground project as a speculative prototype in new frontiers of architectural matter. It examines an engagement between soil and protoplasm as a fertile territory for architectural enquiry.

Overall view, Hylozoic Ground
2010 Biennale in Architecture, Canadian Pavilion
Venice, 2010. © PBAi/ Philip Beesley.

Can soil be constructed? Soil has always been the *prima materia* of architecture. But contemporary soil does not quietly offer itself to the enlightened framing of space. Soil eliminates and eviscerates space. It might seem to stand silently, apparently offering secure mass and compression, available as a plastic, friable resource for framing human territory. Yet soil *desires* collapse. The soil crust of the earth covers and disguises myriad layers formed from condensation and deposition. Soil consumes space, erasing and absorbing daily circumstance within its unspeakably silent, primal fertility. Soil's inexorable infolding of matter within matter negates space, compacting interminably into dark.

Yet soil also desires springing growth. The soil crust of the earth seethes with a myriad of seeded viscera, minuscule fragments gathering and efflorescing, redolent with chorusing oceans of growth to come. Soil's inexorable flowering genesis of matter building upon matter overwhelms and saturates space, riddling voids, boiling and flaming outward. The stuttering oscillation of soil's alternating collapse and expansion sends shivering waves that tangle and choke certainty. Soil's lumpen, sodden masses counter any enlightened world of social construction. The ambivalence latent within soil makes it a monstrous doppelgänger for architecture.

The soil of a fever-laced biosphere speaks of inflamed flux, efflorescent growth oscillating in wild swings punctuated by unspeakable silence. Standing within this tumbling ground, posture pulls toward spasm. The yawing, viscous ground induces queasy vertigo. Legs unconsciously tense themselves, reptile-brain-inflected posture tensed by the inward pulling, elastic meniscus underfoot. The shift of this posture inverts any confidence within an outward gaze. Any bounded territory recedes.

Might an opening appear within this wilderness? Within ancient Greek and Roman texts that dwelt on the origins of cities can be found descriptions of openings amid blood-soaked thickets of darkened soil. Tacitus and other ancient Roman writers pursued their own people's origins in primal dwelling. These texts speak of wilderness, and of an opening within the wild, a 'ludens' that offered sanctuary from the atrocities of unbounded surrounds. The Hylozoic Ground project follows these steps of Tacitus. The project has origins in the site of Rome, in the opening within the metaphorical wilderness that, according to the texts, preceded the bounded eternal city. Entangled within the instrumental systems of this installation lies a sheltering open space of asylum.

Recent finds in Rome confirmed new poignant details of these city foundations described by Tacitus. Excavation work in the past two decades has revealed a labyrinthine topology lying within the Palatine, the artificial mountain that formed the inner sanctuary of the original city. Within this labyrinth are revealed traces of a tiny infant body deposited under Porta Mugonia, the original north gate of the eternal city. The burial appeared to be one of a series of public sacrifices. Following the lot of Remus, the twin-brother alter-ego of Rome who was slain at the edge of the first city by Romulus, the first father of the city,

Breathing pores in motion
Hylozoic Soil, '(in)posición dinámica'
Festival de Mexico, Mexico City, 2010. © PBAi/Pierre Charron.

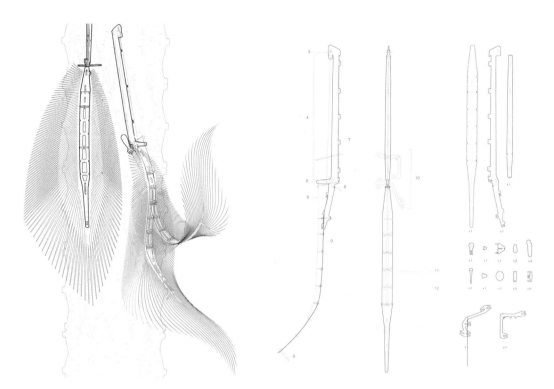

Breathing pore assembly diagram

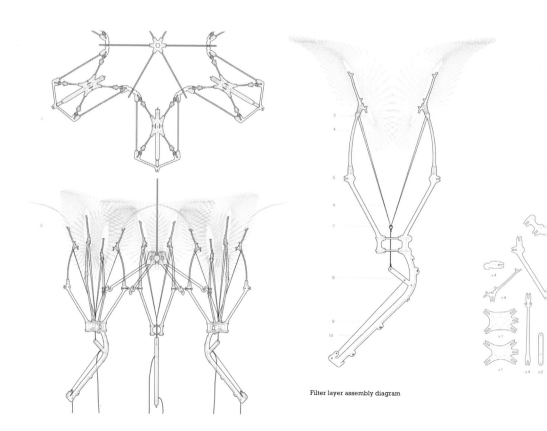

Filter layer assembly diagram

a series of human burials, and literally hundreds of other 'substitution' burials embodied in carved models of swaddled infants – 'first fruit of the first family' – lie within the foundations of ancient buildings throughout Rome. Hovering over these shadows of father and abject twin, and located at the centre of this constellation of burials, a first 'primitive hut' spoke to the ancient citizens of Rome about their own primal origins. A thicket of branches was raised over the sanctuary of Romulus's tomb at the edge of the Palatine. This shelter was maintained for hundreds of years during Rome's years as a republic, bespeaking depths of brimming blood imbued within that earth. The labyrinthine grove that is constructed within the Hylozoic Ground project can be seen as a renewed version of this primitive construction.

In the constructions of the Hylozoic Soil series, sheltering and gently nurturing qualities of construction offer nourishment, while dimensions of darkness and 'alterity' reside just below the surface.[3] A flux of viscous, humid atmospheres creates a hybrid-expanded protoplasm with constantly changing boundaries. The structural core of the Hylozoic environment is a flexible meshwork skeleton of transparent, lily-shaped ribbed vaults and basket-like columns. Dozens of sensors that detect the presence of visitors through changes in space, light and touch are spread throughout the Hylozoic environment. They function like the space-reading sonar employed by dolphins and bats and feed impulses into an embedded network of microcontrollers, working in concert with, and guiding, device movements. Alongside mechanised component systems, a wet system has been introduced into the environment, supporting simple chemical exchanges that share some of the renewing functions of a human lymphatic system. The meshwork stretches and billows, creating a hyperbolic gridshell topology that surrounds occupants in the space. It is assembled from small acrylic chevron-shaped tiles that clip together to form a pleated diagrid textile structure. Columnar elements extend out from this membrane, reaching upward and downward to create tapered suspension and mounting points. Tension rods support the scaffold with toothed clamps that bite into the ceiling and floor surfaces.

Breathing pore assembly diagram

1 Breathing pore assembly actuated position
2 Breathing pore assembly rest position
3 Adjustable shape memory alloy (SMA) clip
4 SMA lever
5 Lever
6 Tensioned tendon
7 Strengthening gusset for main spine
8 Gland clip
9 Copolyester tongue
10 Tongue clip
11 Arm units for attachment to mesh
12 Tongue struts
13 Feather

Filter layer assembly diagram

1 Filter cluster plan
2 Filter cluster elevation
3 Filter feather
4 Leaf spring
5 Connection to adjacent filters
6 Tension cable
7 Tension hook
8 Lever arm
9 Shape memory alloy (SMA) actuator
10 Sled assembly

PBAi Hylozoic Ground 2010 Biennale in Architecture, Canadian Pavilion Venice, 2010. © PBAi.

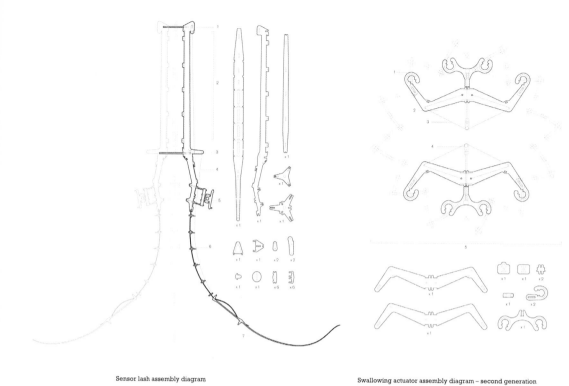

Sensor lash assembly diagram

Swallowing actuator assembly diagram – second generation

Swallowing actuator assembly diagram – third generation

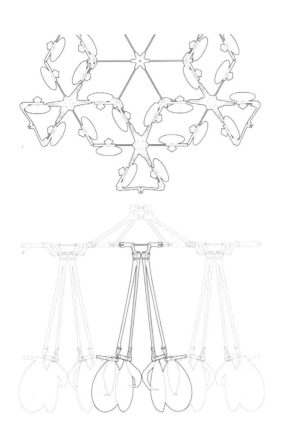

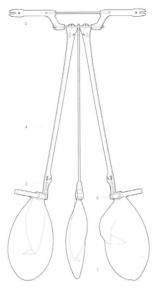

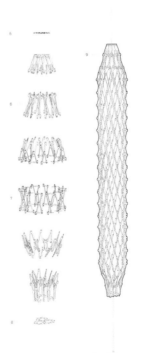

Cricket layer assembly diagram

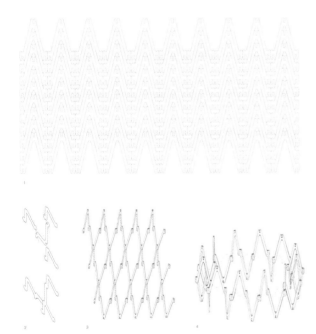

Chevron assembly diagrams

Thousands of primitive glands containing synthetic digestive liquids and salts are clustered throughout the system, located at the base of each breathing pore and within suspended colonies of whiskers and trapping burrs. The salt derivatives serve a hygroscopic function, pulling fluids out of the surrounding environment. These bladder clusters are surrounded by thickened vapours. These design systems provide an expanded physiology akin to the layered envelopes created by nightdresses and bedclothes surrounding a sleeping body.

Pure, distilled spheres and pyramids from Plato's cosmology might hover as ghosts that inform this environment, but that family of reductive crystal forms does not govern. Far from transcendent perfection, the formwork that organises the space boils out of local circumstance.[4] As with the fabric that emerges from the steady cadence of knitting or crocheting, the chevron links are combined in repeating rows, and their numbers tend to drift and bifurcate. Adding links within linked rows crowds the surface, producing warped and reticulated surfaces that expand outwards in three dimensions.[5]

The responsive devices fitted into the expanded Hylozoic topology function similarly to pores and hair follicles within the epithelial skin layers of an organism. Breathing pores are composed of thin sheets shaped into outward-branching serrated membranes, each containing flexible acrylic tongue stiffeners fitted with monofilament tendons. The tendons pull along the surface of each tongue, producing upward curling motions that sweep through the surrounding air. Sensor lashes, carried by the lower tips of meshwork columns, are cousins of the breathing pore. These are fitted with a fleshy latex membrane and offer cupping, pulling motions.

The linking systems that form scaffolds for the filtering systems use a tessellated geometry of self-healing hexagonal and rhombic arrays that readily accommodate tears and breaks within their fabrics. In opposition to design principles of the past century that favoured optimal equations where maximum volume might be enclosed by the minimum possible surface, the structures in Hylozoic Ground prefer diffuse, deeply reticulated skins. These forms turn away from the minimum surface exposures of pure spheres and cubes as they seek to increase their exposure and interchange with the atmosphere.[6]

Although the surface topologies of these forms are generous, their material consumption is reduced to a minimum by employing form-finding textile systems. Strategies include the use of thin tensile component arrays with floating compression elements within interlinked fields of tension fibres. Three-dimensional forms are derived from thin, two-dimensional sheets of material, organised in nested tessellations to nearly eliminate waste during digital fabrication. In pursuit of resonant, vulnerable physical presence, components use materials stretched near to the point of individual collapse. The space formed from these materials expands a thousandfold, filling the volume of the containing building.

The adaptive chemistries within the wet system capture traces of carbon from the vaporous surroundings and build delicate structural scaffolds. Engineered protocells and chells – liquid-supported artificial cells that share some of the characteristics of natural living cells – are arranged in a series of embedded incubator flasks. Bursts of light and vibration, created by the responses of visitors standing within the work, influence the growth of the protocells, catalysing the formation of vesicles and inducing secondary deposits of benign materials. Sensors monitor the health of the growing flasks and give feedback that governs the behaviour of the interactive system surrounding the viewer.

A further kind of swallowing actuator is fitted inside the meshwork columns. Its chained air muscles are organised in a segmented radial system to produce expanding and contracting movements, causing convulsive waves in their surrounding halo of hooked whiskers, while at the same time delivering an incremental, siphoning transport of water within their cores. Wound-wire pendant whiskers are supported by acrylic outriggers with rotating bearings. Tensile mounts for these tendrils encourage cascades of rippling and spinning movements that amplify swelling waves of motion within the mesh structure.

The Hylozoic Ground environment is supported by a resilient, hyperbolic space truss. Curving and expanding both laterally and vertically, the mesh creates a flexible structural meniscus. The meshwork is comprised of flexible, lightweight chevron-shaped components. The chevrons interconnect using snap-fit fastening to create a pleated diagrid, twisting and

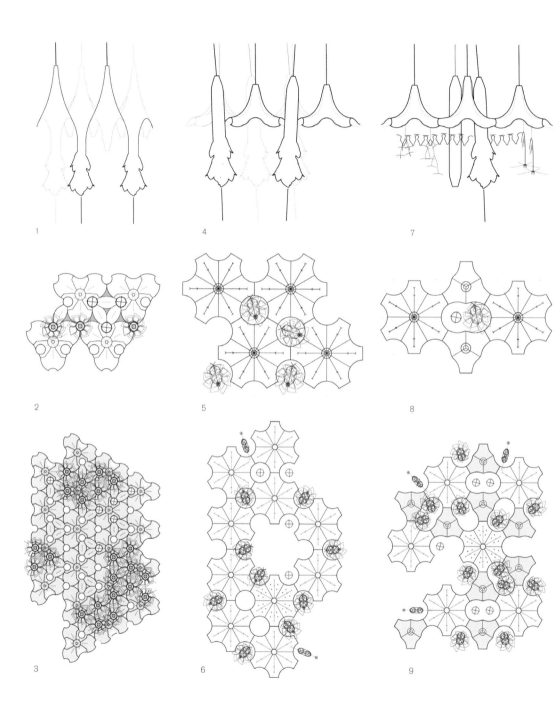

1

4

7

2

5

8

3

6

9

Hylozoic plan diagrams

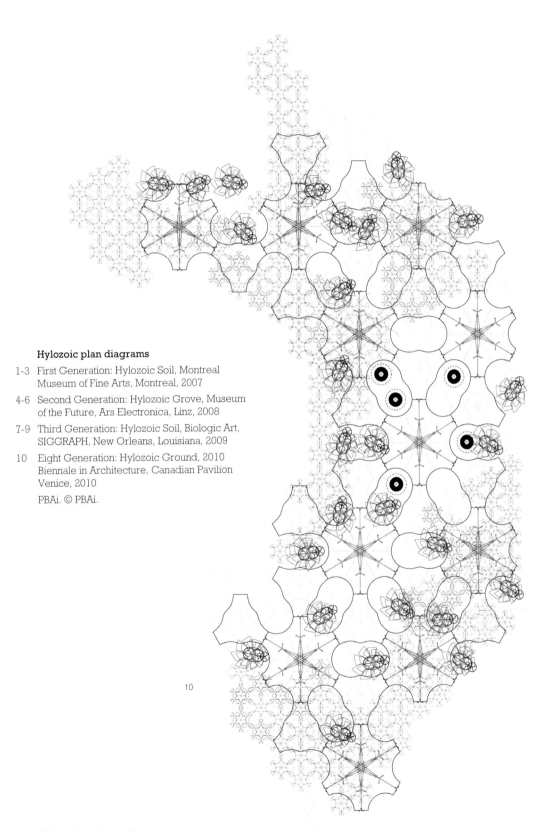

Hylozoic plan diagrams

1-3 First Generation: Hylozoic Soil, Montreal
Museum of Fine Arts, Montreal, 2007

4-6 Second Generation: Hylozoic Grove, Museum
of the Future, Ars Electronica, Linz, 2008

7-9 Third Generation: Hylozoic Soil, Biologic Art,
SIGGRAPH, New Orleans, Louisiana, 2009

10 Eight Generation: Hylozoic Ground, 2010
Biennale in Architecture, Canadian Pavilion
Venice, 2010

PBAi. © PBAi.

10

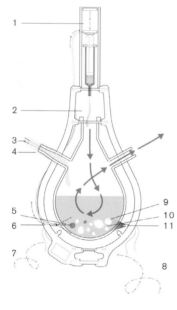

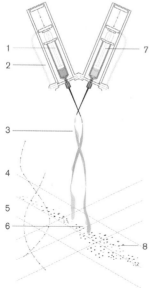

Liesegang ring-like reactions

1 Copper sulphate
2 Ferrofluid solution
3 Attenuated sodium hydroxide solution
4 Magnetite crystal 'seeds'
5 Diethyl pheryl phthalate (DEPP)
6 Complex of various precipitate-forming metal ions
7 Calcium chloride
8 Olive oil
9 Protocell

Protopearl flask

1 Syringe driver with protopearl formulation
2 Air: nitrogen, oxygen, carbon dioxide
3 Venice canal water
4 Filtration unit
5 Copper ions, metal ions in solution from Venice canal water
6 Sensor
7 Agitation
8 The airflow outlet will act as overflow
9 From Venice water: magnesium, barium and calcium ions

Extended Traube membranes

1 Copper sulphate + gelatin
2 Timed release syringe drivers
3 Metal scaffolding to collect and direct traube cell reagents
4 Absorbent matrix to support traube cell growth
5 Agitation from Hylozoic matrix, vibrational forces further extend membranes
6 Traube cell extension (copper hexacyanoferrate with complex polymer scaffolding alginate/gelatin)
7 Copper hexacyanoferrate + alginate + gelatin
8 Hygroscopic attractant permeates absorbent matrix
   PBAi. © PBAi.

wrapping to create the waffle vaulting within the canopy system, and alternately wrapping axially tightly to form columnar extensions. The core unit of the structural mesh is a chevron-shaped link, an optimised laser-cut form with an interlocking 'snap-fit' receiver at each of its junction points. The chevron design contains thickened feet and head, strong shoulders and slender arms that are capable of twisting slightly. The design of this element is coupled to the material characteristics of impact-resistant acrylic, giving the Hylozoic mesh a flexible base unit.

Resilient, flexible materials are used to manufacture components in the environment. A number of features have been developed including snap-fit joints, crack-stop corners and gussets. Cartilage-like layers of silicone appear throughout the Hylozoic Ground environment employed in areas receiving additional stress. Specialised snap-fit acrylic joints are predominantly used for joining mechanisms, avoiding the need for mechanical fasteners or adhesives. Crack-stop detailing involves filleting or rounding off the interior angles to distribute the stress over a greater area. Creating smooth transitions between thinned and thickened sections prevents stress build-up and subsequent cracking. Refinement based on thickening and voiding permits elements to handle substantial torsion forces. In order to use materials efficiently and reduce waste, the shape of the component is refined so that it fits as tightly as possible with duplicates and other components on the same sheet. In the case of the chevrons that make up the expansive mesh lattice, the tessellation of the component has been refined to the point where they are fully nested and share edges. Sharing edges makes it possible to remove overlapping lines, greatly reducing cutting time and reducing material waste to nearly zero.

When the Hylozoic chevrons are snapped together foot to foot, the two-dimensional herringbone pattern thickens to form a structural diagrid of oscillating perpendicular planes. This corrugated sheet material offers a flexible structure capable of acting both in tension and compression. Columnar forms are achieved by assembling rings of diagrid strands in rows. Controlled distortions are introduced into the sheet stock by systematically inserting additional chevrons in progressively lengthening rows. These distortions result in the emergence of doubly curved topologies including conical caps for columnar elements and hyperbolic arched vaulting. The lily-like forms of the Hylozoic Ground mesh-canopy are created by combining sets of hyperbolic arched sheets and conical caps.

What ground, what soil, might be adequate for viable and involved dwelling? Within Hylozoic Ground there lies a diffuse matrix. The trembling, resonant performance of this matrix is rooted in concrete material manipulations. This project offers a design language that prefers thin laminar and tensile dynamic systems over static forms. Resonant, trembling responses are achieved by orienting materials at the outer bounds of their performance. Weakness is, in this design system, a design optimum. The matrix offers a map of a dissociated body moving to and fro across junctures of conception, charged with territory whose gendered roots speak of birth. If, quickened by a humid microclimate and organic atmospheres blooming around human occupation, the vesicles and primitive glands crowding the Hylozoic Ground surface spoke, they might call and lure, voicing abject hunger. This soil is pulling. Its environment seeks human presence as elemental food.

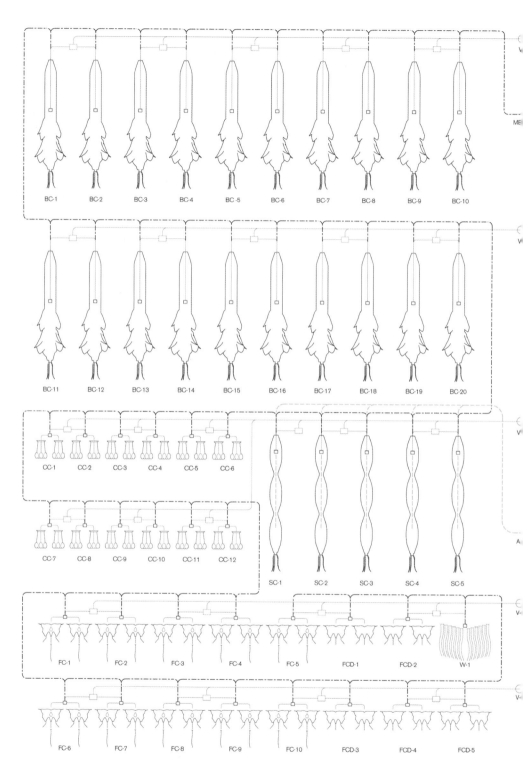

Global system diagram

Notes

1 Hylozoism is the ancient perception of life arising out of material. Following in the footsteps of Grecian and Roman atomists, Hylozoic Ground sees life arising from the chaos-borne quickening of air, water and stone. When the Roman Lucretius watched motes of dust quivering and darting within the sunbeams of his Roman window, he saw atoms play. Rivers of motion took the particles in laminar flows, bringing degrees of certainty into the sight of barely tangible things. Darting and wavering, the dust spoke of possibility, of specious circumstance in flux: corrupted, damaged and dying swerves and a vague, shaded shift of life arising too – the rising semiquaver of living seeds. This quickening leads into the earth.

2 Geotextiles are civil engineering textile systems that provide temporary earthen support for landscapes that will eventually be taken over by organic growth.

3 The text following includes portions of an introductory chapter to Philip Beesley, *Hylozoic Ground: Liminal Responsive Architectures*, Riverside Architectural Press (Cambridge, Ontario), published on the occasion of the 2010 Venice Biennale for Architecture.

4 The ancient Roman writer Lucretius spoke of an approximate geometry within curves shearing away from lines, calibrated within the infinitesimally small angle called clinamen. A clinamen is the angle that occurs when a straight line meets the tangent of an arc. Hylozoic Ground employs the conceptual terrain of the clinamen as a launch into the realm of hyperbolic forms.

5 The geometries of this system are 'quasiperiodic', combining rigid repetition with corrupted inclusions and drift. A tiling system invented by the contemporary British physicist Roger Penrose, based on multiple angles following the 10-way division of a circle, alternates with close-packed regular hexagonal geometry.

6 Such lavish exfoliation has borne disapproval in 20th-century design education. Perhaps inflected by mid-century Cold War preoccupations, North American design has tended to equate energy conservation with heat retention and has prioritised resistance and inert barriers. Reticulated surfaces, despite their inherent ability to foster free cooling and heating through increased energy exchanges with their surroundings, have often been judged excessive and wasteful. The American engineer Buckminster Fuller's 1975 opus *Synergetics: Explorations in the Geometry of Thinking*, Macmillan Publishing Co (New York), exemplifies this view.

'Soil and Protoplasm' was developed by Philip Beesley with assistance and editing by Jonathan Tyrrell.

Global system diagram

BC Breathing column

SC Swallowing column

CC Cricket cluster

FC Filter cluster

FCD Filter cluster drone

W Whisker

MB Masterboard

AIR Main air supply

V+ Main power supply

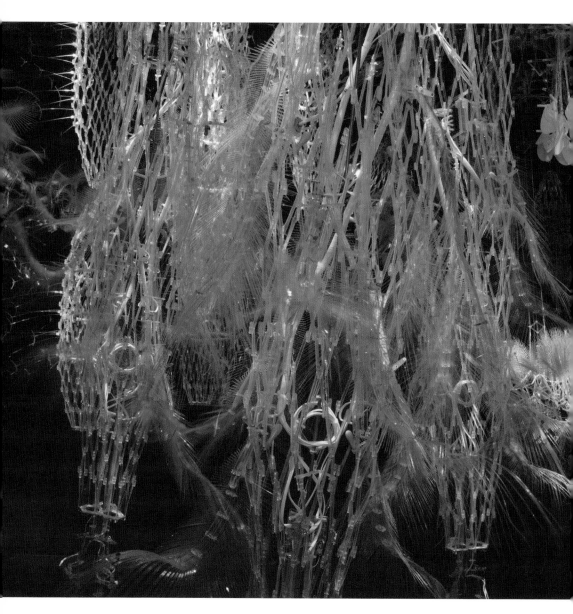

Hylozoic Ground, panoramic view
2010 Biennale in Architecture, Canadian Pavilion
Venice, 2010. © PBAi/Philip Beesley.

Walmer Road

Peter Salter

Are ever more demanding and restrictive building regulations suffocating building construction strategies that are inventive and irregular? Former employee of the Smithsons, and formidable master of building materials and techniques, Peter Salter recalls his experience and ongoing exploration in tailoring bespoke architectural assemblies that stem from an extensive knowledge of the tactile. He advocates a timeless approach of a design methodology that synthesises all scales of design, from overarching strategies of spatial organisation to those of detailed fabrication.

The text is composed of two readings of the bespoke. The first reading, intended as complementary to the second, reflects upon materials and workmanship, and the performance accountability required by the building industry that in some ways stifles invention.

The need to combat climate change has required the UK building regulations to set out increased standards of insulation, and to clamp down on building details that have failed through a system of robust details and performance criteria. The text looks at the way a new common aesthetic has emerged through principles of the rainscreen and the larger section components required for thermal breaks and the elimination of cold bridges. Aesthetic modulation of the facade, shadow and scale have been altered resulting, it is suggested, in the bespoke being lost in such common detail. This 'preamble' begins with Sigurd Lewerentz's daily site visits to determine the course of detail, and goes on to consider the Smithsons' production drawings in which detail was drawn alongside design strategy to encourage a rigorous following of ideas at 1:1. This text equates the relationship between strategy and detail as a means of understanding the bespoke.

The second reading describes certain bespoke pieces of the Walmer Road project that respond to the density of the site. It describes the detail of the external timber room, the 'yurt'-like roof-room snugs, the fair-faced concrete finishes that offer different light qualities, set against the smooth surfaces of carbonised black steel screens that act almost as navigation pieces within the houses. Many of these elements give scale and intimacy to the spaces and are not governed to the same extent by Part L (The Conservation of Fuel and Power) of the building regulations.

1.0: Preamble

Bespoke architecture is synonymous with the invention of detail. The context for such detail in Sigurd Lewerentz's work came from a series of strategies of which layering offered a clear and precise, almost iconic detail. Daily site visits by Lewerentz to agree and adjust detail with long-standing colleagues/craftsmen meant that working tolerances required in drawn construction details were overtaken by the scribed or overlapping of site detail. It could almost be said that such detail became the tolerances of the bespoke.

Alison and Peter Smithson's construction drawings set out full-size details alongside 1:25 scale plans and sections; similarly, 1:200 scale diagrams were sometimes drawn next to such construction detail. In such circumstances, the drawing processes of design explicitly required the simultaneous invention of detail. The adjacencies required thought across scales, where the strategic diagram enabled and required the invention of design rules, a rigour enabling construction detail. Such architectural rules were also set against regulation in a search for an 'economy of means' to enable a total reading of the building, from the strategy of its spaces to detail. Such practice of consistently reading the specificity of space went beyond function, and was an attribute of the bespoke.

The building regulations of the 1970s and 1980s offered a framework within which architectural invention could still be accommodated, and sometimes even flourish. Detail could follow strategy. Lost moments. Today, current building regulations have become a means to drive an agenda for the ratcheting of standards to offset climate change. Insulation standards, the elimination of cold bridges, collateral warranties, prefabrication and robust details have driven new rules and a new orthodoxy towards an architectural vocabulary that belies invention and perhaps also the bespoke. The breadth of detail in relation to strategy has been limited to two broad ways of proceeding. First, that of the performance-based layering of thin economic materials, such as the base and sub-base layers of sportswear, for warmth and 'wicking' structure, and breathable membranes that repel water through the regulation of pores as a rainscreen. The second way, which until recently was not permitted because of changes in the regulations, is a monolithic skin such as brick or concrete. New products have opened the way for new insulating concretes that offer one-pour solutions to Part L. These materials have enabled details to be made that offer shadow to fenestration and identification of scale to the building.

The layering of the performance skin, the science of U values, the position of the dew point, and that of the damp-proof membrane in relation to the insulation and facade engineering, have increasingly reduced detail to keep what is warm inside and what is cold outside. The building form becomes skin and volume. Shadow as a modulation of the scale of the facade through its window reveals has had to be reinvented as larger scale elements. Component details can no longer give scale to the architecture. Regulation has cast new importance on legibility. Dealing with cold bridges and the need to reduce skin surface area has colluded to produce entirely flat facades. The 'Gore-tex' phenomenon of a breathable rainproof skin has further driven this legibility based on scale away from a 'local' component to a much larger element of building.

Computer-aided design, raw material size and its subsequent prefabrication, together with forms of dry construction have enabled components to be aggregated into larger forms. Facade engineering as seen in the repetitive use of components has encouraged the manipulation of fenestration through the use of pattern. Such decoration offers different light qualities and might be said to have replaced shadow as a means of modulating the facade.

Manufacturing tolerances of prefabrication are now better understood and offer a new dimensional control on site. Assembly details offer a precision and consequent reduction of dimensional creep. However the detail of such assemblies, together with

performance warranties, have changed the nature of details. The layering strategy that enabled tolerance as seen in Lewerentz's work is abandoned in favour of a butt-jointed and sealed technology. The invention of detail, which is synonymous with the bespoke, is now largely performance-based. Such invention exposes the architect to risk, as only the largest of projects can afford to undergo prototype analysis as an alternative to manufacturers' warranties. The invention of a bespoke architecture now takes place within a palette of warranted materials and 'robust' details. Strategy and detail are reduced to a poetic reading of the 'ready-made'. What is left of the bespoke is possibly only form.

The dictionary meaning of bespoke is 'specially tailored'. In tailoring this is associated with the measured, the handmade or crafted; in architecture with that which is specifically made for a particular circumstance. Is the violin-maker in the workshop of Stradivarius making a bespoke instrument? Training has enabled the craftsman to copy a template with the greatest precision, using the finest and most delicate of tools, in order to replicate a unique sound. There is no room for minute deviations or the 'workmanship of risk' (David Pye) that we normally associate with the bespoke. A German company makes 'bespoke' precast double-skin concrete wall panels that meet the requirements of part L and the need for a fair-faced finish on both surfaces. Their 'bespokenness' is constrained not only by size and means of transport to site but also by the manufacturing process on heated flatbed forms, and the size and positioning of openings.

Is a radical idea always a necessary component of the bespoke? Does the field of nodes lose its 'bespokenness' by becoming reproducible, subject to production, and does it then set its own conventions and standardisations? The MVRDV high-density housing in a superblock in Madrid uses a mixture of unique spatial elements and standardised apartment forms and components. Its architectural rule system, unique to the design, is another attribute of a bespoke architecture. The building becomes a precedent, a typology, its rarity value an element of the bespoke, a prototype that for one reason or another is not repeated. Much of our social housing, and indeed other prototypes of Modernism constructed within a wider ideal, now carry that tag of bespoke.

opposite: Early sketch showing a courtyard detail of the concrete bench that forms a defensible margin of privacy for each house. The freestanding bulbous lights act almost as a 'companion' to each house entrance, the light fall washes the thresholds and prevents light pollution to the upper storeys. The timber louvres mask window openings and the acoustic render behind, which together with end-grain timber block external flooring capture and deaden any airborne sound. © Peter Salter.

below: Three of the houses have cold moulded timber structures at roof level, either as a dining room, living room or study. As an idea, this follows the country house tradition of placing a dining room at roof level accessed across the 'leads'. These structures are made from laser-cut plywood ribs on to which counter-layered strips of timber are glued and pinned in the manner of the hull of a racing dinghy. © Peter Salter.

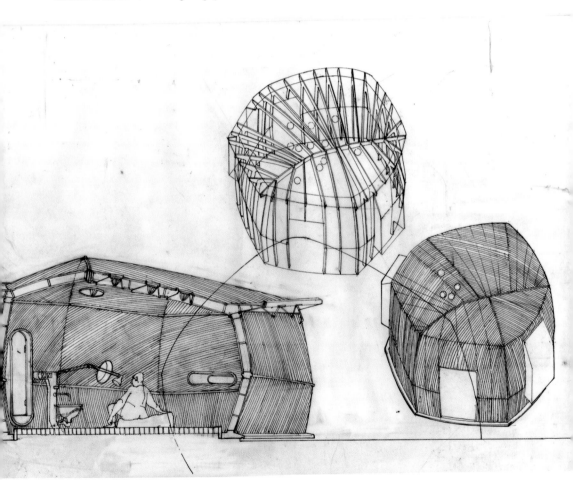

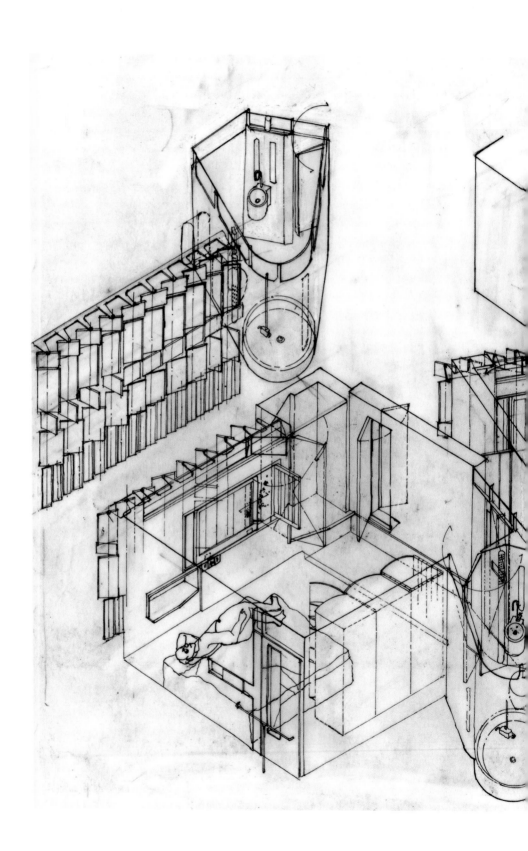

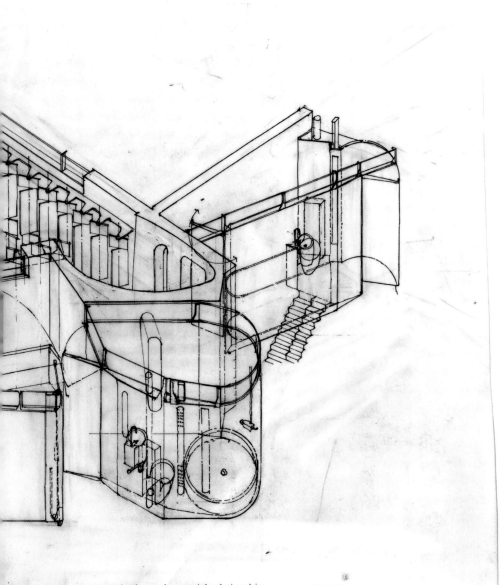

An axonometric shows the spatial relationship between the louvres of each house around the courtyard. The high-level strip window at soffit level is without the louvre screen; this allows light to pass into the room and across the ceiling of fair-faced concrete. Upon entering each floor the visitor will glimpse the remainder of this reflected light across the top of bathroom screens and deep in the section of the house. © Peter Salter.

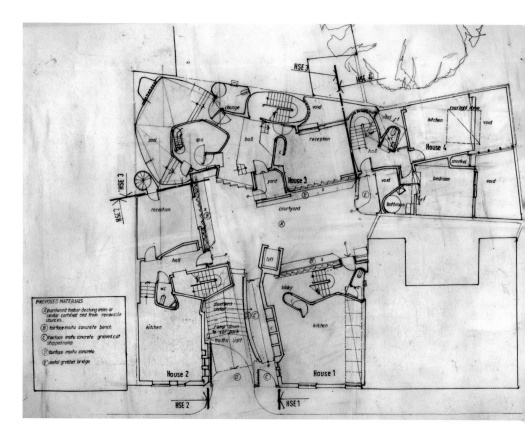

2.1: Walmer Road Project

This project explores the possibilities of a dense urban architecture in West London. Four houses are arranged around a common courtyard that is 5 metres (16.40 feet) wide. This outdoor space enables light to enter the re-entrant balconies and interstices created by the displaced geometries of individual rooms. This is in contrast to the interiors which are single aspect and use the depth of section for privacy. Shadow equates to the privacy of the dwelling.

The courtyard uses a layering strategy to reinforce a sense of privacy between dwellings and is lined in timber. The floor is laid with end-grained timber blocks bedded in a lime mortar. The surrounding facades are built up using small domestic-scale vertical timber louvres. These discourage overlooking, reflect light into the interior and act as sound baffles. Behind these louvres is a patchwork of windows and acoustic-rendered surfaces that trap sound rising from the courtyard below. The louvre boards are constructed off a steel frame that enables banks of louvres to be turned to shut out the sun and gain privacy. Each is a small module, built up as though a bonding pattern, that offers a large surface area and a visual quietness to the space. The courtyard becomes an outdoor room delineated by a perimeter concrete bench, used not so much for people to sit on, but rather for siting flowerpots and plants. The bench width is used to increase the depth of the threshold.

opposite: The planning permission drawing of the raised ground floor shows the four houses around the courtyard. Three of the houses are entered through the depth of section towards the party wall, from which the visitor moves back across the room towards the light. The design introduces a vocabulary of screened accommodation that forces the visitor to skirt such structures, in order to extend the circulation and the privacy in what is essentially a single aspect house. © Peter Salter.

below: The planning permission drawing of the top floor. The re-entrant balconies enable as much light as possible to enter into this top floor. The yurt-like forms in plan offer a varied roofscape in section and complement the external roof gardens. © Peter Salter.

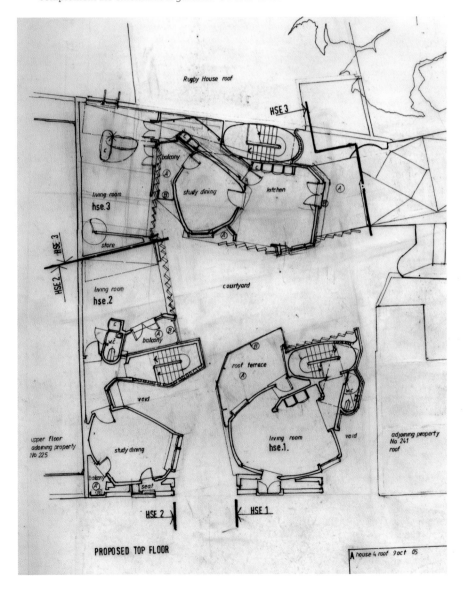

PROPOSED TOP FLOOR

PROPOSED SECTION D-D

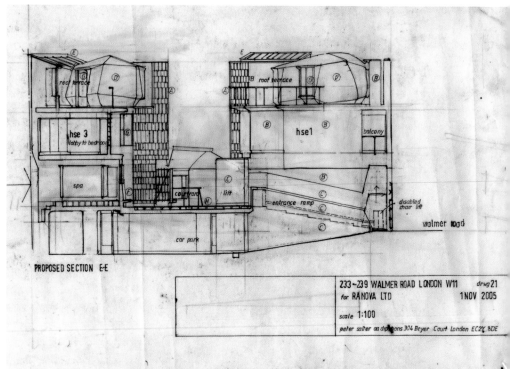

PROPOSED SECTION E-E

233~239 WALMER ROAD LONDON W11   drwg 21
for RANOVA LTD   1 NOV 2005
scale 1:100
peter salter aa dip ngons 304 Bryer Court London EC2Y 8DE

2.2: Concrete

The inner layer of the courtyard wall is constructed of *in situ* concrete. This reflects any stray airborne sound from the dwelling and is part of a patchwork of interior surface finishes. Each of the cottage-like rooms is made of a combination of materials – concrete, plywood, clay board and clay paints – in the manner of the varied interior panelling of the traditional Japanese house. The *in situ* concrete is cast using both phenolic and birch-faced plywood forms set between construction or feature joints. The surface reflection of the smooth concrete cast from phenolic-faced plywood is brighter than the concrete cast from birch-faced forms, the imprint of which provides shadow and a visual darkening of the surface. In certain areas the floor slab is poured in two parts. In such exposed areas, a two-stage structural topping is seeded with rounded river-washed gravels that are subsequently sandblasted to expose the gravel and then ground down to form a flat slab, which is then polished. Additional larger flat rounded stones are occasionally placed in these areas so that the surface finish is like the splitting open of a fossil bed.

Each house is assembled around the concrete frame with a flat soffit transfer slab. Secondary means of escape from the elliptical concrete stair cores enable each dwelling to be a fire compartment. This offers an opportunity for room separation within the dwelling to be formed of screens, counteracting what could have become an oppressive cellular architecture. Movement around the dwelling proceeds from the courtyard through the depth of the house to the party wall from which a staircase gives access to upper floors. On arrival the inhabitant moves back across the section towards the light of the courtyard once again. This quiet perambulation offers a circuitous route around screens, and such distancing enables seclusion between rooms and offers privacy to their inhabitants.

2.3: Black Steel Screens

The screens shut off the spaces to door head height; above this datum a Georgian wired cast-glass panel acts as a fanlight. The screen datum correlates with the high-level clerestory windows on the courtyard facade. These windows at the soffit of the floor slabs are free from louvres and enable light to penetrate across the room at ceiling height. The soffit of the slab is completely flat without construction or formwork joints and fittings. The surface of the concrete is finished to reflect light into the interior, and can be glimpsed from

top: Sectional elevation was part of the planning application. It shows a long section through the courtyard and the pinch of space between the louvred house on the left with the side elevation of the staircase on the right. This offers the courtyard privacy from the street and enables the two surfaces to reflect colour into the re-entrant balcony spaces beyond. © Peter Salter.

bottom: Sectional elevation was part of the planning application. It shows a cross section through the access ramp to the underground garage. Overall height restrictions were a condition of the permission. This prompted a change of strategy; the middle-level floor to ceiling height was restricted to enable the ground floor to become more gracious and the top floor to change its architectural vocabulary. © Peter Salter.

within the depth of section of the dwelling. The screens, which enclose service spaces, are regarded as large immovable architectural 'furniture' sitting on the shelf-like transfer slabs of the dwelling. Each piece demarcates space and through its form directs movement around the house. As a bespoke piece within the frame of the house it 'occupies' and enables tolerance in circumstances of an otherwise dense urban form.

The screens are constructed from carbonised so-called 'black steel'. Such steel is procured directly from the rolling mills so that it retains much of its mill scale and colour from differential cooling processes. The darkness of its material presence conforms to the subdued shadow of the interior much like that of a vernacular dwelling. Its thickness varies according to location and servicing. The basic coordinating dimension of 44 millimetres (1.73 inches) corresponds to the thickness of an internal flush door or flap. From this jamb dimension, the screen geometry curves away to provide stability or in other places widens to accommodate services. The screen surface has very few appendages, relying on cut-outs, multiple drillings and internal pockets to maintain its smooth surfaces. Many of the vertical servicing runs adjacent to the glazed fanlight are ducted through cast-iron sleeveless pipework.

These black steel screens are assembled off site and contain all the pipe runs, extract ducts, soil and vent pipes, electrical supplies and built-in cupboards associated with bathrooms and other servicing elements. Each screen comes with servicing tails to locate the element within the concrete structure. Each becomes a warm wall with embedded radiant heaters that conduct warmth through its steel surface. The screens are built with a minimum of fabrication in order to preserve the carbonised steel finish. The level of precision is similar to that of an agricultural component that might be found on a tractor. The screen is fabricated using exposed and continuous drip welds, spot welds and set screw technology on to a subframe that carries the looped services. No grinding down of welds is permitted, as this would damage the carbonised surface. The screens are finished with beeswax. In places of high humidity, individual surfaces are spray painted using similar multicoatings to that of a tractor part, and using a colour range that can be seen in the low lighting levels of Georgian interiors. In shower areas the screens are lined with a black mosaic.

2.4: Rooftop Rooms – Timber 'Yurts'

The site lies between a terrace of small-scale cottages and a larger-scale office development. The project sets out to reconcile these two scales, while maximising the potential of the site. Planning conditions dictated that the development should not exceed the height of the adjacent office building. This constraint prompted the strategy of inverting the living accommodation and optimising the bedroom heights on the middle floor. This enabled the reception rooms at courtyard level to be of a more gracious height and the living areas at roof level to be liberated, becoming what the Smithsons called 'sky catchers'.

In the manner of a country house in which rooftop dining was accessed across the leadwork, a new architectural language is experienced at the top of each house. At roof level and sometimes embedded within the fabric is a cold moulded and faceted timber room similar in form to the traditional yurt enclosure. This room is used as a formal dining

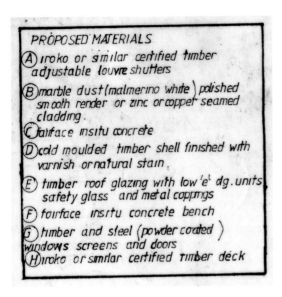

PROPOSED MATERIALS

(A) iroko or similar certified timber adjustable louvre shutters

(B) marble dust (malmerino white) polished smooth render or zinc or copper seamed cladding.

(C) fairface insitu concrete

(D) cold moulded timber shell finished with varnish or natural stain.

(E) timber roof glazing with low 'e' dg. units safety glass and metal coppings

(F) fairface insitu concrete bench

(G) timber and steel (powder coated) windows screens and doors

(H) iroko or similar certified timber deck

Legend of proposed materials for Walmer Road. © Peter Salter.

room, a study room or snug. Like the traditional yurt, the individual rooms have all that is needed for inhabitation, offering an interior quality of comfort and enclosure. In one room there is a sliding opening that resembles the smoke outlet of a yurt hearth and, as in a sea vessel, all the rooms are lit with round prismatic deck lights. As extra-ordinary forms they interact with the privacy of the re-entrant balconies and planted roof terraces.

Prefabricated by boat builders, each structure comes to site partially completed and is lifted into place for on-site copper sheathing. The shell-like form is constructed from a frame of laser-cut plywood studding on to which cold-moulded timber laths are bent, pinned and glued in the manner of sailing boat construction. The cold-moulding process uses counterlayered laths to form bellied and subtly curved shells that are both strong and lightweight. The void between ribs is to be fully sealed with 'air evacuated insulation'. The overall form relies on the subtlety of shape which will need to be evident in the copper sheathing, in the manner of sailing vessels sheathed against Sargasso Sea worm rather than the copper cladding of the standing seam.

The use of the bespoke at Walmer Road is a response to the value and tightness of the site which demands judgement of an appropriate density in relation to place. The project explores dense urban living where a sense of space and privacy is gained within the dwelling by offset views and unexpected shifts of geometry. The geometries of the plan offer liberation to the inhabitant and enable tolerances to be built in without loss of usable space. A complex tailoring to an off-street development.

The Fore Cast

Mark West

Using fabric as a flexible and malleable restraint, Mark West makes extraordinary concrete structures at the Centre for Architectural Structures and Technology at the University of Manitoba. His work is admired by designers, engineers, builders and academics, for its originality, rigour, efficiency and beauty. It has influenced a generation of followers across the world who are inspired by the vast potential his methods have unleashed. Central to his work is the act of speculative and inquisitive drawing. Here he retraces the evolution of his work from its earliest steps, and reviews as much as recounts, how the site and practice of drawing is an integral act in the excavation and search for ideas.

This is a story about the spontaneous eruption of Form, and about techniques for finding the unexpected in the ordinary. It is also a story about how creations in disparate scales, modes and materials can inform each other as an intertwined and linked series of subtle and unforeseen prototypes. This is only a small story, and includes merely a few ways in which such things can happen, but the story may be interesting for restless makers, struggling with the confines of Habit.

Near the end of this story, we find techniques for forming reinforced concrete, freed from the confines of prismatic mould-making. Many techniques have been found for casting wet concrete in flexible fabric moulds, where the materials themselves flexibly negotiate their final form within the gravitational field.[1] In this flexible regime of building, certain boundary conditions are rigidly fixed – for example, the locations and dimensions of edges, or maximum/minimum depths, and so on. The fabric membrane, held to these fixed boundaries, is then left to its own devices to negotiate a precise geometry of stasis between these fixed points and edges while it holds its wet load. The results are a combination of preconceived control and uncontrolled (immaculate) natural events. This way of building runs counter to several deep traditions of architecture, engineering and industrialised construction, yet without surrendering the simplicity and logic that these linked enterprises demand. But all this is near the end of the story, and lest we get too far ahead of ourselves, we must go back to a proper beginning.

Blackout Drawings

This method of building which forgoes forms of rigid control was arrived at by a curious path, more or less unconscious of its own direction. The scent of this trail was picked up through a series of aberrant drawings begun in the early 1980s. Unlike conventional architectural drawings, these have nothing to do with conveying the visual likenesses of anything. In fact, strictly speaking, they are not visual things at all, but rather analogues for a *kind of action* that spontaneously produces unexpected Form.

Thin-shell, spray-concrete 'Curtain Wall' from a hanging fabric mould, 2007. © Mark West.

After a long series of photo collages (a venerable weapon for surprise attacks on the citadel of habit), a method of drawing emerged that takes explicit action on habitual perception. These 'Blackout' drawings start with a photograph or photo collage that is selectively and systematically 'blacked-out' using a soft graphite pencil. The game is to remove the recognisable bits from the photographic reality until some other figure(s) spontaneously emerge to vision. So, for example, faces, hands, or anything else that insists on naming itself, must be removed first. By cutting the moorings to their names, perception is set adrift. In this unnamed indeterminate state, emergent figures will spontaneously appear to vision inside the photographic 'reality', exactly as they do when we stare into clouds, and exactly as Leonardo proposes in his 'Advice to a Young Painter'[2] to stare with similar intent at a stained wall. The figures that appear are then clarified by 'blacking out' the now extraneous portions of the photograph that 'are not them'. This is a game of systematic visual forgetting, an induced amnesia, a renunciation of the already named and recognisable in favour of surprising, unexpected and *nameless* figures and spaces that seemingly arrive of their own free will.

These drawings were an explicit attack on habitual perception, that abiding, steadfast and unshakable enemy of *seeing*. All the works described here represent different attempts to find ways of making that might lift the veil of habit and reawaken direct perception. Of course, one can do this temporarily through novelty, but novel things are an entertainment and, like a drug, wear off quickly, demanding constant replacements with the next and the next new thing. What I wish to describe here is something altogether different from novelty; these are ways to surprise perception through understanding and handling Matter as something *alive*. To clarify what I mean by 'alive' we must take a brief detour into some novel and provocative physical theories.

Understanding all matter as 'living' is, in part, a game. It is a trick of the mind to see a 'dead' material (graphite or concrete, for instance) come alive, restless with its own desires and will-to-form or form-fate. But it is not simply a game of pretend. Putatively 'dead' matter can be understood in an entirely objective sense as truly alive. For this we can refer to the ferocious empiricism of Teilhard de Chardin's physics, where he observes that all matter is everywhere prodigiously active, organised as a kind of protolife (and for Chardin, a protoconsciousness).[3] The truth of this is seen every day in matter's chemical restlessness: the rusting of iron, the peeling of paint, the decanting of odours, all the result of restless and incessant material (molecular) action, though usually at size and timescales far different from our own. Further empirical support is given by contemporary energy flow ecologists who explicitly distinguish between biotic life and non-biotic (or pre-biotic) life.[4] This larger embrace of what constitutes life is based on a broad definition that sees life as the 'negentropic'[5] flow of energy. From this frame of reference, all matter self-organised against entropy is a form of life, biotic or otherwise.

---

top: Anatomy of a Blackout drawing – what is found inside photographic 'reality'. © Mark West.

bottom: (left) Large Blackout drawing, *Everything Falls*, made from collaged photographs. (right) An enlarged portion of this drawing, 1984. © Mark West.

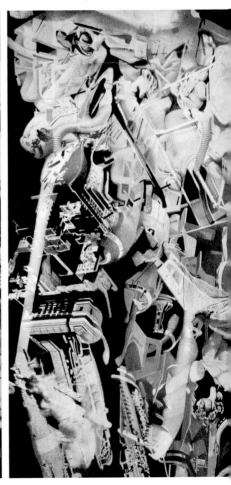

Blackout drawing (detail), 1983. © Mark West.

But let us return to acts of drawing and making. When I found the Blackout method nearly 30 years ago I was filled with an intense youthful euphoria. I felt I had fallen into a deep discovery, something with heavy implications I did not understand, but could only intuit. I drew incessantly, finding ways to eventually free myself of the photographic 'canvas' as a starting point, yet keeping the hallucinatory/amnesic method of production. A long series of 'free' graphite drawings followed, done on blank paper using various versions of collage and Blackout techniques.

But despite their compelling pleasures, these were only images. As a builder I wanted to make actual things, not illusions. Furthermore, these particular images were useless as guides to construction. Despite their compelling realism, they were not descriptions of anything, but rather the found results of a specific kind of action, an action of self-formation. The signal value of the drawing technique was its extreme simplicity – these things almost literally make themselves. Their ease was a hallmark, a temptation. Were there other simple analogous actions suitable to making/finding *actual* things in the world?

The answer to this question came from a sculptural practice that was explicitly aimed at taking the lessons of collage and the Blackout drawings as prototypes of action in construction. During this work I stumbled upon the trick of casting plaster in a thin flexible sheet which was subsequently redeployed in various ways over the years. The solid/fluid, soft/hard, wet/dry things that resulted were truly uncanny. Much like the illusory figures that spontaneously emerge from a Blackout drawing these were, in their own full-dimensional way, self-forming things – intricately defined figures that arrive with no assigned meaning. But unlike the figures that appear to us in clouds (or clouds of graphite), these forms were produced, or 'hallucinated', not by vision but by the materials themselves. Significantly, these objects arrived in full-dimensional material reality with the greatest of ease and, following a builder's intuition, were evidently capable of being built large if the small modelling materials were scaled up to tarpaulins and concrete.

Self-Formation

When the work of scaling up these miniature self-forming casts began, I made a choice to limit the fabric membranes to flat sheets taken directly off the roll – no tailoring or cut patterns. This limitation was an overlay of a builder's sensibility (the imperative of simplicity) mapped on to the freedom of sculptural practice and its search for a particular state of mind.

While the simplicity of these constructions is assured by a reduction in means (flat sheets, simple tools and fasteners), the complexity of the results originates in the *self-forming* nature of the constructions. The final forms produced are found by the materials themselves through their own negotiations/struggles to reach a certain precise shape. In every case this is a singular and inevitable form – a kind of fate. The precise curvatures as well as all the details of buckled folds and stretch marks are calculated by the materials themselves to form the spatial trajectory of their own stability – a one to one, automatic, three-dimensional drawing of their mutual equilibrium state.

Of course, concrete and fabric do not spontaneously self-organise themselves. A builder's hand, attention and energy are all required to contrive these events, implicating a builder's will

top: Early experimental
fabric column mould (left);
filled with concrete (right).

right: Bar Harbor, Maine,
1990. © Mark West.

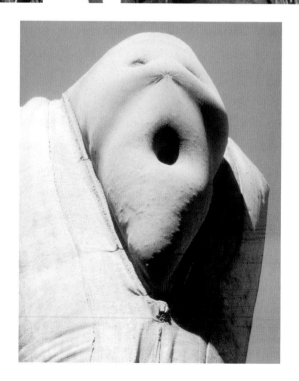

and craft in the process. But this goes without saying. The interesting part is not that craft is required to build these things, but rather that the most beautiful and intelligent bits take place *between* the controlled and crafted boundaries. In this case, the builder's deeper craft consists precisely in learning how and when to get out of the way, how to make a space of action in which the materials can self-organise their own shape of resistance unmolested by human will.

The Immediacy of the Thing
The beauty of these self-formed things, or the self-formed portions of these things, is striking. They are immediately recognisable as natural events rather than as designed form. As such they have a strange *time* about them that entwines their fluid (previous) and solid (current) states. Here are things that refuse to locate themselves in any time except for the moment of their creation which is *held* in an immaculate and permanent form. They may appear to be artefacts of some unknown ancient civilisation that flourished briefly, or something entirely new – some kind of science fiction perhaps? They refuse historic placement while the past of their moment of creation is permanently present. Like something from nature, they somehow remain permanently alive to perception.[6]

The Secretion of Meaning
This is a way of making results in things that are, to some extent, without direct intention. As when you find some realistic form inside a cloud, there is no sense of authorship to its discovery; it is simply 'there'. This lack of intentional authorship changes the basis of meaning found in these forms, freeing them from any semiotic structure; there is no pre-established code, no conceptual key to meaning. Things that arrive by natural processes 'represent' nothing but themselves in their suchness. In this case, perceived meaning erupts spontaneously through the *affect* produced by their presence. Percept displaces concept – or perhaps more accurately, perception *secretes* meaning without intending to.[7]

This kind of *found meaning* is prelinguistic, or nonlinguistic. It arrives unbidden, as in the presence of music, not through interpretation of a code but as a presence. And as with music, the fact that one cannot easily *say* what that meaning is does not in any way diminish the reality and immanence of what has been grasped. It occupies us with the force of an irrefutable argument devoid of language. It is not something one needs to get, but rather something that gets you. In this sense it is allied with and akin to Surrealism's attack on the heartland of intentionality. Do I overstate the case? Perhaps. In any event, an author's testimony should never be trusted – though in this case one's sense of authorship, as such, is nearly disabled.

A Hybrid Method
In the case of flexibly formed concrete, a definite sense of authorship is felt in the craft that is required: choosing the fabric, determining the boundary and support conditions, the connection details and, perhaps, the pre-stress (pre-stretching) of the fabric. Getting these things right is no different, in essence, from any other act of building, except for the fact that these are merely *preparations for an event* that will shape the construction

Fabric-formed column being unwrapped, Bar Harbor, Maine, 1990. © Mark West.

according to its own lights. Everything else that follows these preparations is determined by the materials themselves according to natural law. What emerges in the balance is a composite form of 'design' where wilful control and a surrender to natural events occur in the same space at the same time.

This hybrid methodology has proved to be extraordinarily fruitful. After more than 20 years of innumerable experiments, flat-sheet moulds are still revealing surprising new forms and possibilities, many of which are both beautiful and materially efficient. This unexpected and unreasonable fecundity suggests that within the simplicity and pragmatic constraints of this operation lies something deeper and quite a bit more complex. Here pragmatism does not serve the ends of convention or reduction, but on the contrary induces a kind of constructive metabolism that, as with all natural events, produces complexity as a consequence of extreme simplicity.

The Fore Cast
The work and research recounted here traces a linked series of retrospective 'prototypes', each one replaying a slightly different and more complex version of a similar search; each one a subtle prototype of action suitable to its own materials, size and complexity; each one producing a surprise of its own, and each one subsequently nested within the next incarnation/trial. To recount: this Chain began with Collage, turning into Blackouts, leading to free hallucinatory graphite drawings (early 1980s and onwards), followed by a free sculptural practice (late 1980s), reaching a kind of culmination in the first full-scale flexibly formed concrete structures (1989–92). The project of developing this new way of building has been ongoing since then. Having reached the point where a practical and economical building technology has been developed, one is tempted to start building – and indeed there is no reason not to. But what if the chain or web of linked prototypes is yet unfinished? What if the technical development of flexible moulds is a subtle prototype of action for something more complex again, something with more dimensions than a mere set of building components – another way of thinking about and doing architecture, for instance.

Returning once more to the physics of energy flow, we recall that every bit of matter, caught as it is with us in a temporal flux, plays out its own actions and exchange of energy in the world according to its own timescale and physical/chemical/atomic engagement with everything else around it. These behaviours are not the kind of behaviours mimicked by robotics, 'interactive' architecture, or so-called 'intelligent materials' which are, after all, focused on stimulating (or simulating) our own desires. These are, instead, behaviours innate to the materials themselves according to their own more-than-human[8] requirements, desires and fates. This is the life of the pre-biotic and post-biotic more-than-human world, the actions of the world from which we come, in which we are enmeshed, of which we are made, and into which we will return. When we build we enclose ourselves in another kind of living 'flesh', non-biotic, yet very much alive nevertheless.

Having found all this through these last subtle prototypes of concrete and steel, a series of questions comes to the fore: what if architecture were not made to be so strictly

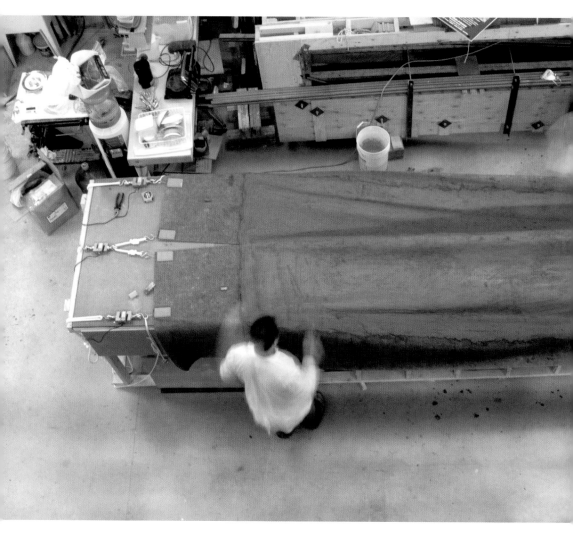

A flat sheet of fabric, loaded with a thin
layer of concrete, self-forms itself into a
funicular compression-shell mould. CAST
lab/studio, University of Manitoba, 2009.
© Mark West.

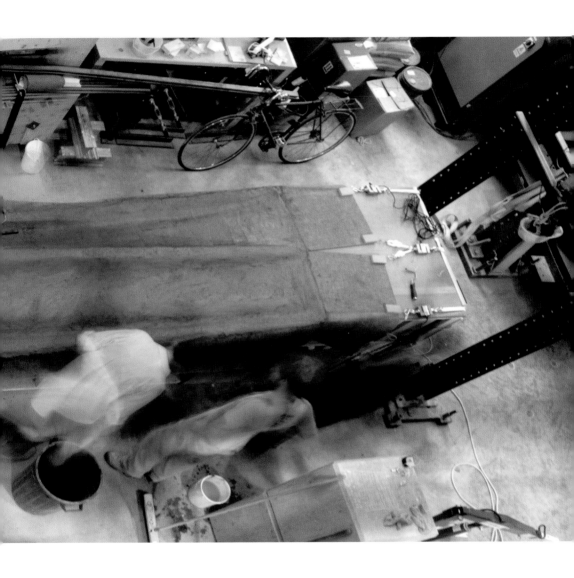

Fabric-formed thin-shell mould and
funicular compression thin-shell cast from
this mould. The deep buckling-resistant
'corrugations', which are spontaneously
formed along principal lines of tension
stress in the fabric mould, provide
buckling-resistant 'corrugations' in the
compression shell cast from this mould.
CAST lab/studio, University of Manitoba,
2009. © Mark West.

about *us*? What would life be like in architecture acutely alive to the events of its *own* existence, quite apart from the rhythm and scale of our lives? Is there an architecture that might assist us in our own living by pointing us not towards ourselves, and what we, we, we, want, want, want, but rather an architecture that helps turn our attention towards the more-than-human world and our role in it?

Notes

1 Fabric-formed concrete research is described at length elsewhere. See, for example: http://www. umanitoba.ca/faculties/architecture/cast/research/fabric_formwork/index.html and http://www. umanitoba.ca/faculties/architecture/cast/resources.html
2 Leonardo da Vinci in *A Way of Developing and Arousing the Mind to Various Inventions* in his '*Advice to a Young Painter*', teaches the following: 'I cannot forbear to mention ... a new device for study which, although it may seem but trivial and almost ludicrous, is nevertheless extremely useful in arousing the mind to various inventions. And this is, when you look at a wall spotted with stains, or with a mixture of stones, ... you may discover a resemblance to ... an endless variety of objects, which you could reduce to complete and well-drawn forms. And these appear on such walls confusedly, like the sound of bells in whose jangle you may find any name or word you choose to imagine.'
3 Teilhard de Chardin, *The Phenomenon of Man,* trans. Bernard Wall, Wm Collins Sons & Co Ltd (London) and Harper Row Publishers Inc (New York), 1959. Originally published as *Le Phénomène Humain*, Editions du Seuil (Paris), 1955.
4 The terms non-biotic or pre-biotic life are commonly used to describe the molecular/chemical foundations of biotic life. Biotic life is differentiated from pre-biotic life by the fact that it can self-reproduce and has memory (its DNA). See, for example, ED Schneider, JJ Kay, 'Order from Disorder: The Thermodynamics of Complexity in Biology', in Michael P Murphy, Luke AJ O'Neill (eds), *What is Life: The Next Fifty Years. Speculations on the Future of Biology*, Cambridge University Press (Cambridge), 1995, pp 161–72.
5 The usual direction of all molecular action is 'downwards' into less differentiated energy gradients, often referred to as disorder or chaos. This is the natural entropic 'flow' of the universe and, according to the second law of thermodynamics, the very foundation of time's one-way arrow. The prime exception to this inevitable flow towards greater entropy is biotic life, which assembles matter *against* entropy and toward greater differentiation, order and complexity, what physicist Erwin Schrödinger called 'negative entropy'. See Erwin Schrödinger, *What Is Life?* and *Mind and Matter*, Cambridge University Press (Cambridge) 1967, first published 1944.
6 Other things, over time, anaesthetise themselves and us, creating a somnambulist's world. The capital-D Design market is predicated on precisely this exhaustion of interest and the subsequent desire for the next and the next new and temporarily interesting thing. As Eric Hoffer has famously said, 'You can never get enough of what you don't really need.'
7 A central lesson of Surrealism.
8 I take the term more-than-human from David Abram, *The Spell of the Sensuous – Perception and Language in a More-Than-Human World*, Vintage Books (New York), 1996.

Instrument Two. A model to produce
paradoxical shadows sits on the folding
picture plane (seen here holding a
printed map). See also caption for
Instrument Three. © Nat Chard.

Drawing Out an Indeterminate Duration

Nat Chard

One of the central contingencies of architecture is that it covers a far broader area than the design and production of the physical and tactile. Key to this understanding is architecture's continued exploration of the role of representation in questioning, revealing, and speculating on the transition of ideas from the drawn to the made. In building the drawing, marks or lines that appear important and firm may often lose an expected status. Likewise, transient gestures may take on a greater significance when translated into tangible matter. Nat Chard experiments with the drawn and the made in a highly inventive and penetrating manner. Here he expands on his latest work, which uniquely resides in a state of constant flux.

Normally when looking at a drawing or painting we become implicated in the content through interpretation. Architectural drawings have been tuned over centuries to be explicit about their exact meaning, through practical necessity prescribing a reliable interpretation by the many agencies that come into contact with them. The architectural drawing typically discusses an ideal state of the architecture, an instant of its life. This paper documents a set of drawing instruments that are searching for other means of engagement, for instance through a more phenomenal relationship to the drawing, with the aim of nurturing a design process and constant enlivening of an indeterminate architecture. Through their engagement with us, the instruments start to rehearse our possible relationships with an indeterminate architecture. The emphasis for the instruments is on their capacity to draw out possibilities and the act of drawing as an analogue to an active inhabitation. All the instruments have folding picture planes to provide a critical acceptance of the ideas that are projected at them, but the means of projection evolves from straightforward observation (where the position of observance implicates us spatially) through fairly normal photographic perspective to the projection of pigment where the trajectory of material disturbs the certainties of optical perspective. After the first instrument, the instruments play on the possibilities of disturbance provided by paradoxical shadows that construct situations outside our normal experience and therefore implicate us in making a new sense of the thing we come across. The sixth instrument concentrates on these possibilities.

Drawing out an Indeterminate Duration

During the period between May 1964 and June 1967, the psychiatrist and psychical researcher Jule Eisenbud[1] observed an extraordinary ability displayed by the American hotel lift (elevator) operator Ted Serios. Serios's gift was the ability to project images from his head on to film, mostly Polaroid instant film. A large number of the prints were 'blackies' or 'whities' where Serios could apparently imbue the print with light when there was none, or produce underexposed or dark images where there would under usual circumstances be a normal exposure, subject to similar conditions and camera settings. Even stranger, he was, according to Eisenbud's research, also able to project thoughts as photograph-like images of absent objects on to the film, a process called thoughtography. The images related to content either in Serios's (often inebriated) consciousness or in hidden packets that Eisenbud was tempting Serios to view psychically. Serios sometimes used a device he called a gizmo to help him with the process. Eisenbud's research concluded when Serios produced the image of a curtain.

Eisenbud was convinced that Serios had a psychic gift,[2] but inevitably there has been much scepticism[3] and suggestions that Eisenbud's research methods were not watertight. Either way, if thoughtography is the direct translation of an idea into a photographic picture, it must also be the apotheosis of the romantic notion of the genius sketch. Such a drawing is the registration of an impulse on to an available piece of paper (conveniently such impulses often appear to happen near to envelopes with unadorned backs, hotel notepaper or paper napkins from an elegant café) and has been massaged in popular culture as an important act of creativity, translating the creative impulse with as little corruption through the medium as possible. As an idea of creative production it assumes that ideas are autonomous and may emerge fully formed. The impulse happens in an instant and its registration is an urgent translation. This clearly differs from the drawing that hopes to find something and uses the process of drawing to find out what that thing might be. This paper discusses a series of drawing instruments developed by the author to draw an indeterminate architecture and support an indeterminate drawing process to the same end.

In an essay recalling a short essay by Barnett Newman,[4] JF Lyotard discusses the question of operating in the sublime in artistic production.[5] He proposes that for the painter or writer who operates in a school of thought, there are supportive prescriptions.

> All intellectual disciplines and institutions take for granted that not everything has been said, written or recorded, that words already heard or pronounced are not the last words. 'After' a sentence, 'after' a colour, comes another sentence, another colour. One doesn't necessarily know which, but it is possible to guess if credence is given to the rules that chain one sentence to another, cue one colour to another — rules preserved in precisely the institutions of the past and future that I mention above. The school, the programme, the project — all proclaim that after such a sentence, such another sentence or at least such sort of a sentence is mandatory, that one kind of sentence is mandatory, that one kind of sentence is permitted, while another is forbidden.

He goes on to explain that for the writer or painter working outside the prescriptions of a school there is not just the question of the empty canvas or the empty page at the beginning of the work, 'but of each instance of something being imminent, which makes a question of every question mark, every "and now what?"' Lyotard suggests that this condition of anticipation or suspense is a positive one that leads to an 'intensification of being'.

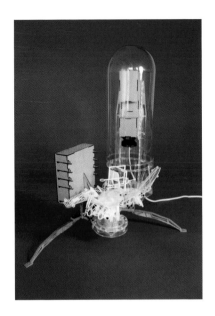

left: Instrument Three. The box in the glass dome contains a model and a light bulb, with a lens from a 5 x 4 in (127 x 102 mm) camera to project the image on to a picture plane that is critical of the projection through its ability to fold. An enlarged replica of the model in the box sits on the picture plane to cast a paradoxical shadow. Glass, MDF, acrylic and cast aluminium. © Nat Chard.

below: Instrument One. Slits in the folding picture plane emit light that can be adjusted for colour and intensity. © Nat Chard.

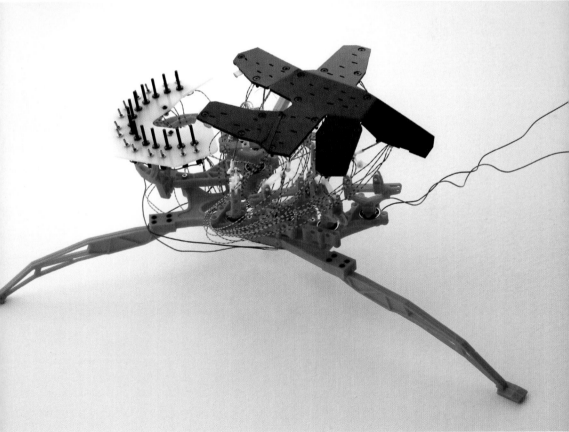

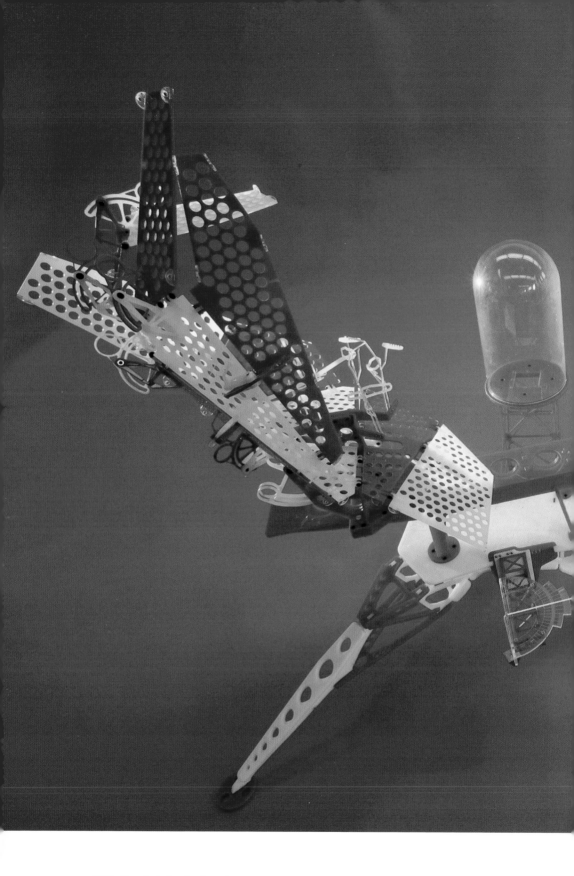

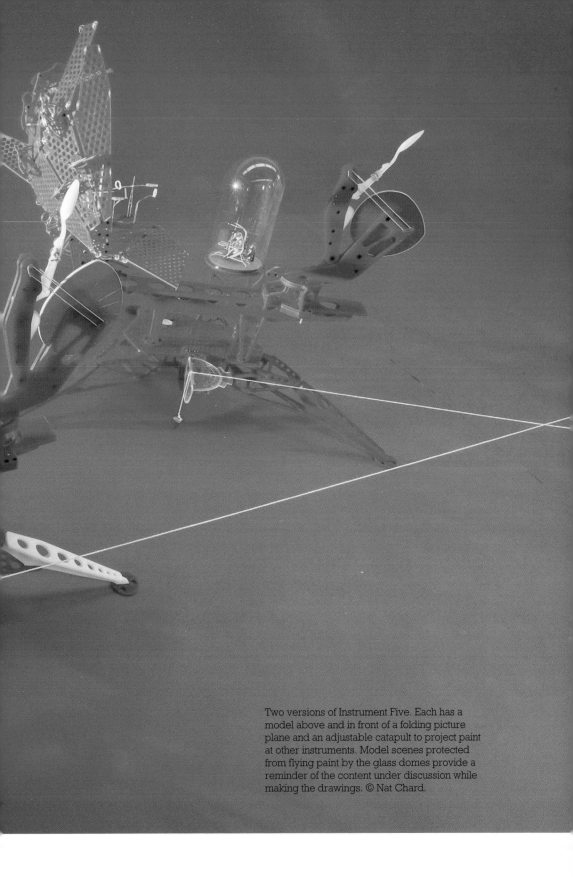

Two versions of Instrument Five. Each has a model above and in front of a folding picture plane and an adjustable catapult to project paint at other instruments. Model scenes protected from flying paint by the glass domes provide a reminder of the content under discussion while making the drawings. © Nat Chard.

Instrument Six. A light bulb on a track illuminates a shadow-maker to cast a shadow on a folding picture plane (bottom right). A camera that slides to take stereoscopic pairs of photographs witnesses the shadow. When the camera is shifting from its left- to right-eye view, the light bulb also moves on the track. As a consequence of this parallax, the shadow in the 3D photograph separates from the surface on to which it is cast. The instrument also works in real time, replacing the light bulb with a pair of candles with polarising filters. © Nat Chard.

In this construction the creative act is not only in the service of an outcome but a pleasure in itself. While an epiphany might provide the satisfaction of resolving something, the condition Lyotard describes is a pleasure in the emergence of something where the something is not established and might not reach a resolution. Ted Serios's thoughtographs or genius sketches compress the emergence of an impulse into the shortest possible time so as not to corrupt its translation into a picture — the representation of something definitive. It is an impulse that wishes to emerge in an instant. The work discussed in this paper is looking for pleasure in the duration of making a drawing, a drawing that is searching for an architecture that supports the very sort of existence promoted in the process of drawing. The act of making the drawing is a rehearsal for the indeterminate condition that the drawing is trying to propose, an emergent rather than resolved condition. Why this should be a productive way of working is a longer story and this paper will concentrate on the tools and technology of proposing such a condition.

Normally, when we view a drawing, we take possession of part of the content through interpretation, or reading the drawing. Architectural drawings are designed to be resistant to any interpretation except that prescribed by the architect, so that the many agencies that come in contact with the drawing all make the same reading. This prescriptive potential makes it essential to question how architectural drawings should be engaged when thinking how to make an indeterminate architecture. The prescription exists both in the drawing's role as an instrument of study (and reflection) for the author and how it is available for others. As reading, or interpretation, has the potential to limit one's indeterminate engagement with architectural drawings or the content discussed in them, this work seeks out other modes of engagement, or more specifically, to spatialise the drawing so that the observer's phenomenal relationship to the drawing is at least as important as any reading.

When we observe a painting we are so familiar with the idea of the frame and the construction of perspective that we read the painting as if we have a frontal relationship even if we have a parallactic view. With anamorphic paintings the observer's position in space implicates them in the nature of the image, for if they are at the point of resolution the image is distinct from that in, say, the frontal view. This is very clear in Holbein's *Ambassadors* (1533)[6] where the combination of normal and anamorphic projection disturbs our normal capability to resolve parallax. Anamorphism has the potential to spatialise the image, even if this is usually in a prescribed way. If we examine Samuel van Hoogstraten's *Peepshow with Views of the Interior of a Dutch House* (c 1655),[7] we find a box with the interior of a room painted inside it and two opposing peepholes from which to view resolved images. One side is left open to illuminate the box. The physical space of the box and the pictorial space of the painted image do not always register at the same place. While looking through one hole, the wall of the box meets the floor in the same place as the painted wall meets its floor. The painted wall continues anamorphically on the ceiling of the box, however. In the opposite view it is the junction of wall and ceiling that registers the physical with the pictorial, but not the wall and the floor. When viewed from the open side the image appears quite

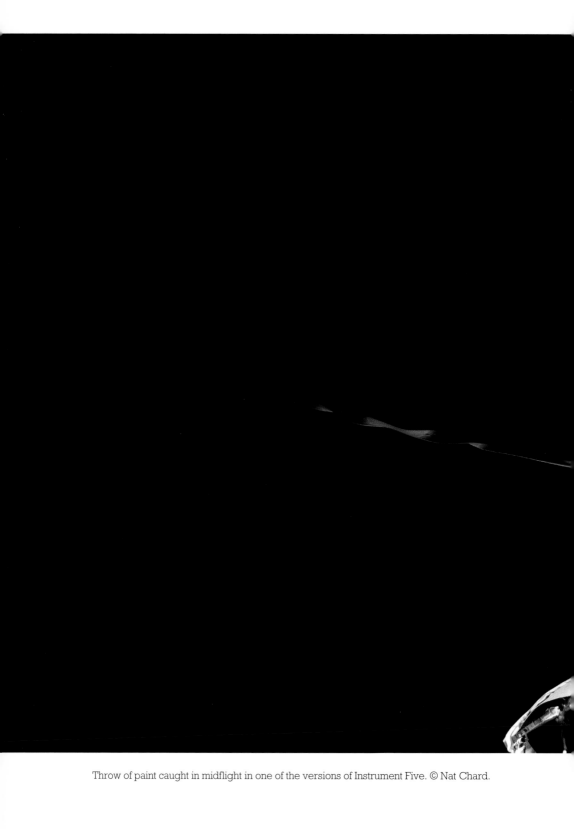

Throw of paint caught in midflight in one of the versions of Instrument Five. © Nat Chard.

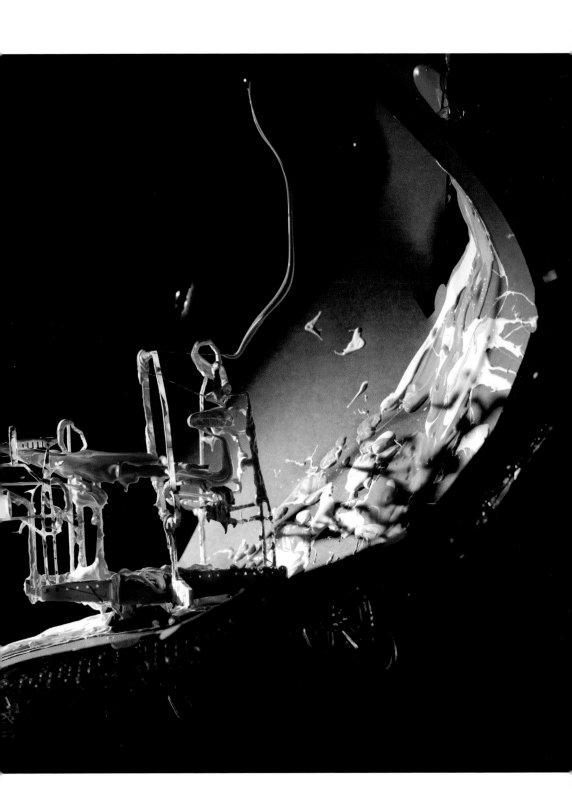

different from the prescribed views, as if seeing the way two people opposite each other are picturing the world but from a distant position. Anamorphism has spatialised the picture and the folding of the box has spatialised the picture plane.

From Leonardo onwards, artists have discussed the potential of manipulating the picture plane to make the painted image more true to our perception. If it is possible to adjust the picture plane to this end, it must also have the capacity to provide a critical understanding of the thing that is being pictured. More than that, the picture plane is a deliciously ungraspable entity between the three-dimensional object and its two-dimensional projection.

How is it possible to make spatial drawings that implicate the observer beyond interpretation through anamorphism, folding and the nether world of the picture plane? There are models that suggest such a thing is possible, for instance the somewhat prescriptive world of the natural history museum diorama or the planetarium projector and dome. In both cases, the discussion between a projection and a three-dimensional screen constructs a realm that implicates the observer spatially and operates in a world that blurs the distinction between representation and experience. Both were studied in pursuit of developing a series of drawing instruments that would support the emergence of an indeterminate architecture through an indeterminate engagement.

What sort of registration would support such a way of drawing? As well as considering how our phenomenal engagement with the drawing might implicate us in its content, there is a question as to whether the drawn content might aspire to such a condition. In her discussion of the *Poetics of Indeterminacy*,[8] Marjorie Perloff argues 'David Antin's definition, in the mid seventies, of poetry as "the language of art" a form of discourse which rather than "saying one thing and meaning something else," returns to the literal but with the recognition that phenomenological reality is itself "discovered" and "constructed" by poets.' If we make the distinction between being absorbed by the image of the picture and observing the structure of picturing, or perhaps picturing the structure of observation, there appears a potential for the content of the image (quite apart from the potential of anamorphism) to touch on such a 'phenomenological reality'. If you examine Canova's[9] full-size plaster models for his marble sculptures you will see a number of registration pins located on the surface. Although some of them register an extremity or generic feature, most of them discuss the local particularity and nuance of a change in surface, registering what matters most for the sculptor. In many of Euan Uglow's paintings[10] he registers measurements that help him to translate what he observes on to a picture plane. Again, what he registers appears particular to his fascination with the body and space he is painting rather than a generic method of location or registration of the figure. When we observe Canova's models or Uglow's paintings we come across both a representation of the body they discuss and a more primary experience of the act of picturing, an engagement that goes beyond a reflexive discussion of the represented and the mode of representation. The registration discusses a potential in the object that is beyond picturing, a reality that the artists have constructed.

Instrument Seven. The picture plane sits adjacent to the flight of the paint (in Instrument Five the picture plane is behind the drawing pieces), while the folds in the plane can protect the area that collects the splatters that come off the drawing pieces from the direct throw of the paint. © Nat Chard.

How is it possible to have an engagement with the process of drawing that makes the duration of emerging ideas significant? The refinement of tools to make them more effective at their intended task clearly makes them prescriptive. Drawing instruments and computer drawing and modelling programs carry prescription through assumptions about how they will be used and how they will draw. The procedural nature of computer drafting exaggerates this. A lack of prescription is not entirely helpful, however. Without any bearings, the person drawing is consumed with the enormity of working out every aspect of what they are drawing and how it should be drawn at the same time. The drawing instruments discussed in this paper are attempts to find a suitable balance in this question, and to develop ways of drawing that involve the issues that were discussed earlier. There are a number of concerns that are consistent with all the instruments. These include: the duration of drawing as a condition that is an analogue for the duration of inhabitation of the architecture that is being drawn by the instrument; the development of anamorphism and folding picture planes as a way to spatialise the observer's relationship with the emerging image; the folding picture plane as a critical device to question the

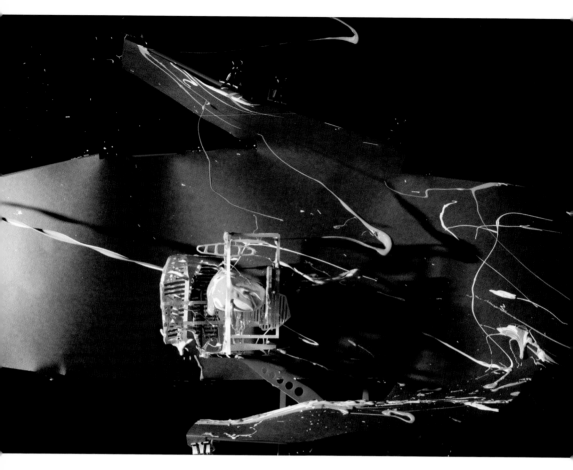

A flight of paint landing on the picture plane of Instrument Seven. High-speed flash photograph. © Nat Chard.

proposal or projection in the drawing; and finally the uncertain realm that lies between two and three dimensions that is partly inhabited by the picture plane, but appears as an ambiguous depth that offers many pleasures.[11] To liberate the drawing process from the prescriptions of generic drawing instruments but to support the act of drawing towards the specific aims of this research, a series of drawing instruments have been built. The first one concentrates on the possibility of the folding picture plane, the second introduces projection with a photographic precision, the third is a development of the second, the fourth is a test and development for the fifth that is a set of four drawing instruments that develop the space between two and three dimensions as well as making the means of projection more sympathetic to the aim of the project. The sixth instrument picks up on the paradoxical shadows in the second and third instruments, and discovers a way to lift a shadow into the space between the object and the surface on which the shadow would normally be cast.

The first drawing instrument was previously discussed in *Architectural Design*,[12] so the description here will be brief. The main concern is the potential of the picture plane, to the extent that the only projection in the piece is in the gaze of the observer, or the camera when making the drawings that came out of it. A folding surface holds a figure of fixed registrations that are illuminated from below with a control panel allowing the colour of the light emerging from the figure to be modulated; the condition of the figure can be adjusted but not the figure, except for a few elements that can be blanked out with sliding shutters. The picture plane can be adjusted relative to the condition being discussed (too long a story for the purposes of this paper), and the picture has two existences, one for the observer and one captured by a sequence of photographs (taken from a number of positions) that are registered on another (but this time fixed) picture plane.

The second instrument learns from the first one and adds perspectival projection. The box in the glass dome contains a model, a scaled-down replica of the one that sits on the folding picture plane below. A light bulb illuminates the model so that the lens at the bottom of the box projects an image of the model on to the picture plane. Moving the box up or down or tilting it can adjust the focus. The wide-angle lens comes from a 5 x 4 inch (127 x 102 millimetre) camera and provides enough shift so that the projection can be reasonably oblique to the picture plane but still in focus over most of it (if the folds are not too great and the lens is parallel to the picture plane). As well as folding, the picture plane can rotate, as can the box. The picture plane is constructed out of acrylic and holds photographic paper to register a negative of the projection as understood by a particular fold. The model on the picture plane is articulated, with the various pieces attached to different folding plates. Normally a perspective projection lands on a surface that appears not to exist (or its presence is replaced by the depth proposed by the image). In this case the shadow of the model on the picture plane registers the picture plane beside the pictorial projection of the identical model in the box, providing a paradox that implicates the observer, as they have to construct their own comprehension of an image that makes no obvious sense. The shadow operates a little like the shadows of the ready-mades on Duchamp's *Tu m'*[13] which also register the pictorial surface rather than land on the images within the depth of the picture, and propose a presence on the observer's side of the canvas in addition to the world pictured behind it. To work photographically, the instrument needs to be played with in a dark room. As a camera it is the reversal of the normal. The world is in the box and the film is in the world.

In both these instruments, the folding of the picture plane makes the position of the observer matter through the varied foreshortenings and occlusions of the image. In the second one the picture plane is much more active in that it provides a critical reception of the projection, anamorphically distorting it and sometimes occluding it, so that whatever it is that the projection is trying to persuade you, the picture plane can accept on its own terms. The third instrument is a development of the second, and both were made to work on a proposal for a house. The registration originates from abstract models.

The fourth instrument is a test-bed for the fifth. In terms of the larger objectives of the project, the perspective projection used in the second and third instruments is such a well understood territory that the anamorphosis caused by the folding can be somewhat predictable. The single projection and receiving surface also limit the ability of the instrument to establish and sustain a dialogue as the parts are set in their relationships to each other. The fourth and fifth instruments shift to a less controlled form of projection. During the Renaissance, a number of European cities and their fortifications were designed or redesigned in relation to the projection of the cannonball. The geometry of projection and receiving was practised through a number of instruments. Some of these, such as the *radio latino* as well as triangulation and surveying instruments[14] were employed by both the gunner (the projector) and the military architect (receiver). Additionally, the military architects who designed the elaborate geometric defences also organised the systems of laying siege.[15] The medium of projection in the fourth and fifth instruments is water-based house paint of differing viscosities (some remain coalesced in flight, while thinner paint develops into a drip). The trajectory can be aimed from one instrument at another with a degree of accuracy but also with more surprises than with the projection of light. The curvature of the projection can also be altered so that the play between the projection and the receiving picture plane can be modulated. The paint is thrown by a catapult and is aimed at a model that sits on the neighbouring instrument. Behind the model is a folding picture plane that accepts the paint or the shadow of the model, if the paint hits its target. The shadow is less the figure of the model than the sort of disturbance the model causes to the flying paint. The accumulation of paint on the model obviously alters it as well as making the drawing, so the play between the two- and three-dimensional continues. The models are adjustable so that they might protect a splat of paint that has landed on them, or protect a part of the model from such a splat. The model starts out with opaque three-dimensional registrations supported by transparent armatures. With the accumulation of paint, the armatures become equivalent to the registrations. All the instruments have a catapult, a model and a picture plane as well as a figurative model of the situation they discuss under a glass dome, as a reminder for the person who is drawing of the content of what is being drawn and discussed. Every time the paint is projected the tone is changed so that the drawing registers the sequence and duration of the conversation. At the time of writing, there is not an equivalent to the paradoxical projection from the model on the picture plane in the second instrument, something that is developed with more focus by the sixth instrument.

The shadow confirms so much about the things we see, especially the relationship of the object to its situation. We understand the shadow so well in this performance that it provides an excellent site of disturbance to keep subject matter alive and outside the reach of easy assumptions. The paradoxical shadow in the second and third instruments tries to play upon this. The sixth instrument is to explore the possibility of the disturbance provided by interstitial shadows. A light source on a track projects light to cast a shadow of an object on to one of the folding picture planes developed for the fifth instrument. A camera that can track from side to side witnesses the resulting shadow to take stereoscopic pairs of photographs. If you take a photograph for the left eye and then move the camera for the right-eye position and move the light source along the track, there are two sets of parallax. The two camera positions produce the stereoscopic image. The two shadow positions provide a second stereoscopy that re-sites the shadow in space (either in front of or behind the surface on which it actually lands, depending on which way you slide the light source) when viewing the photographs. In a second mode, with two candles on the lighting track with polarising filters in front of each and a screen that retains the polarisation of the light on the picture plane, when viewed with polarising glasses the shadow appears directly in the displaced position in space. The flickering of the candles animates the floating shadow.

Drawing with these instruments has the potential to evolve an architectural design, but the greater possibility is that the drawings discuss the current condition, so that authorship takes place as much during inhabitation as in advance of it (and by those that inhabit as well as those who propose). The act of drawing would parallel inhabitation and the instrument would adjust the architecture, not so much as a utilitarian responsive system but as a provocation to save the situation from becoming stale and overfamiliar.

Notes

1 Jule Eisenbud, 'The Thoughtography of Ted Serios', in Stephen E Braude, *The Perfect Medium, Photography and the Occult*, Yale University Press (New Haven), 2005.

2 Jule Eisenbud, *The World of Ted Serios: 'Thoughtographic' Studies of an Extraordinary Mind*, William Morrow & Co (New York), 1967.

3 See footnote 2 in Jule Eisenbud's, 'The Thoughtography of Ted Serios', but there is also material on various websites that attempts to expose Serios as a fraud and to question Eisenbud's methods.

4 Barnett Newman, 'The Sublime is Now', first printed in *Tiger's Eye*, 1948, but currently published in Simon Morley (ed), *The Sublime*, Whitechapel Gallery and MIT Press Documents of Contemporary Art series (London and Cambridge, MA), 2010.

5 Jean-François Lyotard, 'The Sublime and the Avant-Garde', in Simon Morley (ed), *The Sublime*. The quotation is taken from *Artforum*, April 1984.

6 National Gallery, London.

7 National Gallery, London.

8 Marjorie Perloff, *The Poetics of Indeterminacy: Rimbaud to Cage*, Princeton University Press (Princeton), 1981.

9 Antonio Canova, 1757–1822. He came from Possagno in the Veneto but later worked in Rome.

10 See, for instance, Catherine Lampert and Richard Kendall, *Euan Uglow: The Complete Paintings*, Yale University Press (New Haven), 2007.

11 See conversation with Philip Guston in *Interviews with American Artists*, David Sylvester, Pimlico (Yale), 2001.

12 Bob Sheil (ed), *AD Design Through Making*, vol 75, no 4, John Wiley & Sons (London), 2005, pp 22–9.

13 1918, Yale University Art Gallery, New Haven.

14 See J Bennett and S Johnston, *The Geometry of War 1500–1750*, Museum of the History of Science (Oxford), 1996.

15 Most notably Sébastien Le Prestre de Vauban (1633–1707).

The author gratefully acknowledges the support provided by the University of Manitoba's Creative Works grants in the development of this work.

Incisions in the Haze

Kate Davies and Emmanuel Vercruysse; Liquidfactory

If, as Stephen Gage argues, 'The Bespoke is a Way of Working not a Style', then experimental practice Liquidfactory emulate that philosophy stylishly. Offering the reader the first glimpse of a new work in progress, young designers Kate Davies and Emmanuel Vercruysse glide between graphite sketches, molten metal and narrative text, as equally speculative and reflexive processes, with astounding ease. Here, their evolving series of projects known as Prosthetic Mythologies is embellished with a new layer, on this occasion not in a saturated industrial forest seeping with acoustic memories, but a parched and endless desert charged with electric vitality and doom.

This article presents the latest project in the series Prosthetic Mythologies[1] and discusses the role of intuitive gesture within the design process in relation to the bespoke. Set in a Saharan sand sea, deep within endless fields of illusion and hallucination, isolation and repetition, the project is imagined as a series of incisions punctuating an indeterminate landscape. Interwoven within the main body of the article are a number of narrative texts exploring the tactics and context of the project. They discuss our attempts to capture and harness gestural responses to this landscape, exploring our negotiations between writing and making and the importance of the sketch as we search for ways of working that allow a tactile translation from loose idea to physical form.

> In a high wind, the dunes smoke and a low pitched drumming is heard, the spirit of Raoul, the drummer of death, and the Tuareg, the blue men of the desert, draw their veils across their faces and cast their eyes downward.[2]

A Prosthetic Mythology

Prosthetic Mythologies is a collection of speculative projects that explore the cultural and environmental contexts of extreme locations. First in the series was a proposition to release a flock of sonic armatures in a boreal forest, as an enquiry into traditions of folklore and fable that traverse the globe along common latitudes. The works are seen as 'architectural incisions' and 'performative interventions', and are developed through strategic and exploratory drawings, which inform a set of artefacts and site-specific installations. Rather than static objects, these interventions are seen as performances of varying scale and duration, and we see the pieces as the active 'occupants' of a given context playing out a set of choreographic trajectories and sequential disruptions across a given site.

In this latest iteration of the project we explore the desert as an indeterminate landscape, and the work focuses on the sandstorm as an agitator of a shifting terrain. The proposal consists of a set of sculptural and active landmarks for the Sahara Desert, where electrical storms generate huge potential gradients, in essence creating a giant capacitor,

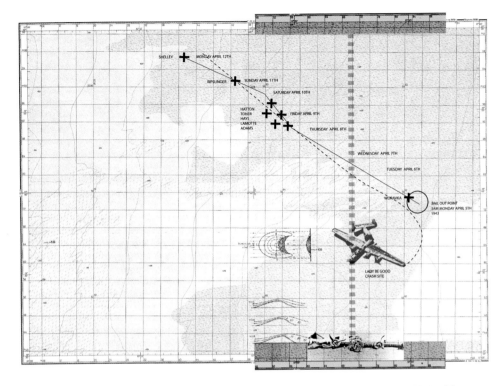

A drawing plotting the crash site of the American bomber 'Lady Be Good' and positions of the bodies found 16 years later. © Kate Davies and Emmanuel Vercruysse.

with the earth and the ionosphere acting as the plates. The interventions we propose are electrically active with various components exhibiting varying degrees of conductivity. The project has developed as a set of prototypes, conceived as agents of interference. In the horizontal plane they modulate the formation of sand dunes by disrupting wind patterns, in this way rearticulating the topography of their immediate context. Vertically they act as a series of conducting nodes within the dielectric of the earth and the sky. Through these prototypical installations we explore notions of disturbance and interference and the way these interventions can shape their own context. Central to the project is the inclusion of narrative texts, excerpts of which are included in this article.

The Fallen Lady

Calanscio, Libya. Dunes whisper and drone sand grain on sand grain creeping in numbers too big to comprehend: Trillions? Quadrillions? Quintillions? Between the two vast fields of sand and stars, ever shifting, eight men hang suspended by parachutes, as their abandoned plane glides silently towards the dunes.

In 1943 the American B-24 bomber 'Lady Be Good'[3] lost its way in a sandstorm and disappeared. It is thought extreme winds blew the plane off course and that

The Shields are a collection of fragmented volumes. They are open, allowing the undulating ground to fold and drape itself around them, revealing and concealing them in turn. © Kate Davies and Emmanuel Vercruysse.

static from a huge sandstorm affected the navigation equipment. The crew was forced to bail out over Libyan Sahara and the wreckage and the scattered bodies lay untouched and mummified for 16 years, awash in the dunes, mapping out the trajectory of an event in a state of suspension. The diaries of the men, perfectly preserved with them in the sands, provide a ghostly account of their last agonising days walking across the merciless emptiness of the sand sea Calanscio, an area so remote that they had no hope of being rescued. The plane was lost to the crew who sought it and lost to the many others who searched in vain. It existed only in the imagination, in an unspecified place, drifting in the desert.

This story of a lost plane and the subsequent late-night conversations spawned a mysterious world for us. The project has slowly woven itself into our imagination and its sands have seeped into the belly of the studio desk. The narrative constructs a world in which the objects we make act as props. We see them as talismans, as agents of interference charged by imagination and aligned to certain intangible forces acting on a place. We were interested in how the making of these objects can be an extension of the act of sketching and the way that a sculptural process can augment digital tools. The project is explored primarily through drawings – formal, tactical and atmospheric. It is the translation of these gestures into physical form that is presented here in relation to the theme of this publication.

When discussing the bespoke, it is natural to refer to tailoring; the bespoke suit, as fitted, unique and made to measure, undergoes a gradual process of refinement through a series of fittings. The word conjures ideas of the specific, the individual and the one-off. A making process not dictated by a specification but beginning with the generic, where the object is designed and made simultaneously without a precise pre-existing plan or pattern through the accumulation of marks and moves – drawing it incrementally towards a 'fit'. We are interested in the wild protean object, and are fascinated by the clay maquettes created by sculptors like Gianlorenzo Bernini, which the Italians call *bozzetti* [from the Italian word 'to sketch']. These sculptural sketches were fragile and not made to last, being regarded only as stepping stones on the way to a finished piece – the 'working out'. Later they were collected as works of art in their own right in an attempt to capture

The drawings describe a moment in time, like a single frame in a film of an explosion; these pieces are in slow flux. We try to capture a brief alignment of one cluster of elements with these drawings. © Kate Davies and Emmanuel Vercruysse.

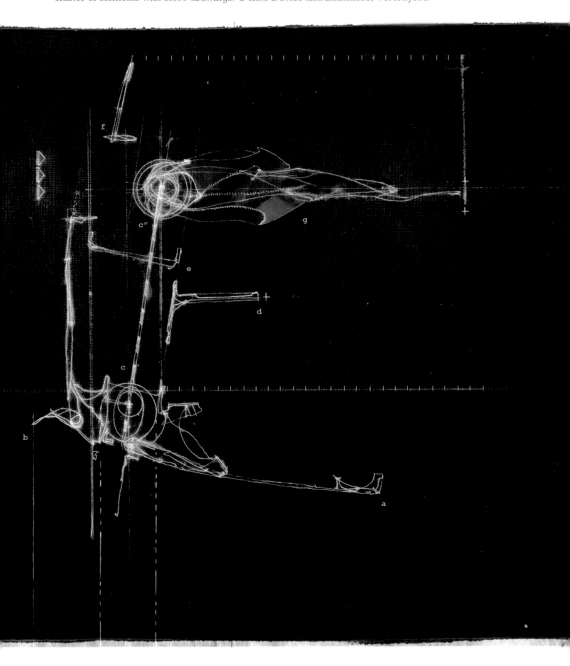

Wrapped in their fabric cloaks, the Hosts form a physical bridge between the electrical 'plates' of sky and earth. During a sandstorm the Host discharges electrostatic sparks into the night sky. Its cloak is animated and charged by the dry Harmattan winds – the 'hot breath' of the desert. © Kate Davies and Emmanuel Vercruysse.

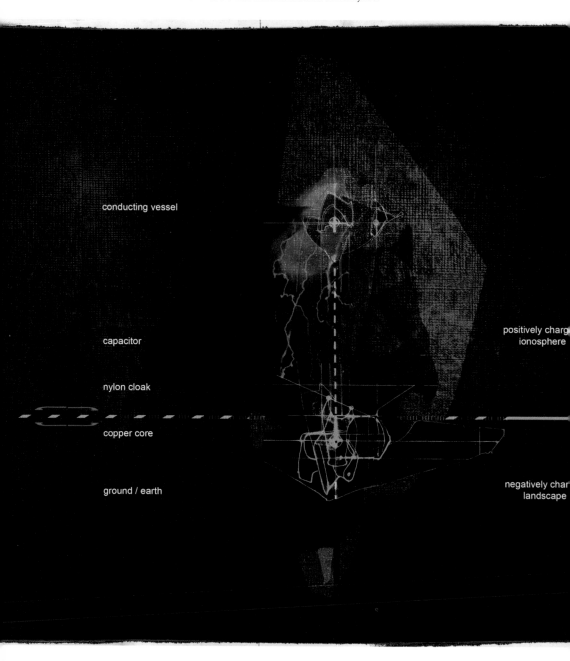

conducting vessel

capacitor

nylon cloak

copper core

ground / earth

positively charg
ionosphere

negatively char
landscape

the *primo pensiero* or 'first thought' of the artist; a stage when handling is loose and intuitive, and the *bozzetti* were often only fired subsequently to preserve them. There is a lucid energy captured in these little protosculptures. Scoops of clay, fingerprints, pinches, sweeping curves the evidence of a fast and loose production. We are interested in that energy, in the frozen gesture. Maps of shifting relationships caught in stasis.

Agile ways of working like these allow the translation from idea to physical form to be tactile and intuitive, and the delicate freedom of the sketch is a natural departure point. A sketch serves to visualise and to test, an accumulation of searching lines evolves towards the manifestation of something imagined. The sketch is fundamental as a means to seduce ourselves; it lures us away from the obvious and is meant to be disruptive – to sneak up and surprise. By its very nature the sketch must leave certain things undefined. In this way the landscape of the desert has become the inspiration for a way of working.

Indeterminate Horizons

The Harmattan haze hangs heavy, a series of incisions punctuate the horizon. Within a matrix of shifting fields these fragments rest on a restless earth, weathering the violent storms and slow creeping of this landscape. Scattered solid and heavy across the dunes, carved by the sting of sand and licked by the sparking tongues of an electric wind, a dark presence is half revealed, like the buried village swallowed by the dunes, huge hulking masses cut the path of the blistering wind, shaping the landscape surrounding them. A surfacing reef corralling the sand like slowly circling sharks.

A sand sea is a landscape like no other, landmarks are few and as all sense of scale is lost there is no reliable perception of distance, the horizon dissolves into haze and illusion. Sand dunes can migrate tens of metres in a strong storm, the entire Sahara is expanding southwards swallowing villages in its wake. In such an indefinable terrain the only unquestionable constants are found in the sky. The cosmos for all its mysteries is a dependable guide in a landscape where there is nothing fixed to be mapped. The Tuareg navigate by day; interpreting patterns of wind and sand they negotiate a realm of uncertainty by learning to recognise those dunes that reveal larger more stable trends among the background noise of a fluid terrain. Maps of sand seas are delicate drawings of imaginary formations and, while the dunes are in flux, their cartographic ghosts stagnate. Maps become sketches of something indefinable; like tentative drawings they are attempts to capture clusters of nebulous and elusive elements in a typical formation, but they can never define the specifics.

As the dunes bear down on it they will collapse the walls. Your last act is to break out the windows, take off the doors. Knock holes in the roof. You allow the wind to work for you. If it succeeds, and fills your house, the walls will stand. Then in a hundred years, when the wind requires it, the dunes will drift on and uncover the village.[4]

Sand seas are surreal and epic, defined by sensory deprivation and physical extremes. To the uninitiated, every horizon looks the same and the terror here is a vertiginous sense of helplessness in an endlessly disorienting space. The desert holds its breath; its sparseness and its extreme horizontality create such a collapsing of distance that to traverse it is to walk on the spot, as if time is slowed. It is a landscape of blinding monotony animated by atmospheric distortions – mirages summon lakes, cities and mountains that are not there – and illusion is embroidered with delusion. Dehydration and a high body temperature can cause short circuits in the brain and with little for the senses to grasp an already untrustworthy horizon is laced with hallucinations. The traveller quickly learns to be suspicious of this deadly, beguiling landscape.

> Sandstorms can be black as night or lurid yellow or a bleak grey the colour of old ash; they may hiss or roar. Or rumble like thunder; the air is oven hot and crackles with static and a hand run over a canvas tent pops and sparks like methane breath on a smouldering coal tip; nerve ends tingle with electricity and firefly sparks jump and snap.[5]

The sandstorm forms the crux of the project as a moment of extreme disorientation, tension and violence. The notorious Harmattan haze – thick clouds of dust disturbed by hot, dry Harmattan trade winds – accumulates into sandstorms of colossal scale. We are interested in how the terrain is reconfigured by these vast storms and an entire landscape can change overnight. Saharan winds are fierce. The nomadic Tuareg have a huge array of descriptive words for the wind – as they do for thirst – and they craft amulets and talismans to appease its malevolent spirits. In the extreme low humidity of the desert, during these sandstorms the air becomes highly charged with atmospheric static. Clothes spark, hair stands on end and electrical equipment fails.[6]

> *Above, in the storm-darkened sky, the flighty whip of wind in a cloak, and crack of static. A field of conducting vessels or Hosts act as collectors within the dielectric of air and Earth, forming a vertical bridge. Like buoys animated by the forces around them, they are violently shaken by fiery desert winds. Scattered, shattered among them across the vastness are the fragmented remains of something once whole – shrapnel in the sand. Changing the dynamics of dune formation around the Hosts, the Shields are a measure against which to read the landscape, a datum in the flow. But they are untrustworthy players on this illusory stage, ambiguous in scale and on the move. These drifting cadavers with their soft compliant bodies may be swallowed up in a giant dune for years or laid bare like wrecks, performing a slow re-articulation of the landscape while the tethered Hosts thrash in the storm and lie motionless in the hot calm.*

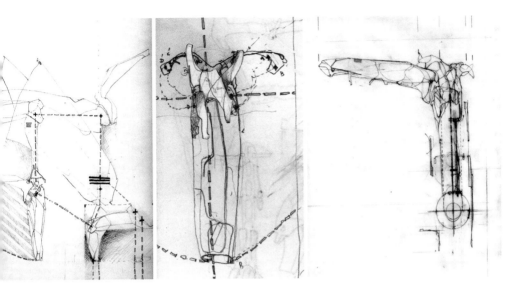

Initial sketches for the Shields: loose sketches allow the initial ghost of an idea to be captured on paper and these fragile little collections of lines become the seed of a project; an intangible and mysterious target to steer the made work towards. In this way the work is never fully determined on paper. © Kate Davies and Emmanuel Vercruysse.

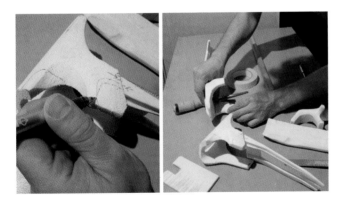

The aluminium fragments begin as hand-carved foam patterns, using the initial sketches as a guide for sculpting. These become positives for sand-casting. The foam is a gentle material; it is light on resistance and working it is close to drawing. It is soft directionless matter and it suits the fluidity of the molten metal. © Kate Davies and Emmanuel Vercruysse.

i

ii

iii

iv

Untamed Gestures

The made fragments, created in response to this illusory terrain, exist with no predetermined composition; once made they are ripe for reinterpretation. Inspired by this landscape, the aim of the project is to leave certain things unknown and – rather like a lucid dream – to consciously allow space for uncertainty while maintaining a level of control over the process.

Finding the desiccated bones of a sheep on the side of the road, I am struck by how beautiful they are in their gentle occupation of the sand. They lie where gravity, wind and fortune dictate. Together these pieces form an accidental composition, caught in a slow drift of fragmented anatomy.

The sketches are a starting point for the making, which is the true site of exploration. We fight to capture the gentle gestures of those original pencil lines in the shadow of the final pieces. Unlike a precise drawing that acts as an instruction, the sketch is a wilder thing from which to work. It brings with it a certain liveliness, an indeterminate horizon to steer the work towards.

In sculpture, like dance; skill, timing and agility are honed, and the physical act itself is central to the creative process. We are interested in what we can learn from exploring how dextrous and intuitive acts may be integrated within the measured logic that defines much architectural production. The distance between the drawn and the made is a territory we are particularly keen to explore. Using making as a mode of drawing we employ a sequence of malleable processes that alternate between control and freedom. We are interested in how a dialogue between the analogue and the digital can inform the translation of the gesture of sketching into the physical, specifically the integration of the handmade within CAD/CAM, so we tend to work back and forth between the two. Handmade objects are translated into digital 'copies' through 3D scanning; reworked, milled by machine and then reworked by hand. This allows the pieces to be handled throughout the process and understood in tactile terms.

Gesture is not talked about often enough when describing the act of making in architecture, which is more often described in predefined terms – logic, rule systems, diagrams. We talk with incredible confidence about all the ways in which we are certain about something. The more interesting elements are likely to be those that are uncertain.

Image showing the evolution of Shield 1 from sketch to carved foam, to 3D scan, to cast aluminium. When cast, the originals are sacrificed, burned away by the molten metal, and so we scan them in 3D before they are used for casting. If the cast is unsuccessful we have a digital 'backup' of the original. We are interested in the digital ghost of the 'one-off'. Like the cast, the scan creates a cloak of the original but it is a virtual one. These digital duplicates can be adjusted and begin a new iteration of their own, cut in foam on CNC machines and recast or used as digital overlays to rework a cast piece directly. The translation of such a material and physical object into a computational model interests us as a fusion of the tactile and the digital. A finite object becomes imbued anew with infinite possibility. © Kate Davies and Emmanuel Vercruysse.

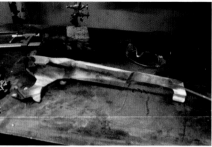

Sand-casting aluminium in our backyard foundry: inspired by the traditional bronze talismans cast by the desert-dwelling Tuareg, the sand-casting process has become an integral part of the project. The alchemy of the process is magical. The foam form is buried in sand, packed down and engulfed in its cocoon, molten metal is poured into it, dissolving and replacing the foam – transfiguring it – and when the form boxes are opened a fiery hot object shrouded in smoking burnt black sand emerges. In this way the cheap, temporary foam that accepted so easily the gentle gestures of the hand is transformed into solid aluminium. These smouldering castings are then excavated from the sand to be reworked, refined and polished. © Kate Davies and Emmanuel Vercruysse.

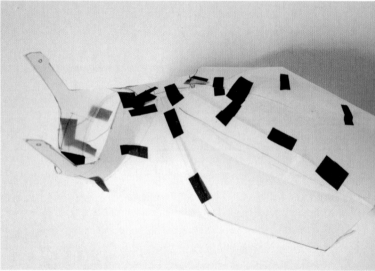

The Hosts' internal shell structures and external fabric cloaks are explored through the construction of paper forms, which are taped together, constantly reworked and handled roughly. Like the foam pieces, these are about a process of sketching in three dimensions. These patterns are unwrapped, scanned and redrawn in CAD, laser-cut, adjusted, rescanned and recomposed. We are interested in the way in which these two parallel processes of pattern making – in foam and in fabric – condense acts of gestural form-finding. © Kate Davies and Emmanuel Vercruysse.

The sculptor can happily be intuitive and wilful; the architect it seems is more comfortable with logical and measured. And this tendency to cling to the rational and to make-by-numbers – neglecting the intuitive gesture – is exaggerated somewhat by computer-aided design. The determinism and accuracy of digital design tools can seduce us into thinking that everything we design with them should follow a rational set of parameters throughout, allowing no leakages, no mess, no ambiguity or subtlety of interpretation, any uncertainty being seen as a flaw.

Sketches and words are dextrous and often irrational, they are beautiful in their ambiguity and can slip into the spaces between things and pull out invisible threads; they provide a scaffold in the mind for the possibilities of the made work, teasing it with the ease of their simple accumulation. Our aim is that the energetic freedom and the nuances of their ambiguity be carried from these generative modes of imagining into the physicality of the final work, that they may fulfil that promise held so delicately by a nimble collection of words or the agile dance of a sketch.

Notes

1 Kate Davies and Emmanuel Vercruysse, 'Prosthetic Mythologies', Bob Sheil (ed), *AD Protoarchitecture: Analogue and Digital Hybrids*, vol 78, no 4, John Wiley & Sons (London), 2008, pp 56–61.

2 Marq de Villiers and Sheila Hirtle, *Sahara: The Life of the Great Desert*, Walker & Company (New York), 2002, p 67. A reference to a phenomenon known as 'singing dunes', the noise made by the shifting of millions of grains of sand.

3 The story of the missing plane is described in Dennis E McClendon, *The Lady Be Good: Mystery Bomber of World War II*, Aero Publishers, Inc (Fallbrook, CA), 1962.

4 William Langewiesche, *Sahara Unveiled: A Journey across the Desert*, Random House (New York), 1996, p 44. Here Langewiesche describes a futile struggle with the dunes as the Great Eastern Erg threatens to engulf a man's house in the village of El Oued, Algeria.

5 Marq de Villiers and Sheila Hirtle, *Sahara*, p 81.

6 The ionosphere – a highly charged layer above the atmosphere – is made up of positively charged particles emitted continuously by the sun's solar winds. This positively charged layer in turn induces a negative charge in the Earth's surface. The Earth and the ionosphere act as two plates of a giant capacitor with a powerful electric field generated between them. Huge potential gradients have been measured above the ground in a sandstorm and there are reports of sandstorms that cause extreme headaches unless a metal rod is used as a walking stick and electrical earth.

References

- Ammen, CW, *Metalcasting*, Mcgraw-Hill (New York), 2000
- Bagnold, RA, *The Physics of Blown Sand and Desert Dunes*, Methuen (London), 1941
- Chastain, Steve, *Metalcasting: A Sand Casting Manual For the Small Foundry*, vols 1 and 2, Chastain Publishing (Jacksonville, FL), 2004
- Davies, Kate and Emmanuel Vercruysse, 'Prosthetic Mythologies', Bob Sheil (ed), *AD Protoarchitecture: Analogue and Digital Hybrids*, vol 78, no 4, John Wiley & Sons (London), 2008
- Langewiesche, William, *Sahara Unveiled: A Journey Across the Desert*, Random House (New York), 1996
- Pallasmaa, Juhani, *The Thinking Hand*, John Wiley & Sons (London), 2009
- Saint-Exupéry, Antoine de, *Wind, Sand and Stars*, translated from the French by Lewis Galantière, Harcourt Brace Jovanovich (New York), 1967
- Thompson, Rob, *Manufacturing Processes for Design Professionals*, Thames & Hudson (London), 2007

from top left to right:

'Putnam House', Buffalo, New York, 2007, with University of Buffalo Graduate School. The facade on this house was cut away from the building and hinged to allow it to spin freely. It was eventually reconnected to the house in a 90-degree shifted position. Photograph: Frank Fantauzzi. © Frank Fantauzzi.

'Big Orbits', Big Orbit Gallery, Buffalo, New York, 2000, with Mehrdad Hadighi. This exhibition was in two parts: in the gallery space, an elliptical void was carved from a large stack of industrial wood pallets, using tools orbiting around two centres. In the mirror space of an adjoining courtyard, the process was reversed generating an elliptical solid. The work functions as a scale, balancing positive and negative, apogee and centre. A lever of space. Photograph: Frank Fantauzzi. © Frank Fantauzzi.

'Big Orbits', Big Orbit Gallery, Buffalo, New York, 2000, with Mehrdad Hadighi. Photograph: Frank Fantauzzi. © Frank Fantauzzi.

'Big Orbits', Big Orbit Gallery, Buffalo, New York, 2000, with Mehrdad Hadighi. Photograph: David Misenheimer. © David Misenheimer.

An Interview with
Frank Fantauzzi from Iceberg Project

Natalija Subotincic

Within a catalogue of over 35 works spanning more than 25 years, the Iceberg Project, a collective of experimental architects who met at the Cranbrook Academy of Art, Michigan, choose solitary and bold terms to name many of their works: 'Ortho' (1988), 'Resistance' (1990), 'Landmarks' (1994) or 'Wraps' (1996). Theirs is a highly critical form of architectural practice engaged in what lies beneath the physical and tactile materials of dynamic urban environments. Acts of building or 'un-building' are set against questions of meaning on the condition or form of building materials and the processes put upon them in the course of construction and demolition. Here, Iceberg Project member Frank Fantauzzi talks to Natalija Subotincic about the ideas behind the actions. Projects that are referred to in this interview may be viewed at: icebergproject.org

This interview discusses the foundations that have been opened up by the work of Iceberg Project. This 'cultural research' discloses and engages repressed aspects of our culture, reaching deep into what we don't want to or can't confront directly. It bespeaks of an ever-present but unconscious terrain hovering just below the surface of our built environment. As projects surface, they displace expectations and comforts in the act of making a place for themselves. By tapping into the unconscious, they connect us with the foundations underlying existing sites or built conditions. Much like a dream compiles its manifest content from incomprehensible fragments, this research lures us out of this obscurity by revealing to our consciousness a latent content that arrives through the process of the work.

This work is about seeing
This work is about doing
This work is about opening
This work is about touch
This work is about tools
This work is from the inside
This work is about nothing
This work is section
Not a project, a utopia of form, a hope, nor an image
Not an argument, a goal, a directive
Not a commission
Not subject
Not beauty, angles, shape
Not designing

Not compensation
Not solution
We want insight
We want ideation
We want less
We want to open the foundation
We want the joints
We want to assemble facts
We want silence[1]

NS Let's begin with how the collaborations started.

FF We met at Cranbrook Academy of Art in Bloomfield Hills, Michigan. The first collaboration, 'St Cyril', was done with five people: Jean-Claude Azar, James Cathcart, Terence Van Elslander, Michael Williams and myself. It occurred just as we were graduating and bridging away from school into various forms of practice. For me it has become a touchstone project, especially for how it engages architecture as an embodiment of social and cultural forces. In effect, 'St Cyril' was an attempt to register the single-family house somewhere between myth and economics.

NS So 'St Cyril' was driven by a preconceived idea and then you went out and found the building?

FF Yes. We were invited to do a gallery show with the assumption that we would exhibit work that we did at Cranbrook. However, we didn't want to show objects and products made in the studio. We wanted to work directly with the city, to engage real-time conditions. So displacing a house into a gallery was an immediate idea and dealt with the size of the gallery, the condition of Detroit and its derelict buildings, and the fact that we could access a house as raw 'valueless' material. The logic of how everything was put into the gallery and how people circulated around it was simple and direct, and came from the material itself. For example, plaster was most easily carried in 55-gallon (250-litre) drums as opposed to insulation fitting into plastic bags. We wanted to avoid any formal interjection or expression.

NS So the initial act was about an approach to building from its opposite, an un-building? What did this reveal?

FF That un-building is a positive, proactive gesture and is as legitimate as building. By editing or un-building you are actually constructing a new second condition that can reveal and index situational forces in culture and the built environment. With 'St Cyril' we realised that the single-family house is temporary and fragile. If you can't pay the mortgage, or don't fix the roof leaks, it evaporates. All these 'outside' forces are far more powerful than the house itself. The process also revealed some disturbing coincidences, such as, it turns out that a single-family house fits exactly into a 35-cubic-yard (26.7-cubic-metre) dumpster. These dumpsters are units of measure, based on the value of how we build cities, but they also end up registering the elimination of a house and all the lives that inhabit it. The house was a mask that was gutted with all its life, in this one simple gesture.

NS What's the difference between your experiences of taking the building apart versus the viewer's experience of the materials in the gallery?

FF There was a temporal dimension to our experience. Given the simple logic of un-building, the house presented itself as many houses in time. Like a Russian doll, it morphed into separate layered houses of differing materials. When we were removing the plaster it seemed that the entire house was made of plaster. The same happened for the insulation and so forth. Each layer of the house became the site, experience and preoccupation of the work. Over nine days, the house was displaced into the gallery, mirroring the order and process of the demolition. For the viewer, the installation engendered a varying and shifting set of responses. Discussions ensued about loss, family, time, melancholy, economics, politics, and so on. Unlike our experience-over-time with the house, the viewer was confronted with a stark, even existential, final condition of house vs nonhouse.

NS You've said that a house normally comes down in a single day but this project took nine days?

FF Yes, a bulldozer is the usual method of demolition and it often takes just a few hours. They used to knock houses right into their own basements and then cover over the site, but they've stopped doing that. Perhaps here, Duchamp's notion of the 'delay' comes to mind. When you slow things down to an almost frozen state, then you can actually see and index the changes taking place. One might say that there was also a ritualistic aspect to the work, given its duration and process.

NS If we consider your collaborations over time, did this initial un-building idea develop into a way of working?

FF The notion of un-building branched out into a range of oppositional strategies for engaging architecture. 'St Cyril' apart from engaging the act of un-building was more broadly a displacement activity, a theme that reappears in the work in different ways. For example, 'Still' is a project where we cut a portion of a ceiling in a gallery and hinged it down to become a wall dividing the gallery space in two. 'Displacement' is also the name of a project we did at Carleton University School of Architecture in Ottawa, Canada, where we took apart a set of Post-Modern brick arches that had been added to the main entryway and stacked them in a solid mass in a small side room. This project was intended to erase what we saw as a troubling symbol or sign of the state of the school. To explain, there had been a huge shift in attachment to these arches, from when they were constructed to the time we did our project. Initially they were a 'subversive' act, built by students who thought the Modernist architecture building was too machine-like and considered their installation a way to humanise the space. Years later, I came across a group photograph of the entire faculty standing in front of the arches – the very faculty who swore to get rid of them when they appeared. For our work we wanted to expose the nostalgia that had developed around them, and to erase them, leaving behind a vacuum. We felt that this would provide a more appropriate condition for a forward-thinking school of architecture.

Another type of displacement found in the work involves manifesting invisible or neglected dimensions and facets of architecture. 'Resistance', for example, made the electricity available to a building visible by hanging live resistance wires from the ceiling of a gallery space in the building. One could say that architecture should also be expected to bring about the presence of things unseen or unfelt.

NS You've mentioned rotations, resistances and inversions. Do these leveraging devices offer mechanical advantage to the work?

FF Yes, leveraging is an accurate way to put it because it has to do with shifting, breaking or wedging open conditions. The meaning of something changes as soon as you reverse or reposition it. Although mechanical gestures often play a central role in the work, it's really the semiotic or cultural 'advantage' that we are particularly interested in. This brings to mind 'Putnam House' a project where we rotated the facade of a house 90 degrees. The immediate focus of this project was how we were going to gain mechanical advantage over the construction of the building, but alongside this we also desired to leverage a broader discussion about housing and conformity. By directly engaging and confronting a basic aspect of a single house, we indirectly implicated all houses in the city.

In 'Big Orbits' we built two elliptical forms with industrial wooden pallets – one negative and the other positive – side by side. Here, there was a deductive interest in having people experience a space and its reverse. The project leveraged latent aspects of the site – a square gallery space located right next to a courtyard of almost exactly the same size and proportion. The site presented this dual condition that we made more emphatic with the installation.

Reversal was central to the 'Toilets' project at the Storefront for Art and Architecture in New York City. The site presented a very strange triangular sliver of gallery space. Its name was appropriate because it was all 'storefront'. For this project, we inserted five portable toilets through the facade that were open and available to the public for the duration of the installation. So they were inside the gallery, but accessed from the outside. This introduced a strange spatial complexity that most buildings never have to contend with. The project activated basic and problematic questions about private and public property, inside/outside, merchant/buyer, the space of high culture and low culture, etc.

NS Did you see this transgression of the facade in a prophylactic way?

FF Yes, to a degree. When you're inside the gallery all you experience is the back of the toilets (the residue) without any functional access to them. When you're outside, you have the use of the toilets without engaging the gallery.

NS Could you smell them?

FF Well this was a small oversight given our improvisational way of working. When the toilets arrived we realised they had vents on the back. So we used flexible duct and re-vented them outside. In photographs of the installation, you'll notice small 4-inch (100-millimetre) circular holes directly above each toilet.

NS Much of this work, in both content and method, engages resistance to culturally accepted ways of making architecture.

FF The work is primarily interested in cultural exploration and indexing. By indexing, I mean that the built environment has the ability and responsibility to honestly reflect and articulate the myriad forces that underlie it, rather than masking those forces and presenting illusions. In this regard, the work certainly questions the role and methods of architectural production, particularly seen in the context of an increasingly codified profession and discipline. The tools, roles and cultural spaces accessible to architects risk being ever more emasculated and limited. Resistance is an implicit and necessary part of our work.

NS How do you reconcile this 'work of resistance' with its venue often being the gallery?

FF The gallery as an institution offers a very particular site. Our engagement of these spaces attempts to gauge the very nature and dimension of their role in our society. To put it a little differently, our work resists thinking of the gallery as a neutral container.

NS Many projects engage drawing in space or on and through materials and surfaces (ie, hole saw, car that spins, plumb line, and so on). Can you talk about drawing in the work?

FF Drawing is very important in our projects. Our work doesn't project, it reveals. We draw out and make evident what's already there. When I build, I'm constantly aware of drawing through space, time and material. The ideal space of a piece of paper or the computer screen is replaced with the imperfect and reciprocating space of the site. So, drawing is problematic for us, let's say even political, yet we draw all the time and couldn't do this work without understanding drawing as a way of being, and making sense of the world.

NS You've mentioned that you're looking for 'the cracks'?

FF Absolutely. Charged conditions that can be wedged open to reveal unvarnished views and measures of contemporary life. The Storefront 'Toilets' engaged the fact that there are no public restroom facilities in New York City for those without money. By linking the toilets to a nonprofit public gallery we also found a culturally acceptable vehicle to provide for the homeless. At the time, New York was experimenting with a French pay-toilet design. They wanted to see if it would be vandalised, but the politics were such that after all the experimentation it never panned out. The crack in this case was a moment of humanity's disregard for human dignity. So, in an activist way, it was remarkably satisfying to put public toilets in place without going through the politics or economics of it.

NS What is it about architecture that is too safe or comfortable? I ask this because risk appears to be an essential component of your work.

FF Architecture in our society has become synonymous with safety and comfort. This limited and instrumental view has marginalised the discipline in so many ways. The real problem is regarding architecture's complicit role in psychological and cultural compensation. Everything in our society has been organised into a constellation that serves capital and architecture has become a capitalist instrument with specific agendas, assumptions and rules. Our institutions are focused on comfort and predictability, and the prophylactic is the street system, the work schedule, things we have that make us feel like everything is under control – it's a psychosis. It's sad that society is not interested in opening things up and allowing them to breathe but prefers to keep unpredictability at bay. Life is not fixed or predictable – it's much slipperier. Entropy is the most natural process yet our culture cannot allow it to take its course. We see this as a loss of control. We really have a need to bring things back to new. What's truly risky is not questioning and remaining open to change.

NS What's the riskiest project you've ever done, the 'Putnam House' facade?

FF Yes, primarily because we could not anticipate how the city or public would respond to the project – only that they would. There's a striking conformity to housing in our cities – a house 'out of sorts' seems to be a problem for everyone. In this project everything was done empirically as there was no precise way to pre-engineer the project. So the structural and mechanical aspects were invented and tested in the process. This led to a considerable amount of physical risk. For example, at full height during the rotation the facade was 20 to 30 feet (6 to 9 metres) off the ground. If it had become disconnected, it would have fallen into the street and probably taken out some cars, if not people. As well, it was a collaboration done with untrained students and the project involved money – the house was worth something. So, it was incredibly risky and we treated the risks very seriously.

NS The work is often open-ended at the same moment that it folds back in upon itself. Is this part of its impermanence? In other words, is the work not able to be 'fixed' because it is crossing itself out?

FF   This folding back is part of the goal of the work. It is constantly referring back to itself – commenting on itself. It's interesting the way you've asked this because I agree that the work does start open-ended but at some point there's a soft spot that's found, and when you push this it tends to fall back on itself. Thinking about 'Putnam House', one thing that unsettles me the most is that one day I will be driving by and see that the facade has been 'righted'. Actually, I made sure to remove the critical pieces from the mechanism behind the facade so it couldn't be turned back. In some projects the work is pushed to such a limit of exposure or vulnerability that it eventually perishes. There's something beautiful about that.

NS   In many ways your work taps into the unconscious of architecture. By drawing it out and playing with it you make us aware of it.

FF   Architecture is almost always conceived in the cold light of day. It reiterates the known and the predictable. It holds at bay instability, uncertainty and the essential ephemerality of being. As an ultimately conservative instrument, it obsessively compensates for change and the unknown. Yet the built world as a reflection or calcification of consciousness also contains a fulcrum to the unconscious. To put it differently, the conscious and the unconscious are always linked. When architecture dares to rotate away from the former it tilts into and reveals the latter. To transgress this link one must approach architecture in an unscripted way guided by alternate orientations, contexts and frameworks. Our work, free from professional mandates and obligations, has the opportunity to redirect material practices in order to tap into their latent potentials. But let's be clear, we are not interested in an expression of imagination or fantasy. We believe that engaging and wrestling architecturally with our culture's unconscious tendencies provides a vehicle to a deeper understanding of our consciousness and being.

NS   Do you see 'Resistance' as a prophetic dream or nightmare that the gallery must have had?

FF   The gallery was in a building next to an electric substation. The amount of resistance that the building could provide (23.7 ohms) is also a measure of its ability to consume electricity from the substation – a minuscule amount comparatively speaking. The tilted relationship between these two architectural structures must have certainly, over the years, inspired the strangest dreams for each of them. There's a lot to unpack here ...

Note

1   J Cathcart, F Fantauzzi, T Van Elslander, *Pamphlet Architecture 25 – Gravity*, Princeton Architectural Press (New York), 2003, p 76.

Grymsdyke Farm
An Enquiry into Making on Site

Guan Lee

Processes of mould making and casting have engendered a prolonged fascination among artists, architects, designers and makers. Both have an intrinsic relationship to form, space, time and materiality. Some 56 kilometres (35 miles) northwest of central London, architect and maker Guan Lee is establishing an experimental workshop within a group of former agricultural buildings in Buckinghamshire's Lacey Green. Like the majority of their neighbours, the original purpose of these buildings and their relationship to the surrounding land has been lost, while they have since become highly desirable residences for city commuters. Lee's preliminary works are developed as a means to reinvent the site as a place of production and enquiry. In this regard, he makes a series of beautiful and poetic links between materiality, process and place, and forms a fascinating parallel between the physicality of mould making and the intangibility of the design process.

The builder is indispensable. In fact, the project for a building is not really complete if it does not consider how it will be built, and the ways in which a building can be built have a notable power of inspiration. All viable new structures are intimately related to construction methods, and these methods are visible in the finished building.

Eladio Dieste[1]

This enquiry states the case for the relevance to design inspiration of physical experiences in making. These experiences are based on three personal and collaborative projects developed and constructed at Grymsdyke Farm in Lacey Green, England: projects which focus on processes of making, and which specifically engage with processes of mould making and casting.

As digital processes prevail in contemporary architectural practice, inspiration taken from nature, mathematical constructs and abstract ideas lacks a necessary relationship to the physical reality of making and place. How can design ideas taken from an intimate interaction with materials and a site remain relevant? Ever-evolving modes of construction, fabrication and craft inform design executions, yet are less integrated into contemporary architectural practices. Is this becoming an innate disposition in design?

Ideas and Making

My design enquiry follows the assumption that new and valuable knowledge can be acquired through developing an intimate and personal relationship with materials. Intimacy is not simply a factor of physical distance or proximity – one can imagine having an intimate moment with the stars in the night sky, for example. It is also not just by

Fig 1: 'Drying Raw Wool', view of the paddock from the farmhouse, Grymsdyke Farm, Lacey Green, 2009. Photograph: Mark Pantrey. © Mark Pantrey.

physically handling or touching something that one can experience intimacy. Developing an intimate relationship with a material, and with a place, involves bringing everything 'closer' – in the sense of a 'close' observation and an advanced cognitive scrutiny, with all five senses engaged. Intimacy also precipitates the question of time: prolonged engagement can create intimacy, closeness and familiarity through repetition of motions and through revisiting an experience. There is a fine line between this and a sense of endless engagement, which can lead to indifference and habit, and thus create distance.

Intimate knowledge of how something comes together, that is, the fundamental make-up of a material, also provides us with insights on how it can come apart,[2] an examination that is a question of scale. Design decisions, which include considerations of how something can be made and the physical execution of making, are complex and often nonlinear. These decisions require very different modes of thinking, which are not merely cognitive. Findings and design decisions may travel back and forth many times before any satisfactory outcome is achieved. To be able to execute even the simplest of operations takes practice, and experimentation with materials is a direct and immediate way to push design processes further. The process should not only include information gathered from what works; errors, mistakes and failures can also contain a myriad valuable clues.

This design enquiry proposes to establish a spatial relationship that exists between the experiments and the specific places in which they are carried out. These spatial conditions develop over time as the experiments progress. The starting point of these design projects is the restoration of Grymsdyke Farm in Lacey Green, a small village set in the Chilterns in Buckinghamshire, about 56 kilometres (35 miles) northwest of London (Figure 1), which began in 2004. The properties on the site comprise a series of farm buildings, stables and cottages, surrounded by a paddock and a small orchard. At the turn of the last century, this was a large working farm that was later divided and sold off over time: the manor house was separated from the farmhouse, and eventually the farmhouse and barns were sold off separately. Only then did each of these buildings acquire their separate names: Grymdsyke Manor, Grymsdyke Farm, Grymsdyke Cottages, and so on. My aim is slowly to restore the cottages as living quarters, and to convert the current dilapidated outbuildings and stables into usable workshops.

The set-up of Grymsdyke Farm is intended as residence for an architectural and fabrication practice with workshops for personal and communal use. A shared-workshop model presents many challenges: how can it be financially sustainable in the long run? How can it be more than just a purely commercial facility? Can it be ideologically driven, or is this merely a fantasy? Existing models of working environments – Open City in Valparaíso, Chile; CAST in Manitoba, Canada; Rural Studio in Alabama, USA – are each inspiring and viable, and provide potential clues. Over time, as more projects – personal, academic or commercial – are carried out at the farm, the practice and residence will slowly take shape.

A series of recent works in progress at the farm, which I will go on to discuss, have provoked a number of guiding questions. Are building processes simply the means to an end? Is there such a form that is true to a particular process or materiality? Can we allow form to create itself by designing and manipulating the process? Is there a form which materials have the tendency to become? Architecture is built and un-built not out of one, but from many interrelated materials, at various stages of stabilities and rate of change. Like chemical processes, the interaction of materials can be reversible or irreversible. The environment itself, as well as the maker and any other inhabitant of the space, must also be part of this architectural equation.

In discussing his work, engineer and architect Eladio Dieste wrote that his designs were guided by more than mere functionality: 'I have also been guided by a sharp, almost painful, awareness of form.'[3] His modesty appears linked to his lack of formal academic training in architecture or visual art, which, Dieste believed, hindered him 'from talking about form since I have studied almost nothing of all that has been thought and written about the problem that it poses.'[4] With these words, Dieste extricated himself from the design process as the decider of forms: instead, the materials and building processes form themselves.

For architectural historian Adrian Forty, the very definition of the terms form and shape creates confusion in architecture of the 20th century: 'What "form" itself has been taken to mean has been rather less important that what it does *not* mean.'[5] Forty seems to suggest that the very interpretation of the word 'form' can be slippery, flexible, even contradictory.

In my own undertakings, I have decided not to be limited by the meaning of form, or to concern myself with what form can mean. My focus on 'forms' is linked to the desire to make, to find and to form. Grymsdyke Farm situates and thus provides the environment in which the investigations can take place, take hold and take shape. Decisions on the suitability of materials to be used for such undertakings are made based on their pliability, their adaptability and, most importantly, their ability to transform or change shape.

Fig 2: 'The Other Room 1', interior view of project 'Cast', Grymsdyke Farm, Lacey Green, 2006. © Guan Lee.

Three projects: 'Cast', 'Ring', 'Hole'

'Cast' (Figure 2)

In 2004, I set up one of the outbuildings at Grymsdyke Farm as a personal workshop. This room houses ongoing casting experiments and a resulting collection of objects. From the outset, I focused my efforts on different casting methods, and specifically experimented with the use of flexible material as a mould. Casting processes often involve working to a predetermined shape or design, or as the means to reproduce or copy an existing form. My interest in fabric formworks was triggered by the possibility of the mould having a more dynamic relationship with the cast. I was intrigued by the challenge of making moulds that could be shaped by the casting material, or even the mould's own material. Alongside my own experiments, I researched the works of Miguel Fisac and Mark West. For both, the flexible mould acts as the construction material's extremity, able to express concrete's 'paste-like' mouldable origins.[6] The considerations that led to the production of the objects in this room were seemingly divergent, yet the objects produced and collected within the room share a certain physical commonality, as though they naturally emerge from the same family. This inspired my current enquiry: to establish the theoretical, material and transformative connections that essentially bind these objects together.

The work in this room was contextualised through considerations of preservation and representation, moment versus permanence, and materiality undergoing change versus the rate of change. Yet, it was the experiences acquired and knowledge gained through a prolonged period of experimentation that informed my theoretical enquiries into these themes. One result of this was the use of photography and film. Photographic documents and representations of the projects became integral parts of my enquiry, and ultimately became viewed as works in themselves.

'Ring' (Figures 3, 4, 5)

With the redevelopment of the farm's workshop spaces, I set out to understand how issues in processes of making, and specific theoretical considerations, can be effectively integrated into an architectural practice that also includes digital fabrication. In 2005, I set up a collaborative architectural practice called Multiply Studio (2005–09) with two colleagues.[7] In 2008, I introduced a computer numerically controlled (CNC) router, and Multiply Studio developed various projects, which culminated in 'Ring' (2009), which was presented that same year in the *PhD Research Projects 2009* exhibition at the Bartlett, UCL. Thematically, the issue of reproducibility in casting and mould making employing digital design and fabrication processes was the focus behind the work. Repeated forms in prefabricated concrete construction were prevalent from the 1950s through to the 1970s, when a number of innovative projects harnessed the efficiencies of casting and elaborated the possibilities of it as a construction technique. 'Ring' directed my attention to the work of engineer and architect Pier Luigi Nervi, and specifically on understanding

Fig 3: 'Ring', side view of concrete 'Ring' at the *PhD Research Projects 2009* exhibition, Wates House, Bartlett UCL, London, 2009. © Guan Lee.

the construction of his large-scale dome structures using repeated tiles. Nervi's concrete tile constructions of highly complex geometries were achieved with great precision, due to his technique of building full-scale guides and jigs for his mould construction.

'Ring' employed digital means to provide a system of construction and allow us to build an enclosure with repeated elements. Together with a geometrical system of tiling generated through digital means,[8] I designed and constructed test elements and prototypes in the workshop. Ideas for the fabrication of moulds travelled back and forth between computational and physical investigations. The geometry of these tiles was not predetermined but generated through a dialogue in design and making which subsequently could be multiplied and reproduced. This project became a way for Multiply Studio to explore and understand the possibilities and limitations of digital fabrication. Our experience in Ring's construction was that intimate relationships still exist between digital fabrication techniques and manual processes. The involvement of digital processes does not render physical making abilities obsolete. These two processes can, and must, inform each other.

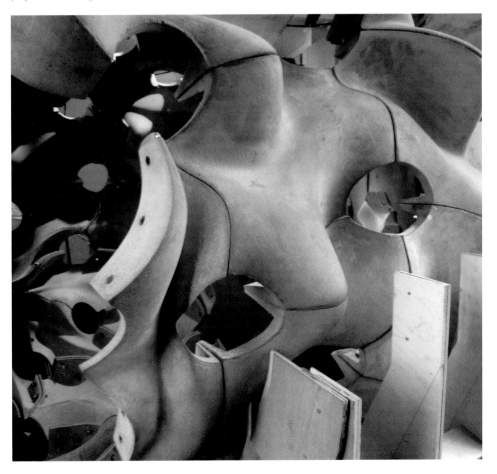

Fig 4: 'Ring', close-up view of concrete 'Ring' at the *PhD Research Projects 2009* exhibition, Wates House, Bartlett UCL, London, 2009. © Guan Lee.

Fig 5: 'Tiles Swimming', interior of the woodworking shop with casts for project 'Ring', Grymsdyke Farm, Lacey Green, 2009. © Guan Lee.

'Hole' (Figures 6, 7, 8)

'Hole' was constructed for the *PhD Research Projects 2010* exhibition at the Bartlett, UCL. This personal space, a room underground, was built within the paddock of the farm, and made from material emptied from the ground, which was then reconstituted and placed over a series of wooden guides to shape its walls. The project was inspired by a series of findings in 'Cast', and incorporated digital design and fabrication techniques from 'Ring'. At the exhibition, I presented a series of photographs and a film of the making of 'Hole', and introduced two fictional characters – 'He' and 'She' – as a way of discussing the construction process. 'He' is in the film, and 'She' is in the photographs.[9] With the use of these characters, 'Hole' is firmly situated in the larger context of the site: beyond Grymsdyke Farm to the nearby villages, and taking in the landscape of the Chiltern Hills. Their story includes a discussion on the geology and ground formation of the site and the region, as a way of elaborating the findings during the excavation. This approach offers a vertical study of the site and its history, and places the discussion of the landscape in a different timescale. The geology and the materiality of the excavated site remain visible, offering the hole an added relationship to its surroundings, as its construction materials reflect the very fabric of the nearby villages. The hole within the ground becomes an aperture, a lens through which to consider interior versus exterior, reversibility and the idea of negative form.

Mould and Cast

Within these projects, the work focuses on material investigations and experiments into the processes of making, and specifically on methods of forming material.[10] Material can take shape in specific ways: it can be subtracted from (like carving or chipping away), or added to (through the use of joints). A form can also be created without adding or subtracting, but by forming the material through processes like folding or bending or moulding.

The making of a mould is not an end in itself. It is used to produce something else; a cast, sometimes repeatedly, and sometimes only for single use. In architecture, large-scale moulds, also known as formwork, are required to cast elements in parts (usually precast in a workshop environment), or a building in its entirety *in situ*. The quality of the resulting cast often depends on the design and craftsmanship of the mould; an enormous amount of effort can be invested in an object which, in the end, may lie dormant in a workshop or simply be thrown away. This is not dissimilar from an architectural design process, which is not seen or experienced; instead it is embodied and imprinted on architecture itself. In this sense, a mould can represent the complex process where the designer's energy and effort will ultimately go. It is not the finished product that will be considered, examined, appreciated or interpreted; yet traces remain.

In mould and cast, the process of making can only be attributed to the mould – one does not 'make' a cast. It is the construction of the negative that achieves the positive. The process requires a particular spatial understanding, as it involves imagining that which is not there. The maker requires a comprehension of voids and solids. The operation also involves a transformation of materials. Working through a process where materials change properties can have a profound effect on the maker.[11] To be able to make a successful

Fig 6: 'Her Horizon and Hole', view of Jessie Lee in project 'Hole' looking west, Grymsdyke Farm, Lacey Green, 2010. © Guan Lee.

Fig 7: 'Her and Hole', aerial view of Jessie Lee in project 'Hole',
Grymsdyke Farm, Lacey Green, 2010. © Guan Lee.

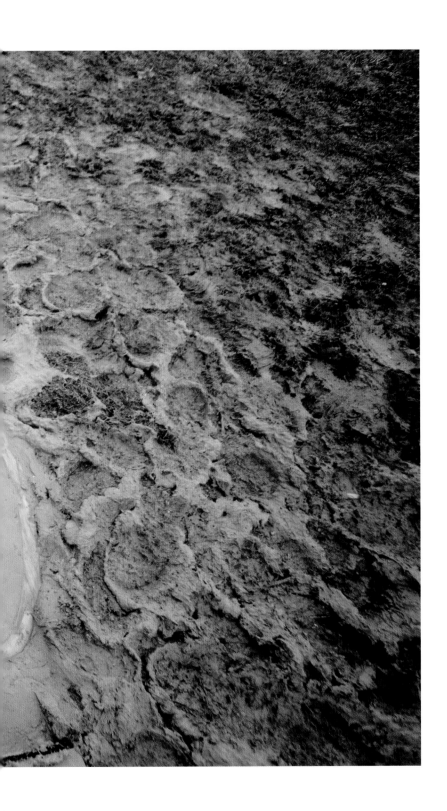

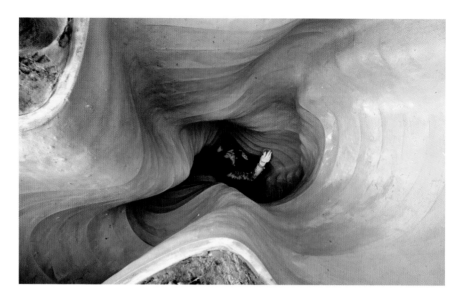

Fig 8: 'In-Hole-Down', interior view of project 'Hole' looking down, Grymsdyke Farm, Lacey Green, 2010. © Guan Lee.

mould, one must fundamentally understand and accommodate a material's properties as it undergoes change, and moves from, for example, liquid to solid form. Moulding is a multifaceted process requiring a maker to be knowledgeable about the fundamentals of material. Yet, at the same time, it is a process that produces a void as a product. Until something is actually cast using the mould, nothing has actually been made.

Part of the potency of mould and cast as a making method is the way it influences how we see space, and particularly in-between spaces. A cast object is the positive of the negative space of a mould. The cast object forces me to consider the space around the object, and the relationship this has to the space within the room. The cast is within the mould, which is within the workshop, which is on the site of Grymsdyke Farm. The relationship between these spaces and their boundaries is a constant consideration provoked by the mould and the cast process.

The possibility of multiples is another enriching element of mould making, where an origin form is reproducible, and can be cast over and over again. Casting as a method of reproducing works of art is as old as Western civilisation.[12] The question of reproducibility can be considered negative, as a reproduction of something does not have the same inherent value as its original. In architecture, reproducibility is associated with efficiency. Buildings can be constructed of modular units, which can be reproduced in a shorter period of time, possibly even requiring less labour, which can lead to a more economical, accessible way of working.

The realms of inspiration, execution and place are not distinct, but inseparable. My enquiry engages with these ideas by working with materials in a direct and intimate manner through the processes of mould making and casting. Casting engages the maker with issues of time; positive and negative space; materiality in fluid and solid form; traces; copy; and reproducibility. Grymsdyke Farm was established in order to understand the possibility of creating a situated architectural practice as a way of living and working with others. The projects on Grymsdyke Farm initiate essential connections between personal and collective activities and the site. The resulting work demonstrates how working environments, people and space are inextricable elements of the final product.

Notes

1 Eladio Dieste, 'Architecture and Construction', *Eladio Dieste: Innovation in Structural Art*, Princeton Architectural Press (New York), 2004, p 185.

2 Kenneth Frampton: '… something has to be said about the signification of "break" or the "dis-joint" as opposed to the signification of the joint. I'm alluding to that point at which things break against each other rather than connect: that significant fulcrum at which one system, surface or material abruptly ends to give way to another. Meaning may be thus encoded through the interplay between "joint" and "break", and in this regard, rupture may have just as much meaning as connection.' 'Rappel a l'Ordre: The Case for the Tectonic', first published in *Architectural Design*, vol 6, no 3/4, 1990, taken from *Labour, Work and Architecture*, Phaidon (London), 2002, p 102.

3 Eladio Dieste, p 191.

4 Ibid, p 191.

5 Adrian Forty, *Words and Buildings: A Vocabulary of Modern Architecture*, Thames & Hudson (London), 2000, p 150.

6 Miguel Fisac: 'Architecture is limited space and as such it needs a material limitation, and this, just like our own bodies, must have a skin. I have also always thought in my desire for truth that, if at all possible, that texture or skin should be made from the same enclosing material. (…) For a long time now, I have been thinking about how to achieve a texture which shows traces of its paste-like state and the fact that it was poured into a mould, and to try to make sure that the flexible material into which it is poured is very polished and completely smooth, like a sheet of G800 transparent polyethylene fill.' Francisco Arques Soler, *Miguel Fisac*, Ediciones Pronaos (Madrid), 1996, pp 249–50.

7 Guan Lee, Andrew Fortune and Olivier Otteveare founded Multiply Studio in 2005. The practice dissolved in 2009.

8 For details on the digital origin of the project, please refer to Olivier Otteveare's master dissertation (Olivier was one of the founding members of Multiply Studio, 2005–09): Olivier Otteveare, 'Quasi-Projection: Aperiodic Concrete Formwork for Perceived Surface Complexity'. Dissertation submitted for the degree of Master of Science in Adaptive Architecture & Computation, from University of London, September 2008.

9 My aunt Jessie Lee posed for all the photographs as 'She'. My partner Paul was featured as the character 'He' in the film for project Hole. Director of photography for the film was Clara Kraft Isono.

10 My approach to 'naming' the processes of changing the shape of material varies from those used by David Pye, who divides these methods into six categories: processing, wasting, connecting, forming, casting, polishing. 'Forming means changing the shape of a piece by bending, pressing or forging etc. Casting means pouring a liquid into or over a mould, which liquid subsequently hardens having taken the shape of the mould.' David Pye, *The Nature & Aesthetics of Design*, Herbert Press (London), 1978, p 44.

11 I recognised the potential and significance of mould and cast as a making process when I cast my first object in my early years at architecture school. I cast a site model from plaster, instead of stacking pieces of cardboard or cutting a profile out of plywood. The idea of having the site as a solid object attracted me, but in the end, it was the physical experience of the process of making the mould that left a lasting impression.

12 'The Greeks had only two ways of technologically reproducing works of art: casting and stamping.' Walter Benjamin, 'The Work of Art in the Age of Its Technological Reproducibility' (third version), from *Walter Benjamin 1938–1940: Selected Writings Volume 4*, Harvard University Press (Cambridge, MA), 2003, p 252.

Student team and Andrew Freear inspect the original fire tower prior to it being taken down, regalvanised and rebuilt at Perry Lakes Park. © Timothy Hursley.

The Rural Studio
Between a Twister and a Hurricane

Anderson Inge

In its 17-year history, Rural Studio, an outpost of the School of Architecture at Auburn University in Alabama, has attained a mythical status in international architectural education. The decree of its visionary co-founder, the late Samuel Mockbee, to 'Proceed and be Bold', towers over the aspirations and ambitions of its staff, students and local community. As an outsider enterprise located in the town of Newbern, Hale County, participation in Rural Studio is a chosen path requiring absolute commitment and an unambiguous attitude towards the ideology of an architecture school in relation to its immediate and wider context. Here, the purpose is nothing less than to build and be engaged in the fundamental challenges defined by a location overlooked by building control and progressive economic investment. In this regard, the creative legacy of Rural Studio is delicately balanced between the relative transience of its membership, the ingenuity and optimism of its portfolio, and the stagnation of its deprived surroundings.

In the 17 years or so since it began erecting buildings in the forests of western Alabama, the Rural Studio has gained international notoriety as a uniquely successful experiment in architectural education. Known as much for the benevolent ethos of its founders as for the buildings realised there by its students, the Rural Studio has become a paradigm for a special breed of architectural education.

A great deal has been written about the Rural Studio, most of which accurately reflects a journalistic strategy, revealing the ethos of the place through quotes and anecdotes of persons involved there. This essay, though, looks from the inside, 'from the heart' in a different way, to shed light on the less tangible side of how the Rural Studio 'builds'.

Surprisingly, the Rural Studio is not an exemplar of emerging digital methods of design and fabrication. The students there do use CAD to draw and visualise their projects, but the place has almost no evidence of rapid prototyping or numerically controlled manufacture. There is no struggle with or against digital modes of production, but the scale of these self-build student projects seems to get incrementally larger with each academic year, and recent projects have attained a truly incredible size.

The Rural Studio is fuelled, instead, by a powerful mix of ideals that are an unusually strong part of the student experience. It is an inseparable blend of American *frontier mentality*, contemporary *win/win* aspiration, lots of good old *can do* spirit, as well as fundamental religious beliefs now provoked by post-9/11 anxiety. The result is a palpable, self-renewing ambition that energises students afresh each academic year, to not only design, but also to build, the formidable 'thesis projects' that are the focus of their final year of formal architectural education.

The Rural Studio

Fact is, students at the Rural Studio build. What's more, they get their work published. Every architect is driven by the desire to build. Architecture students even more so, since they haven't yet had their excitement quashed by contractors and clients who often transform over the life of projects into bull terriers. Students at the Rural Studio find themselves in the privileged situation of knowing from the outset that they are about to begin their first building, what will probably also be their first published building, while still a student.

The simpler part of the RS story marries a remarkably unfettered situation with the unbridled ambition of young wanna-be architects, in a situation that has a huge legacy of goodwill lending momentum at most levels.

I first travelled to the Rural Studio in November 2002, as a guest of the Architectural Association School's Diploma Unit 8.[1] In the preceding year or so there had been several high-profile publications, and the RS was being discussed regularly by students and staff (essay in *AD* magazine by co-founder Samuel 'Sambo' Mockbee;[2] feature article in *Architectural Record*;[3] Mockbee's appearance on *The Oprah Winfrey Show*;[4] the first of two books that

Pavilion, Perry Lakes Park, Perry County. © Timothy Hursley.

have now been written by Andrea Oppenheimer Dean).[5] All the right elements were in place to create an impressive mythological image: a school of architecture set in the rural Deep South, where students actually get to build their design projects! The publications were also making it clear these were not simply banged-together temporary kiosks; they were achieving, as students, proper permanent structures that had scale and flair. It had to be seen to be believed, so, like groups of architecture students from all over the planet, 'Dip 8' organised a 10-day 'unit trip' that began with a collaborative project *in situ* with RS students, went on to tour the Mississippi Delta, and finished with a high time in New Orleans.

We arrived in Greensboro, Alabama, after dark, and followed cryptic instructions to a ramshackle building just off Main Street for an opening of sculpture by RS students, work that had been generated in relation to their current project 'Music Man House'.[6] Through a brick warren, expanding toward the back as a metal shed with high ceiling and concrete floor, we were finally delivered out at the rear through open sliding metal doors into a works yard complete with raging bonfire. The enthusiasm and engagement of these students was intense, joyful and contagious. The work: youthful. But something was working here, to get, or enable, students to get on with expressing themselves through making and building, and we were delighted to have arrived, to have an opportunity to check it out.

The more visible output of the RS comes from the sixteen fifth year students who work in teams of four for the entire year to design and build their final 'thesis projects'. As important but somewhat less visible are the sixteen third year students. This group stays at the Rural Studio for only one semester, but they work as a group on a single project that typically runs for the full academic year. In the second semester, a new group of third year students will carry on where the first semester group left off.

Sambo Mockbee, had died about a year before that first trip of November 2002, and the first person we were taken to meet was Andrew Freear, the first director to follow the visionary co-founder at the Rural Studio. Andrew, a Yorkshireman with an accent now confused by a love of the South, gave us a great 'Alabama welcome', and our look-in had properly begun. What we came to learn in that week was this: the RS is simply one of those rare places still driven by ideologies. The balance of power in what pushes the place forward swerves between mission statements, ideals, even morals, and ignores bureaucracy and the mandates of the latest technologies. Europeans love to describe Americans as 'naive', and they're right, but the payback may be that Americans simply do *do*, and the RS is a perfect example.

I've taught at the Rural Studio each September and January since that first visit in 2002, and I have been impressed on each journey, confronted really, with the presence of *big weather*. September is considered to be the height of the hurricane season in the Gulf and Atlantic, and hurricanes often send big weather well up into the southern states. In addition to hurricanes, the autumn is also tornado season – tornadoes being a different natural phenomenon from hurricanes. It seems like most evenings in west Alabama are preoccupied with checking the television for tornado watches or warnings. It's popular conversation, the weather, for good reason. Any given day can be swelteringly hot, torrentially rainy, or threatening a tornado to dip down and suck you into the sky.

When tornadoes do threaten, the conversation turns naturally to a personal version of *risk assessment*, and people begin to talk about exit strategies just in case. In hindsight, if nothing really happens, one usually feels slightly embarrassed at having been afraid. When our AA group left the Rural Studio by driving north, it was less than an hour before we had crossed not one but many paths of total destruction.[7] The tornado warnings we had been keeping an eye on the evening before by radio and TV had not become a reality in Greensboro, but they certainly had for the folks up the road.[8] The tornado watch had not been regional theatrics after all. For the next hour of our drive, we repeatedly crossed swathes of destruction, each about a 30 metres (100 feet) wide. Home after home had simply been smeared across the landscape.

An uncomfortable feeling has remained with me since, about the meaning of *home*, and the quality of the homes there in that part of Alabama. It's different seeing a well-constructed home destroyed, as compared to seeing a sheet metal mobile home simply laid open. Sure, a sense of physical vulnerability arises, but the message to me has been bigger than that. Here in the Black Belt of Alabama where the RS has made its home, the homes of the people are particularly insubstantial, and this keeps the homeowner vulnerable as a result. When a tornado makes a direct hit, it's a coin toss whether or not the quality of construction will make much difference, but these very modest homes were likely to have also been poorly insured, and harder for these families to replace. There was a disturbing sense that these folk had lost nothing, but had also lost everything.

It's always striking when notoriety is accompanied by misunderstanding. I came once to the Rural Studio a few weeks after Hurricane Katrina[9] had devastated New Orleans and much of the Gulf Coasts of Mississippi and Alabama to the east of there. It's only 273 kilometres (170 miles) from the Rural Studio in Hale County to Mobile, Alabama, which is on the south coast and suffered severe damage during the hurricane. I was meeting with Director Andrew Freear when a call came in from a community leader in New Orleans, asking if the Rural Studio would mobilise and come help rebuild.

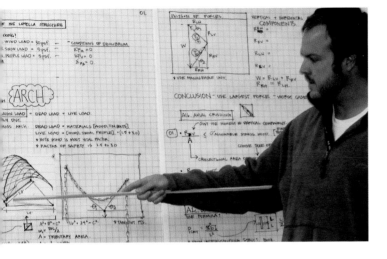

opposite left: Window detail of Lucy House, Mason's Bend, Hale County. The walls were made from carpet tiles. © Bob Sheil.

opposite right: Concrete Bridge. 'Design, make, test workshop', led by Anderson Inge. © Anderson Inge.

left: Hale County Animal Shelter. Anderson Inge with the student presentation of the results of the initial workshop. © Anderson Inge.

My first thought in overhearing was 'Well, of course', a new important project had just come over the line. What a perfect challenge for young, energetic, problem-solving architects. Just get 'em to come down the road a ways and give a hand to folks in need. I was very surprised when Freear politely declined the request! To not mobilise in the aftermath of Katrina initially seemed to me hugely inconsistent with the Rural Studio's broad reputation to help communities in need through design and build. However, that decision actually points to a strength and clarity of the Rural Studio vision. It is not about helicopter aid, dropping in to deploy novel emergency shelters or temporary fixes. The Rural Studio is about working within communities, over long, committed periods of time.

The in-and-out of the Rural Studio is a 'day in and day out' involvement with the host community, sharing the form of wealth known as education to assist communities in helping some of the members break a cycle of poverty, through the design and construction of homes, public spaces and community buildings. The RS is a local thing.

Most schools of architecture today are wrestling with how to keep up with the rapidly changing digital technologies that are now an integral part of design practice. A huge percentage of available resources, of time, money and know-how, are required to implement, maintain, integrate and keep current with the latest 3D modelling software and rapid-prototyping machinery. Architectural practice now routinely uses these tools, so most schools are making efforts to integrate them into the design processes of their students. But at the Rural Studio you won't come across even a whiff of rapid-prototyping solvent, or the whisper of any CNC cutters. In the great Alabama tradition of being left behind,[10] these modern tools are not a part of the magic that enables RS students to actually build their student design theses.

Indeed, it's hard to actually identify any tangible special elements in the way projects are designed or physically realised at the Rural Studio. To a visitor, the design processes might appear traditionally linear and relatively protracted. About all the visitor will see of the *processes* of how the RS students achieve the fantastic works published annually is

Rolling gantry system: as used to build both Hale County Animal Shelter and Akron Boys and Girls Club. © Bob Sheil.

a lot of hand tools, trucks and journeys to the lumberyard. As an example, despite the implicit deadline of 'graduation' looming a mere 10 months after the thesis students arrive, projects usually unfold at a pace that is comfortable in the South. I've never seen at the RS anything resembling *fast-tracking*, a common industry strategy where elements of the design, procurement and construction processes have been overlapped to compress the overall duration of the project. Director Andrew Freear makes a point of not harassing the students about schedule. He's intent on supporting first and foremost the imagination that makes the results visibly sing.

Architecture schools routinely use a rota of visiting lecturers to spice up their annual educational offering, and the Rural Studio does as well. But the lecturers who are brought annually to the RS have been carefully selected to provide a complementary set of inputs to the project teams. Lecturers here are referred to as 'consultants', and they typically spend several days working sequentially with the individual project teams, helping them to design and implement those aspects that fall within their area of expertise.

Since my teaching began there in 2003, my work has frequently dovetailed with several of the other regular visiting consultants: Xavier Vendrell,[11] architect based in Chicago, visiting approximately monthly and focusing on architectural design and planning; Steve Badanes[12] of Jersey Devil Design/Build comes regularly from Seattle to share his career-long experience in design and build; Paul Stoller[13] of Atelier Ten's New

York office, focuses on issues of energy, daylighting and planning for sustainability; Tim Macfarlane,[14] structural engineer with offices in London and NYC, goes out approximately biannually to give fresh impetus to the really ambitious structurally oriented projects; and Joe Farruggia,[15] structural engineer from Chicago, goes several times a year to prepare and finalise structural designs for construction.

I go to the Rural Studio twice annually as one of the consultant team, for a week at the beginning of each autumn semester, and again at the beginning of each second semester. As an architect with additional trainings in structural engineering and sculpture, I undertake to erase the barrier that scale often puts on the ambition of young architects, and to help these students integrate the materiality and aesthetics of architecture with the physical opportunities of structure.

For the autumn trip, I usually devise and deliver a workshop for the fifth year thesis students that is primarily intended to excite ambition, stimulate creative thinking about different building strategies and raise confidence for building *at scale*. My workshops usually require the students to combine design, analysis, model-building and testing (usually to destruction). By January when I return, the student teams have been working for some months on their chosen projects, and I focus on the team that is working on the project that has the most ambitious size, the group that may well be overwhelmed or confused about how to achieve the best balanced solution. This is often a time for a workshop that allows the team members to see for themselves the implications of their design as it stands, and this often becomes a sharp reality check as to what can and should be built with the resources available.

Part of the formula for how the Rural Studio builds has to do with simply nurturing the ambition to build that is bubbling up naturally in these students of architecture. From the outset the ambition is high and the goal is clear: you come here to build. Co-founder Sambo Mockbee is regularly quoted as having encouraged students to, 'Proceed and be Bold'. This part of the formula, then, relies simply on setting a high ambition, to a highly motivated group, and then (key step) GET OUT OF THE WAY. In most cases, it is far from magic, and it couldn't be less sexy in the sense that achieving the goal involves a staggering amount of difficult physical work, what is affectionately referred to at the RS as 'neck down work'.

One of the ongoing roles of the director is to cultivate projects that the community needs, and which make a suitable challenge for project teams made up typically of four architecture students. Each new academic year at the Rural Studio is begun by introducing the new group of fifth-year thesis students as a whole to the new set of available community projects. Then commences the courtship, exciting as any, with the students undertaking a number of inaugural workshops aimed at introducing them to each other, as well as to the several projects.

The Rural Studio has been working in and around Hale County, Alabama, for about 17 years now, and each new student group benefits. They inherit the communities' appreciation of their predecessors' results, as well as working relationships between the Rural Studio and community leaders who are all keen to see the projects succeed. Numerous other practical benefits accrue in support of simply getting things done,

Opening of Akron Boys and Girls II, Akron, Hale County. © Rural Studio, Auburn University.

such as contributions of materials, tradesmen, equipment, cash from benefactors and helping hands. The various forms of collaboration that go into Rural Studio projects are impressive. From the mayor to the lumber supply yard, Rural Studio student projects now benefit from a significant, broad-based support. But these relationships and gifts can't be taken for granted, and it often takes a long time for such things as donations in kind to actually show up on site. It's nearly impossible to demand that someone who has kindly offered to donate something (like welding services or helical 'earth screws') drop what they're doing and *deliver*. Donations in kind are an essential part of project success, but they are often accompanied by significant delays.

It is surprising in this day and age to come across places, particularly in the First World, that lack the fleet of control mechanisms we've grown to resent with tired acceptance. The Rural Studio is located in one of those rare places in North America where there is no enforcement of building regulations or planning controls. It's not that no one cares – it's more a matter of the communities not being able to *afford* to police them. The absence of building controls does not end up being helpful in the obvious way by enabling student project teams to flout good practice. The Rural Studio takes pains to police its own projects, particularly through the timely involvement of its several structural consultants at regular intervals to ensure safety and compliance with the applicable building codes. The real and significant advantage of no building controls, though, stems from the *time saved* for the project by not having to go through the usual process of submitting plans, waiting for a response, and possibly having to resubmit. With students attempting to design and build in one academic year, this timesaving is significant to the Rural Studio.

The Rural Studio is actually a satellite campus, separated from its parent, Auburn University, 225 kilometres (140 miles) to the east. There is a strong sense among RS students and staff that it benefits from a 'rural remove', with fewer distractions and compromising pressures on their imagination from peers and other tutors alike. The student experience at the Rural Studio is uniquely unfettered in many ways, and this is complemented by the exceptional amount of open space one sees in rural west Alabama. Space to spread out, to leave things lying about, and to experiment with full-sized elements and mock-ups. The lack of constraint and scrutiny are significant boosts to the students' efforts to tackle the challenge of physically building.

The part of the Rural Studio story that is most interesting, and the most difficult to explain, is really the American story, the story of a young place driven by simple ideologies that mingle the individual, country, freedoms, lots of open space and God. The settlement of America westward and southward from the original 13 colonies was realised through a set of attitudes that could largely be summed up as the 'frontier mentality'. Like most of America west of, say, Virginia, the frontier mentality is still palpably present in Alabama today.

Americans are somehow particularly mindful that the Book of Genesis entitled man (read 'America' in America) to 'Be fruitful, multiply, fill the earth, and subdue it [not necessarily in that order]. Have dominion over the fish of the sea, over the birds of the sky, and over every living thing that moves on the earth.'[16] The apparent idleness of land that can be seen in rural areas, particularly poor rural areas, fuels the American imagination to

Hale County Animal Shelter, Greensboro, Hale County. © Timothy Hursley.

dominate and utilise God's gifts. Among university students in the American South there is an abundance of evangelical, fundamentalist belief. While not often overt, there is an ethos among these students that resonates with these commanding religious tenets.

One of the many things that is striking about the few published writings by, and interviews with, Sambo Mockbee is how little emphasis is given to the act of building, which is really what the Rural Studio has become best known for. His writings are preoccupied, instead, with a larger ideological mission that intertwines strong moral objectives with the power of architecture to affect lives. Mockbee wrote that he had been inspired by southern American civil rights activists, ordinary people who had taken action for change, action that often risked their lives in pursuit of broader humanitarian goals. Mockbee's action for the improvement of social conditions was realised through building, with architectural knowledge as the vehicle. For individuals and communities trapped within a cycle of impoverishment, the action of designing and physically building provided a form of resource that couldn't be afforded by money alone, because there was no money available.

Mockbee writes of countering the elitist tendencies of the architectural profession and its patronage routes by training architects to embrace an 'affection for people and place'.[17] For him, these were the things that mattered. He recognised knowledge and professional training in architecture as a form of wealth that could be shared to positively influence the quality of life for people and communities that were impoverished. His focus was almost exclusively on the goal of connecting the architect-in-training with a 'client' who quite simply needed fundamental help, help with homes or community buildings.

Sambo's 'Proceed and be Bold' resonates strongly with the religious beliefs prevalent in the southern United States. It also resonates well with an optimism that seems to accompany the low cost of living typical in rural America. The scale of projects completed in recent years clearly shows this *can do* attitude, as seen in the large RS projects such as the Fire Station,[18] the Animal Shelter,[19] and the several Perry Lakes projects of the Pavilion,[20] Birding Tower[21] and Bridge.[22]

For those who know the RS only through its reputation, it will be surprising that there is nothing particularly special in its design and fabrication methodologies. If anything, it's a bit retro on these fronts. If you're one of the masses of moderns who has become embarrassed talking of beliefs, and even more so of ideals, the RS will never make sense. But it's worth giving some quiet thought to how these intangibles can underpin physical action. Building at the RS is afloat in a cocktail of ideals. And students there build, in large part, simply because they can. But the vision and beauty of the works that are realised there come from the ever-present, regularly discussed ideals of that place, that community, the school, the South and God.

When I close my eyes and think back over my times at the RS, I first feel the weather hug me, and scare me, in equal measure. And I see open space, to stretch the arms and exercise the eye. My imagination quickly follows, with the belief that anything can be realised on that relatively blank physical canvas. Students aren't supposed to drink on campuses in America any more, but what could be more intoxicating than this? What could be more motivating than the invitation to build, early, in an unencumbered environment, with your mates, your design, knowing it's likely to get published? It is magic after all.

Notes

1 Diploma Unit 8, Architectural Association, Unit Masters Peter Thomas and Mark Prizeman.
2 Samuel Mockbee, 'The Rural Studio', *AD The Everyday and Architecture*, AD Profile 134, vol 68, no 7/8, Jul/Aug 1998, pp 72–9.
3 Andrea Oppenheimer Dean and Christine Kreyling, 'Sam Mockbee: the Hero of Hale County', *Architectural Record*, vol 189, no 2, February 2001, pp 76–82.
4 On the 19 February 2001, *The Oprah Winfrey Show*, Rural Studio co-founder Sambo Mockbee received the 'Use Your Life Award'. With millions of viewers for each episode, this was a significant boon to the reputation of the Rural Studio and its mission.
5 Andrea Oppenheimer Dean and Timothy Hursley, *Rural Studio: Samuel Mockbee and an Architecture of Decency*, Princeton Architectural Press (New York), 2002.
6 'Music Man House', Greensboro, Alabama, 2003, second year project.
7 'The 2002 Veterans Day Weekend tornado outbreak was a large, widespread and rare outbreak of storms that occurred from the late afternoon hours on November 9 through the early morning hours on Veterans Day, November 11, 2002. Eighty-three tornadoes hit 17 states. Twelve tornadoes

killed 36 people in five states.' Wikipedia, 2002 Veterans Day Weekend tornado outbreak, http://en.wikipedia.org/wiki/2002_Veterans_Day_Weekend_tornado_outbreak (as of 3 September 2010).
8   'November 10, 2002 8:50 PM CST: About one third of the town of Carbon Hill, Walker County, Alabama, [161 kilometres (100 miles) north of the Rural Studio] was completely destroyed. At least 11 people were killed and 50 were injured. The tornado ripped through the very center of town.' Tornadoes in the Past, http://www.tornadoproject.com/past/pastts02.htm (as of 4 September 2010).
9   Hurricane Katrina began forming in the Gulf of Mexico on 23 August 2005 and began to dissipate on 29 August 2005.
10 Demographic figures for Alabama reflect a state that comparatively lags behind most others in many important indices, with low literacy rates and a high incidence of diabetes related to poor diet.
11 Xavier Vendrell, architect and landscape architect, Xavier Vendrell Studio, Chicago and Barcelona (www.xaviervendrellstudio.com).
12 Steve Badanes, architect and professor, Jersey Devil Design/Build, Miami, and University of Washington, Seattle (www.jerseydevildesignbuild.com).
13 Paul Stoller, environmental design consultant, Atelier Ten, New York (www.atelierten.com).
14 Tim Macfarlane, structural engineer, Dewhurst Marfarlane (www.dewmac.com).
15 Joe Farruggia, architect and engineer, GFGR, Inc, architects and engineers, Chicago.
16 Genesis 1:28.
17 Samuel Mockbee, 'The Rural Studio', p 75.
18 Newbern Fire Station/Town Hall, Newbern, Alabama, 2004 thesis project.
19 Hale County Animal Shelter, Greensboro, Alabama, 2006 thesis project.
20 Perry Lakes Park Pavilion, Marion, Alabama, 2002 thesis project.
21 Perry Lakes Park Birding Tower, Marion, Alabama, 2005 thesis project.
22 Perry Lakes Park Covered Bridge, Marion, Alabama, 2004 thesis project.

References

- Forney, John, 'Learning in Newbern: Rural Studio in Year Ten', *AD Design through Making*, vol 75, no 4, July/August 2005, pp 92–5
- Moos, David and Trechsel, Gail (eds), *Samuel Mockbee and the Rural Studio: Community Architecture*, Birmingham Museum of Art (Birmingham, AL); Distributed Art Publishers (New York), 2003
- Oppenheimer Dean, Andrea, *Proceed and Be Bold: Rural Studio after Samuel Mockbee*, Princeton Architectural Press (New York), 2005
- Oppenheimer Dean, Andrea, *Rural Studio: Samuel Mockbee and an Architecture of Decency*, Princeton Architectural Press (New York), 2002
- Oppenheimer Dean, Andrea and Christine Kreyling, 'Sam Mockbee: the Hero of Hale County', *Architectural Record*, vol 189, no 2, February 2001, pp 76–82
- 'Rural Studio: Interview with Andrew Freear of the Alabama Based Practice, by Giacomo Borella' (includes Cedar Pavilion, Perry Lakes Park, Alabama; Mason's Bend Community Center, Alabama; The Lucy House), *Lotus International*, no 124, June 2005, pp 116–23 (text in Italian and English)

Fractal, Bad Hair, Swoosh and Driftwood
Pavilions of AA Intermediate Unit 2, 2006–09

Charles Walker and Martin Self

Bedford Square, London WC1 has been host to many of architecture's most curious and experimental temporary constructs: John Hejduk's 'Collapse of Time' (1986), 'Urban Pavilion' by Mary Miss (1987), or 'Open House' by Coop Himmelb(l)au (1988). In recent years, a new generation of architectural structures has began to appear annually, designed and assembled by students of the Architectural Association's Intermediate Unit 2. Unlike previous generations of Bedford Square installations, these were clearly structures that talked about the influence of digital techniques on the design and manufacture of building components and assembly methods. In most cases, this was explored through one material, usually timber. Here, the unit's tutors expand on the pedagogic trajectory that led to the series, and offer a detailed insight into four of the projects.

This article describes and analyses the mechanisms of design and production explored through the Architectural Association's Summer Pavilions of 2006–09. Designed, fabricated and constructed by groups of second and third year architecture students, each pavilion was an experiment in maximising a formal architectural effect through inventive use of digital design and fabrication tools. Pedagogically, the aim was to take students through an exercise that exposed them to the full experience of a project from conception to completion. In wider terms, the projects formed a small research programme into the built possibilities of new design tools and timber technologies. Although student-designed, each pavilion was developed with the input of engineering consultants, the timber industry, and many architectural critics and tutors, who hopefully also drew lessons from the projects. In this tentative way, these projects demonstrate how the relative freedom of the educational project can be valuable as a research activity for wider practice.

In this paper, the technical explorations of each pavilion are discussed. That the pavilions were each a response to the same brief and common material and production constraints, yet delivered four very different outcomes, is seen as illustrative of the freedom engendered by digital production. Also, that each project employed digital tools at differing stages (switching in each case between 'digital' and 'manual' modes at different points) presents an argument for fluidity in the application of the computer in design, and acknowledgement that a craft approach is needed to find the appropriate (and potentially still labour-intensive) tool for the job at hand.

Pavilions of AA Intermediate Unit 2, 2006–09

The AA's Intermediate Unit 2 was established in 2003 by Charles Walker, with Lip Chiong, as a year-long design-and-documentation exercise that followed the brief of London's Serpentine Gallery Summer Pavilions. Charles and Lip were part of Arup's Advanced

Geometry Unit (AGU), a specialist group of architects and engineers who collaborated on geometrically complex projects including the Serpentine Pavilions.[1] This meant that the students were able to relate their fictional projects to the parallel development of the actual pavilions in Hyde Park. Similarly, students were able to engage with AGU colleagues to access their specialist technical knowledge (mathematics; programming; engineering analysis) that had allowed projects such as the pavilions by Daniel Libeskind, Toyo Ito and Álvaro Siza with Eduardo Souto de Moura[2] to be realised.

In 2003–04 and 2004–05, the unit's projects were hypothetical (rather than built) design but each student was required to develop a set of fully defined technical drawings of their pavilion proposal. The basis of the unit was to 'get real' – to fully understand the material implications of an architectural proposal by defining it down to its nuts and bolts. Although the pavilions remained as paper projects, they were grounded in engineering practice and were treated as genuine design works for construction. In 2005, Martin Self took over Lip's position as tutor. As an engineer who had just completed the Serpentine Pavilion by Álvaro Siza and Eduardo Souta de Moura, the unit gained both the capacity to deliver built projects and a material sponsor in Finnforest Merk who had sponsored that pavilion. This, combined with the availability of the wonderful timber workshop at Hooke Park (the woodland campus that became part of the AA in 2002)[3] led to the proposal that Inter 2 become a design and build unit, realising student-designed pavilions for the AA's end-of-year show. The programme for the unit followed the three academic terms, loosely splitting the project into concept generation, design development and construction. The first term was used for skill building and idea generation ('50 Ideas in 50 Days') that led to an identified pavilion concept from each student. These concepts were developed through the second term into scheme designs and then (following competitions to regroup the student team around the strongest proposals) the fully detailed documentation, for construction, of a single pavilion.

Through the ideas phase students were encouraged to explore techniques and architectural propositions without prejudice, building a palette of approaches and, ideally, to develop a research agenda that led them to a strong and definable pavilion concept. Deliberately, the design brief for the pavilions kept concerns of context and programme to a minimum; the requirement was for a 80–100-square-metre (861–1076-square-foot) event pavilion that would be sited in the corner of Bedford Square outside the AA for its end of year *Projects Review* exhibition. As tutors, our aim was to enable the students to be as ambitious and autonomous as possible while ensuring the pavilion would be deliverable on time. The constraints of each pavilion were consistent: materially, we used the product that Finnforest could supply (mainly Kerto laminated veneer lumber)[4] and that could be worked in the Hooke Park furniture-scale workshop. In terms of fabrication we were limited to the three-axis CNC machine[5] at Hooke and the capabilities of a generally unskilled set of students in the workshop for five to six weeks. On site in Bedford Square, professional contractors worked with the students in erecting the pavilion. This arrangement allowed students to have hands-on engagement through to completion of the project, maximising the tactile experience of construction.

The other key constraint was the level of students' ability and motivation to engage deeply with the tools of digital production. The hope was that by explicitly learning scripted modelling techniques at the very start of the academic year, students would develop a comfortable relationship with them. The aim was not to produce expert skills, but to introduce the philosophy of a craft-like approach based on understanding the correct tool for the job and to have confidence as a 'tool-maker' in that realm. Individual students, driven by particular responsibilities within the project, would take ownership of developing the specific digital tools needed to tackle the problems they needed to solve. The early simple exercises were chosen to help prompt wider individual explorations at the ideas stage. These opened up discussions over more sophisticated design tools and the potential for direct control at fabrication. Despite students often initially fearing these techniques, in the end each project fundamentally depended upon them.

2006: The Fractal Pavilion

This pavilion's geometry was based on a branching algorithm through which the structural elements multiply and are dispersed volumetrically, generating the fractal system's characteristic self-similarity at multiple scales. Simon Whittle, who authored the pavilion concept, spent his first term learning the techniques of scripted geometric modelling (using RhinoScript),[6] exploring the mathematical basis of fractal geometries and branching algorithms (L-systems)[7] and testing ideas for their spatial application. The unit's reading list included the chapter on 'Recursive Structures' in Hofstadter's *Gödel, Escher, Bach*[8] which prompted Simon to search for meaningful applications of self-similarity. The early pavilion proposals were effectively two-dimensional branched screens arranged to enclose a space. It was the later realisation that the symmetrical single axis rotation at each branching node (through a +/-60 degree angle, in this case) could also include an asymmetrical rotation on a different axis, that allowed the branching system to become truly three-dimensional.

The pavilion consists, in principle, of two component types – the stick-like 'beams' and the shield-shaped 'flanges' that are repeated over nine 'generations' of scale. Each generation's dimensions are a golden-ratio reduction of the preceding one's. At each flange, one larger beam is connected to two smaller beams in a complex slotted joint that sets the angle changes between generations. Theoretically at least, every component is exactly similar, varying only in dimension, so that every connection shares the same geometry and therefore need only be designed once. In reality this was not the case: the Kerto sheets are supplied in discrete thicknesses that do not correspond to exact golden ratios and the structural design imposed different conditions (footings, bracing, bolt numbers, etc) on each joint. As a result, in detailed design the connections at each generation became bespoke, painstakingly defined individually in the digital 3D model, the paper drawings, and later in the slot-cutting jigs in the workshop.

Fractal Pavilion

- 42 sheets 6000 x 1500 mm (236 x 59 in) Finnforest Kerto-Q laminated spruce 33, 39, 51, 57, 69, 75 mm (1.29, 1.53, 2.01, 2.24, 2.71, 2.95 in) thick
- 45 sheets 2450 x 1225 mm (96.45 x 48.22 in) exterior birch plywood 6, 12, 15, 24 mm (0.23, 0.47, 0.59, 0.94 in) thick
- 124 mild steel flat connection plates 8 mm (0.31 in) thick
- 120 mild steel folded connection plates 5 mm (0.19 in) thick
- 664 M12 galvanised steel bolts, lengths 80, 90, 100, 120, 160, 260 mm (3.14, 3.54, 3.93, 4.72, 6.29, 10.23 in)
- 28 M12 galvanised steel threaded rods 300 mm (11.81 in) long
- 872 M12 nuts; 112 M12 60 mm (2.36 in) washers; 1216 M12 25 mm (0.98 in) washers
- 800 M12 single-sided tooth-plate timber connectors 65 mm (2.55 in)
- 3136 brass CSK slotted wood screws type 203.2 x 44.4 mm (8 x 1.75 in)
- 1 Type 1 PVC welded membrane
- 20 6 mm (0.23 in) diameter steel cables; shackles; turnbuckles

top: Test assembly of components for the Fractal Pavilion in the Hooke Park workshop. © Eli Lui.
above: Detail of the Fractal Pavilion, 2006. © Martin Self.

The glue-laminated elements of the 2007 pavilion, during fabrication and staining at Hooke Park. © Martin Self.

The completed Bad Hair Pavilion in Bedford Square, 2007. © Sue Barr.

2007: The Bad Hair Pavilion

This was conceived by student Margaret Dewhurst as a geometrically freeform collection of timber 'strands' that flowed over a central space for social gathering. Probably in a reaction against the deterministic mathematical rigour of the Fractal Pavilion, the ambition was for an informal arrangement of structure that appeared to have been designed and constructed in a more ad hoc manner. The solution developed into a system of large-section solid laminated timber elements that were straight, singly curved, or doubly curved in various ways. These were arranged asymmetrically over the central space in concentric spherical layers and then allowed to flow freely outwards. Structurally, the primary dome was constrained to one of the middle spherical layers (with straight legs) off which the other, nonstructural, layers are carried. Technically, the interesting part of the pavilion is in the geometric definition and CNC fabrication of the doubly curved laminated beams. Two of these beam types were developed; one in which each laminate strip is initially a straight element, and another in which each laminate has a unique, CNC-cut, curved profile. In both cases, steel moulds were fabricated upon which the 6-millimetre (0.23-inch) thick plywood laminates were laid up, nailed and glue-laminated to form the freely twisting beams 400 millimetres (15.74 inch) square in section.

In the first type, a geodesic 'ribbon-laying' script was written in RhinoScript to determine the volumetric form that would be developed when layering many straight strips on to an initially curved and twisted surface. As each strip's path is determined by the offset surface from the previous layer, the overall cross section is forced to shear (from square to a parallelogram); this shearing was mapped to allow the correct initial mould form to be made. In the second type, the target curvature was defined first and then the doubly curved path of each laminate found so that at all points centre-line offset was kept perpendicular to the local plane defined by the previous layer. In this way the beam's local cross section was kept square along its length, rather than shearing. Each laminate's individual profile was then extracted, flattened, labelled and laid out for CNC cutting from the plywood sheets. These scripts were developed by student Adel Zakout (whose own pavilion proposal had used a scripted method to generate a semi-random 'tornado' of timber elements). In contrast to the Fractal Pavilion, where scripted methods were used in the global definition of the geometry at an early design stage, here the instrumental use of scripting came late in the construction documentation.

Bad Hair Pavilion
28 sheets 6000 x 1500 x 39 mm (236 x 59 x1.53 in) Finnforest Kerto-Q
600 sheets 2450 x 1225 x 6 mm (96.45 x 48.22 x 0.23 in) birch exterior plywood
116 M16 Grade 4.4 bolts, lengths 200, 300, 400 mm (7.87, 11.81, 15.74 in); nuts & washers
440 shear plate timber connectors 102 mm (4 in) in diameter
Resorcinol glue
Laminating staples
9 mild steel fabricated layer–layer connection brackets size 8 mm (0.31 in)
4 mild steel folded anchor plates size 8 mm (0.31 in)
14 mild steel routing templates size 6 mm (0.23 in)
4 fabricated doubly curved laminating moulds

2008: The Swoosh Pavilion

Students started their year with pattern-generation exercises, exploring in two dimensions the geometric principles of pattern and tiling, and forming a vocabulary of their effects. They were encouraged to test the potential of generative scripted techniques to produce and control their patterns, an approach which many of the students extended into their individual pavilion proposals. Valeria Garcia's concept of Op-Art-influenced spiral patterns developed into a rotationally symmetrical flowing grid of elements that formed a sequence of occupiable spaces (from bench, to tunnel and canopy). Her student colleagues took the early pattern scripts and 'three-dimensionalised' them to test a large series of options in the arrangement of the pattern elements. Curiously, in the final stages of optimisation of the structural pattern, the students switched to 'manual scripting', a term that they coined for the meticulous refinement of the pavilion's arrangement of elements. At this point, the rigid script structure became too constrained to deal with the local specifics of the structure and was abandoned.

As the number of special conditions grew, the manual approach of adjusting each element in the 3D model became the best way to complete the detailed design. These special conditions were largely driven by issues of constructability – for example, the need to allow access for hand and spanner to make bolt fixings on site, requiring local adjustments not consistent with the rules of a prescriptive generative algorithm. In the fabrication workshop, a similar interweaving of the digitally controlled and manually worked was needed. The structure consisted of cantilevering 'column' elements that, due to their large size, were cut by hand-held jigsaw, whereas the secondary 'beam' elements were small enough to be produced on the CNC router. The sequence of workshop operations to produce these elements, with their angled cuts, bolt channels and spanner access pockets was complex and depended on integrating the accuracy of the CNC production with the flexibility of the manual tool. Crucially important were the early phone conversations and exchanges of sketches with the Hooke Park workshop supervisor, Charles Corry-Wright, through which the student teams determined what would be possible with the tools available.

Swoosh Pavilion
11 sheets 6000 x 2400 x 51 mm (236 x 94.48 x 2.00 in) Finnforest Kerto-Q
53 sheets 2400 x 1200 x 51 mm (94.48 x 47.24 x 2.00 in) Finnforest Kerto-Q
205 sheets 2400 x 1200 x 24 mm (94.48 x 47.24 x 0.94 in) Finnforest Kerto-Q
1894 M12 bolts, lengths 150, 160, 170, 180, 190 mm (5.90, 6.29, 6.69, 7.08, 7.48 in); nuts, washers
1240 M6 bolts, lengths 100, 150 mm (3.93, 5.90 in); nuts, washers
1760 wood screws, size 100 mm (3.93 in)
480 tooth plates 76 mm (2.99 in) in diameter
8 weld-fabricated base plates of 8 mm (0.31 in) thick mild steel

Students checking components of the Swoosh Pavilion, 2008. © Martin Self.

The completed Swoosh Pavilion with the shadow projection of its originating 2D pattern. © Sue Barr.

2009: The Driftwood Pavilion

This was probably the most ambitious of the four projects, appearing as a *'millefeuille'* of thin plywood layers freely flowing in a ring that rises and falls to allow access to its central space. All 28 of the 3.5-millimetre (0.13-inch) thick bent plywood layers comprised CNC-cut panels – about 1600 in number – that were held by slotted diaphragms that were in turn supported by a primary central structural box-beam. The key challenge in the project was in developing suitably rational interior construction geometry that allowed the apparently completely free geometric form. Surprisingly, given that it is not read as such in any oblique view, the plan of the pavilion has a pure three-axis symmetry.

As with the Swoosh Pavilion, Driftwood's flowing effect was conceived during two-dimensional scripted pattern studies. One of the tutorial examples was a method for generating vector-field flow lines that produced timber-grain-like effect. Danecia Sibingo studied the potential of this method and made a pavilion concept proposal based upon carving a vertical extrusion of the pattern. This was developed further by student Taeyoung Lee who established the technique for controlling its full geometric definition. This included using T-Splines software to make the smooth carving surfaces, and the logic for defining their labelling, positioning and fixing. A series of geometries was proposed and tested in parallel with the development of the interior structure by student colleagues. Once again, the integration of CNC fabrication with manual work was key to maximising production in the workshop. Particularly tricky was the slotted 'diaphragm' pieces, each different in shape, that were CNC-cut in outline and CNC-labelled with precise cut marks to allow subsequent manual operations to saw the angles' surfaces and slots that were not possible to make using the CNC.

The core lesson of the pavilion programme is that digitally driven design and fabrication is not a tidy or linear process. In none of the projects was it a case of a distinct design-phase of computer modelling being followed by a button-press to realise a physical artefact. The popularity of the rapid-prototype machine in architecture schools risks reinforcing that fallacy. Rather it is a complex series of cycles in which the craftsman-like knowledge of material, tooling and other know-how is used to pre-empt the real-world issues of making and construction.

Notes

1 Arup's Advanced Geometry Unit was founded in 2000 by Cecil Balmond and led by Charles Walker. See *Architecture and Urbanism*, special Issue, *Cecil Balmond: Architecture and Urbanism*, A+U Publishing Co, October 2006.
2 *Eighteen Turns*, Daniel Libeskind with Arup, 2001; Serpentine Gallery Pavilion 2002, by Toyo Ito with Arup; Serpentine Gallery Pavilion 2005 by Álvaro Siza and Eduardo Souto de Moura with Cecil Balmond – Arup.
3 Hooke Park is a 141.6 hectare (350-acre) forest in Dorset, southwest England, that includes a small campus centred around a woodworking workshop.
4 Finnforest Kerto is an engineered timber panel product made of glued 3-mm (0.11-in) softwood veneers, produced in continuous billets up to 90 mm (3.54 in) thick and 2.5 metres (8.20 feet) wide.
5 The Hooke Park workshop CNC machine is a Wadkin CC100 three-axis router with a bed size of 2450 x 1225 mm (96.45 x 48.22 in).
6 RhinoScript is a programming plug-in for McNeel's Rhino 3D v4.0 modelling software.
7 An L-system (Lindenmayer system) is a formal language developed by Aristid Lindenmayer that is used to model growth processes including branching structures.
8 Douglas R Hofstadter, *Gödel, Escher, Bach: An Eternal Golden Braid*, Basic Books (New York), 1979.

Fitting the CNC-cut plywood skins to the Driftwood Pavilion's Kerto armature, June 2009. © Valerie Bennett/ Architectural Association.

Driftwood Pavilion
10 sheets 6000 x 2400 x 51 mm (236 x 94.48 x 2.00 in) Finnforest Kerto-Q
40 sheets 1200 x 2400 x 51 mm (47.24 x 94.48 x 2.00 in) Finnforest Kerto-Q
65 sheets 2450 x 1225 x 9 mm (96.45 x 48.22 x 0.35 in) exterior birch plywood
499 sheets 2450 x 1225 x 3.5 mm (96.45 x 48.22 x 0.13 in) exterior plywood
92 M20 Grade 4.4 bolts, lengths 80, 125, 350, 650 mm (3.14, 4.92, 13.77, 25.59 in)
128 shear plate timber connectors, diameter 102 mm (4 in)
475 M12 bolts, length 80 mm (3.14 in); washers, nuts
8 M12 bolts, length 250 mm (9.84 in); washers, nuts
2500 wood screws, size 35 mm (1.37 in)
37 mild steel connection plates, each 6 mm (0.23 in)thick
77 75 x 75 mm (2.95 x 2.95 in) mild steel angles typically 2 metres (6.56 feet) long

The completed Driftwood Pavilion, 2009. © Valerie Bennett/Architectural Association.

Microstructure, Macrostructure and the Steering of Material Proclivities

Phil Ayres

The Persistent Modelling Project, based at CITA (the Centre for Information Technology and Architecture) at the Royal Danish Academy of Fine Arts, School of Architecture, Copenhagen, is an investigation of novel design strategies that exploit the potential of digital technologies applied to design, fabrication and use. The project seeks to reconsider the relationship between architectural representation and architectural artefact, and proposes to investigate the opportunities of a circular relationship through which intent is translated into artefact. Here, author of the project, and member of sixteen*(makers), Phil Ayres, provides a detailed analysis of recent experiments in hydroforming, which are providing vital insight into the development of new theories of design and representation.

Both separateness and continuity are interwoven, each necessary to the other and demonstrating the relationship between different features on a single scale and between units and aggregates on different scales.

Cyril Stanley Smith[1]

The most complete change an individual can affect in his environment, short of destroying it, is to change his attitude to it.

Mark Boyle[2]

This article reports upon recent and initial explorations by the author in the hydroforming of steel. The material processes involved and the resulting artefacts are reflected upon, providing a ground from which to speculate about implications for architecture as both artefact and practice. The particular hydroforming procedure employed bears close similarity to that under investigation by the chair for CAAD (Computer-Aided Architectural Design) at ETH. This article therefore also seeks to identify how the work presented differentiates itself from that being conducted in Zurich.

The simplicity in execution of the forming method belies a complex matrix of interactions occurring within, and between, scales of material organisation. Within certain limits, these interactions dramatically and irreversibly transform material and component attributes towards increased performance potentials and formal complexity. These transforms are steerable but not exclusively dependent upon profile geometry. The definition of geometry leading to physical outcome is familiar design territory.

The forming method can be arrested and resumed arbitrarily. The notion of an extended forming process presents interesting implications to the linear relationship that tends to bind the commonly distinguished phases of design, fabrication/construction and occupancy/use. It suggests a potential for active response in relation to demand. This, in turn, presents challenges to a design practice that is reliant upon methods of representation that tend towards the ideal, predictive and predetermined. This is less familiar design territory.

This work begins to define both a material language for, and a nondeterministic design paradigm of, *steered proclivity*. A conceptual framework for this paradigm is sketched out and presented in the form of the *Persistent Model*.

The ensuing examination commences with an anecdote.

Shocking Material

About a year ago, during the summer of 2009, I was taking a stroll with my wife and son down one of the pedestrianised streets in our home city of Copenhagen. It was (and still is) littered with chichi outlets selling all manner of designer-branded manufactured goods. Within this miasma there was one object which, having been strategically positioned out on the street, caught my attention from afar – a three-legged inflated stool glistening with glossy black vinyl shininess. It was a ridiculous proposition. Curiosity aroused, I ventured towards it in order to reaffirm my assumptions that it couldn't possibly sustain any semblance of structural integrity under the impending 90 kilogramme (198 pound) point load test. The object's *actual* materiality and method of manufacture offered itself only – but instantaneously – upon haptic interrogation.

I purchased a *Plopp* immediately.

'Wonder En Is Gheen Wonder'

The axiom inscribed beneath Simon Stevin's 16th-century proof of *the law of equilibrium on an inclined plane* translates directly as 'magic is no magic'.[3] Rather than being interpreted as an expression of sour grapes, the more optimistic and didactic view is that Stevin was conveying an understanding in which the construction of scientific explanation does not lead to the destruction of wonder – indeed comprehension can amplify the sense of wonder through a deepened appreciation of the physical world's capacity for constructing complexity out of simplicity.[4] This wonder can be further sustained and extended through an examination of the consequences and implications such *magic-that-is-no-magic* poses to a particular domain of application.

Every *Plopp* is nuanced through its method of forming – a technique patented as FIDU (Freie Innendruck-Umformung or Free Internal-Pressure Forming).[5] The FIDU process is a derivative of hydroforming which is commonly used in the automotive industry. Hydroforming involves the application of fluid into a closed blank at sufficient pressure to cause material deformation and conformity to a confining die. The *FIDU* process distinguishes itself from hydroforming in that no die is employed; rather, two sheets of material are welded at the seam to form a sealed cushion into which the fluid medium is introduced. This material organisation inflates as the internal pressure increases. The substantial tooling cost for the die is therefore eradicated, but so too is the die's influence on the production of repeatable and accurately predictable results.

Clearly, the variety and differentiation between individual examples is conceptualised as an attribute for the *Plopp*, playing on the association of uniqueness with value. But I think that there is much more at stake here. This process unsettles certain assumptions and particular established principles that manufacturing has come to exemplify by disassociating it from the pursuit of fully predetermined, highly specified, dimensionally accurate and predictable outcomes. Furthermore, it provides a viable, wonderfully simple and strangely poetic analogue counterpart for exploring notions of variety, difference and unpredictability within the familiar and digitally saturated discourse of *mass customisation* – a paradigm which is also predicated upon the established values of manufacturing stated above.

To be clear – I am not arguing against these established values, as there are very apparent and valid reasons underlying them; I am arguing that techniques such as the one under consideration should not be dismissed from serious investigation out of nonconformity to these ideals before a thorough evaluation of their potentials and implications.[6]

Furthermore, this article will certainly not be promulgating the digital Luddite's guide to novelty and variety with a take on mass customisation through quaint unpredictability. As will be described, the interest in this method of fabrication is conceptually congruent with a broader scope of research that fundamentally implicates digital tools and procedures in an effort to search out and develop new design strategies that support the consideration of sensitively dependent, dynamic and transformable architectures.

Most importantly, I see significant and valuable potential in examining how this simple forming procedure begets complex potentials and implications when considered within the context of architectural practice and at an architectural scale. This article sets out to describe what these might be through reference to some recent explorations by the author and the broader research scope referred to above. But first, a more detailed examination of the inflation process, and the consequences on material behaviour, will provide some useful and fascinating conceptual insights for this consideration.

'Ut tensio, sic vis' and Beyond – Material Dynamics

In 1679 Robert Hooke published his findings on the linear proportionality between stress and strain exhibited by most materials.[7] An interesting implication of Hooke's findings and their contribution to the theory of elasticity is that any solid is attributed with an inherent dynamic in the face of applied mechanical force. That is to say, all solids will change shape under loading through contraction or stretching and this occurs *through* the material, down to the scale of atomic bonds.[8] Hooke's law only holds up to a certain amount of stress (*the proportional limit*) under which material behaviour is considered *elastic*. Within the elastic phase, energy introduced through loading is held as potential energy and is therefore recoverable through unloading. The direct consequence of this *resilience* is that deformations are temporary and reversible (Figure 1a).

When inflating metal, the material behaviours of interest commence once we go beyond the elastic phase. In testing, the proportional and elastic limits are exceeded very quickly with less than 0.1MPa internal pressure. Our inflating metal cushion now enters a phase of *plastic deformation* in which introduced energy is nonrecoverable and permanent forming

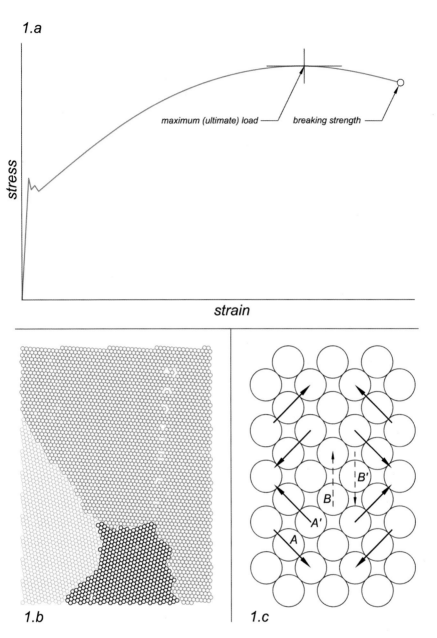

1.a

stress

maximum (ultimate) load —

breaking strength —

strain

1.b

1.c

Fig 1a A notional stress/strain curve for steel. Two principal material behaviours in relation to loading are clearly observable. Elastic behaviour is described by the linear portion of the graph to the left, and plastic behaviour is described by the extended curve. Metal inflation exploits the material potential for strain hardening that occurs as the material is driven along this curve. Inflation should be arrested before the maximum load point is reached and material failure begins (drawn by the author after DeGarmo et al). © Phil Ayres, CITA.

Fig 1b A geometric approximation of a photographic plate appearing on the inner leaf of Smith's *A Search for Structure*. Smith's caption reads: 'An aggregate of bubbles illustrating the structure of metals on an atomic scale and serving as a visual metaphor for the hierarchy of interactions of all kinds. Note the formation of regions of order that tolerate a few internal local anomalies but conflict on a larger scale to produce linear boundaries of connected disorder.' (Drawn by the author.) © Phil Ayres, CITA.

Fig 1c Schematic showing how atomic planes A, A' within the lattice show greater atomic density with wider interplanar spacing than planes B, B', thereby offering less resistance to the shear deformation of plastic forming (drawn by the author after DeGarmo et al). © Phil Ayres, CITA.

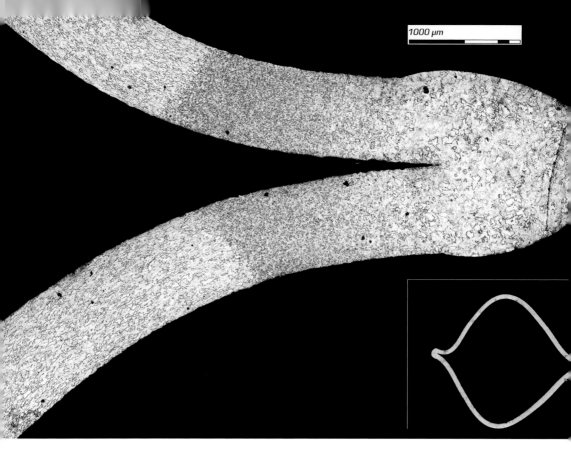

1000 μm

Fig 2 Microscopy reveals the granular microstructure of the inflated sample (detail bottom right). Individual grains and their boundaries are clearly visible and act as material witnesses to various forming processes inflicted upon the material. The elongation of grains to the left of the image are a witness to the process of rolling the sheet, whereas the welding of the two sheets to construct the 'cushion' composite has caused a very evident zone of recrystallisation. Microscopy preparation and imagery by Sarat Babu, UCL Bartlett School of Graduate Studies and Jonathan Warwick, Imperial College London. © Phil Ayres, CITA.

is induced. The ease with which this occurs belies a complex series of interactions within and between scalar hierarchies of material organisation established, in turn, through a complex series of prior interactions occurring during the processing of the raw material and its solidification from a liquid state. During solidification, atoms aggregate in a geometric lattice around a solidified particle of material – *a crystal nucleus*. In polycrystalline metals, which are the most general case, *nucleation* occurs independently at numerous sites throughout the solidifying material. These are the seeds of the heterogeneity observable within the next hierarchical level of structure because the *nuclei* randomly differ in their three-dimensional orientation with respect to each other. As a consequence, the developing discrete lattice eventually encounters a geometric incompatibility with its adjacencies causing a cessation in crystalline growth and establishing bounding surfaces of weaker atomic bonding (see Figure 1b). The surfaces formed at the geometric disjunction to adjacent lattices are termed *grain boundaries* and the bound region of continuous lattice is defined as a *grain* (Figure 2).[9]

These two levels of organisation – the lattice and the grain – are instrumental in determining the transforms to mechanical attributes of the material under applied loading. Within the plastic phase, the material attempts to reduce imposed loads by permanently dislocating planes of atoms through shear deformation, or *slip*. Being arranged in a lattice there are inherent planar relations between atoms. Depending on orientation these planes vary in their density of atoms, and the interplanar spacing between parallel planes. These two attributes define the plane's relative resistance to slip (see Figure 1c). The direction of the loading force privileges the slip plane that offers the least resistance and is most favourably aligned to induce the shear deformation. Being a consequence of the lattice's periodicity, slip planes are local to the grain. They do not transgress the profile boundary of the grain and thereby constrain the motion of dislocation. Furthermore, each dislocation within a grain constructs increased potentials of interaction with subsequent dislocations, constructing resistances to motion by symmetry breaking of the lattice. The net effect on the mechanical characteristics of the material is a strengthening and hardening – a phenomenon known as *strain-hardening*, to which Stevin's notion of rational magic surely applies. This material behaviour continues to be exploitable as we travel up the stress/strain curve and constitutes a harvesting of material performance capacity. The highest point of the curve marks the limit of benefit. Exceeding this begins the descent of material failure (see Figure 1a).[10]

Macrostructures Given v Macrostructures Driven, and the Reliability of Their Relative Representations

The behaviours described, and their associated transform on the mechanical and physical attributes, are native material responses to loading irrespective of imposed artefact geometry.[11] Imposed geometry plays a principal role in steering the extent, and under which conditions, these behaviours are exhibited. This introduces a further level of material organisation at a macro-scale to which architectural design might more readily contribute.

The morphology of steel sections for use in the construction industry is well established and its relationship to representation is such that a high degree of correlation is demanded, and can be expected through controlled manufacture. This high correlation between representation and physical artefact continues to hold as the morphology evolves from the rigidly standardised to the possibilities of the bespoke.

The freeform inflation explorations do not conform to these ideals. A discrete component begins as a 2D idealised digital geometric definition of profile. This geometry is used to instruct the laser-cutting of two sheets of 22-gauge steel which are then welded by hand using the TIG (tungsten inert gas) process.[12] As this composite is inflated, the profile geometry plays a significant, but not exclusive, role in steering the extent of deviation from the initialising representation. The two profiles shown in Figure 3 overleaf illustrate how deviation is slight in the case of the bar and extreme in the case of the chevron forms. These results suggest that our methods of representation must extend into simulation of the inflation process in order to better predict outcomes. This has been attempted, but to date these simulations have met with limited success at the component level, and the lack of correlation between representation and physical artefact is compounded as we investigate aggregates (see Figure 4).

1m

above: Fig 3 The initialising representation, employed to instruct the laser cutting of the profiles, becomes redundant through the transformative procedure of inflation. Deviation is slight in the case of the bar and extreme in the case of the chevron forms – profile geometry plays a significant role in steering the extent of deviation. Note the subtlety of formal transforms in the case of the bar – the shrinkage in length and the slender necking towards the centre. © Phil Ayres, CITA.

opposite: Fig 4 Attempts at simulating the inflation process have met with limited success. In the component comparison (top), note how the digital simulation produces carefully blended curvature and remains proximate to the original profile, whereas the physical artefact exhibits well-defined yield lines that produce regions of single curvature. The extent of closure between the two arms is also significantly more pronounced. The lack of correlation between representation and physical artefact is compounded as we investigate aggregates. This disparity is seen as an opportunity for the proposition of the Persistent Model, which operates through error-controlled regulation. Digital inflation studies by Anders Holden Deleuran, CITA. © Phil Ayres, CITA.

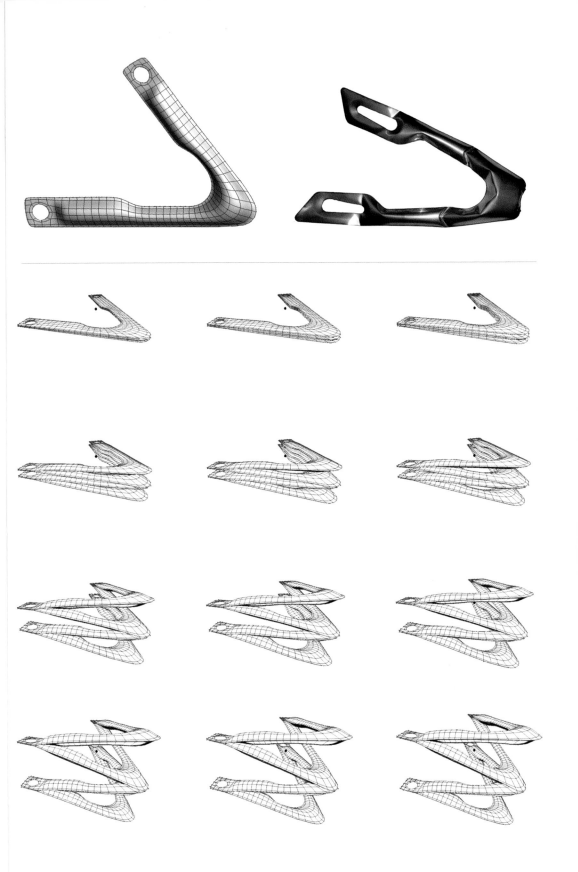

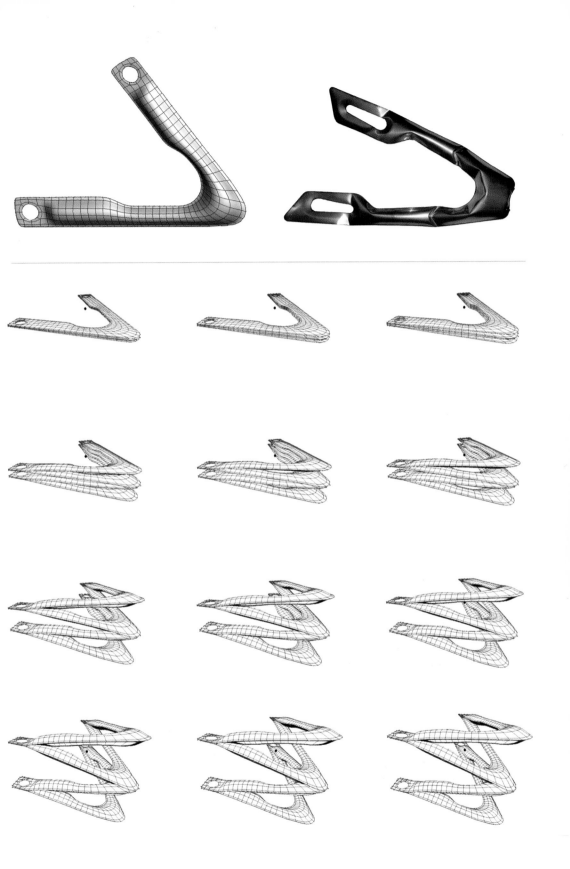

If one accepts Evans' assertion that a principal role of representation is to provide a 'complete determination in advance',[13] then this position poses challenges to the use of a fabrication method that contributes significantly to artefact attributes in a manner that is difficult to predict. Two avenues of resolution immediately suggest themselves; the first is to dismiss the procedure for use in any instrumental capacity due to nonconformity to particular established methods, concerns and values of practice; the second is to re-examine particular methods, concerns and values of practice to determine how such a procedure might be accommodated. It is assumed that the latter would be the more rewarding and contributory approach, but perhaps only worth the effort if other values beyond the managing of arbitrariness can be identified.

Progressive Material Capacity and the Conjecture of Material Economy

As the interactions within and between micro- and macrostructure of our cushion are driven by increases in internal pressure, the principal deformation of interest at the macro-scale occurs with the increase in cross-sectional separation of the sheets – a result of the composite organisation. The transforms to the formal characteristics of the component are dramatic, but the potential performance capacities are more so. A beam profile similar to that in Figure 3 deflected considerably under its own weight when uninflated, yet after inflation to just 0.3MPa the component passed the aforementioned 90 kilogramme (198 pound) point load test with ease when simply supported. A celebratory comparison of the inflation pressure can be made with that of a bottle of champagne which lies in the range of 0.4–0.6MPa. Furthermore, the relationship between material weight and load-bearing capacity shows promise for greater material economy. In a prototype pedestrian footbridge fully composed of inflated components, manufactured and more rigorously tested at ETH, the 6-metre (19.6-foot) span structure outperformed expectations sustaining almost 2000 kilogrammes (4409 pounds) for a material weight of only 170 kilogrammes (374 pounds).[14] Material economy certainly provides a potent incentive in favour of searching for methods of integration within a palette of available and employable techniques.[15]

A parallel but more speculative opportunity that segues into interesting conceptual, theoretical and practical implications presents itself through the possibility of easily arresting inflation within the plastic regime. The internal pressure can be returned to atmosphere without a deflation of form and arbitrarily resumed to induce further transforms. The speculative notion that proceeds from this fact considers the process of forming not as one occurring discretely and isolated from the site of use, but as a process that occurs in exchange with an environment of demand; doing so with active intent rather than simply passive response and progressively driving the transform of material and component capacities. It is through this proposition and the consideration of its considerable implications that the work presented differentiates itself from that being conducted at ETH.

The proposition of active and responsive forming in relation to demand unsettles established demarcations between the commonly distinguished discrete phases of architectural activity. Design, fabrication/construction and occupation/use become coupled in a complex matrix of sensitively dependent and circular interactions rather than linear consequences.

The shift from a linear progression of consequences to a circular paradigm of exchange between the making-of-information, the making-of-things and the making-use-of-things, demands new roles, relationships, capacities and conceptual underpins to be defined and established between the realm of representation and the physical artefact.

Persistent Modelling

The underlying premise of the broader scope of research, to which the enterprise of metal inflation contributes, is the construction of a conceptual framework and design strategy through which to consider architectures of persistent and active transform.[16] A prerequisite to the notion of active transform in an architectural context is the capacity for the artefact to represent critical variables of its dynamic environment over time. Establishing this primary coupling permits the consideration of active exchange, active temporal and contextual sensitivity, and the potential to extend beyond, yet still incorporate, passive modalities of response.

A conceptual basis for this proposition can be found in the discipline of cybernetics which draws its name from the Greek term *kybernetes*, meaning *steersman*. Cybernetics provides a variety of models for goal-directed systems that operate within dynamic and endemically contingent environments. These models are defined through abstract principles of organisation, control and communication. They define how their goals are managed in relation to information about change in their environments but do so independent of specifying material details and composition, thus permitting their generalisation to both biological and synthetic systems.[17]

The *Persistent Model* is conceived as an *error-controlled* regulatory system. Such systems employ feedback as the principal means of control. Feedback systems operate by assessing disturbances to their critical variables caused by perturbations in their environment. These disturbances cause a deviation (actual state) from the goal (ideal state) and therefore produce a measurable difference, or *error*. This information informs a response in the form of corrective action, or *control*, which aims to mitigate the effects of the disturbances on the goals of the system.[18]

Adhering to this system, the *Persistent Model* comprises both artefact (the actual – performing in the physical world and being disturbed by it) and representation (the ideal – specifying the goal and dealing with the modelling of change over time), coupled to a dynamic and unpredictable environment. This presents a radically consequential shift in the relationship between representation and built artefact, as established practice tends towards a linear progression from representation (the ideal) to the built (the actual). The *Persistent Model* reconfigures this relationship into one that is circular, such that the ideal is tempered by the actual to become both a record and the ground for iteration and transform (Figure 5). The potential instrumentality of the representation in relation to artefact can therefore be extended beyond design and construction, into use and occupancy. Of course this can only be considered in relation to the instrumentality of the artefact on the representation – the relationship between the two is coupled, in feedback and circular. Control is persistently passed and shared.

The theoretical basis of the proposition rests upon certain issues revolving around the procedures and aims of the architect, and offering a possible means of resolving the disparity arising between them. First, if one accepts that a central concern of the architect must be the human use and occupation of buildings, as pronounced by Gropius, then Forty points to a contradiction that must be acknowledged between this architectural concern and the reality of architectural practice. The contradiction revolves around the fact that the architect's role is generally complete the moment occupation begins.[19] Second, as previously referenced, in his examination of the translation from drawing to building Evans asserts that a principal role of representation is to provide 'a complete determination in advance'. The status of such representations must therefore be considered as entirely ideal, prescriptive and predictive. In relation to our contemporary understandings and experiences of the realities we inhabit, those that impinge upon us and those that we construct, being fundamentally open to the dynamic, complex and unpredictable, the notion of the 'complete determination in advance' can be considered as being somewhat at odds. It certainly places considerable responsibility on the predictive and anticipatory capacity of the architect, with all the repercussions this has on framing the limits of design scope. Hill identifies a further issue regarding the medium of representation that Evans is principally referring to – the drawing: 'Most architectural drawings offer only a limited understanding of use. Their primary purpose is to describe an object and, as they refer to only certain aspects of the physical world, they limit the types of object architects usually design.'[20]

These issues lead to the technological basis of the *Persistent Model* which relies upon the capacity for digital representations to sustain explicitly time-based attributes compared with more traditional means of architectural representation. Located within a broader milieu of digitally mediated analytic and synthetic procedures which enable *contribution-to* (modification) or *operation-from* (instruction), such representations are endowed with the potential for potent forms of instrumentality applicable to the various phases of design, fabrication/manufacture and construction. The repercussions of this non-neutral time-based representational medium are to be seen in transforms of practice and extensions to our craft. Evidence of this is apparent across the domains of architectural research, practice and education. The premise of the *Persistent Model* is reliant upon technologies that are already deeply embedded within the various practices engaged in the production of the built environment.

Fig 5 The *Persistent Model* proposes a shift from the familiar and established linear progression from representation to artefact. Instead it proposes a circular relationship permitting the artefact to re-inform the representation after disturbance from the environment. Representation and artefact co-exist – the ideal feeds into the actual and the actual feeds back to the ideal, tempering and steering its predictive nature. Control is passed and shared. Image by Anders Ingvartsen. © Phil Ayres, CITA.

Persistent Model #1

This project initiates a synthetic phase of investigation into the research territory sketched out above. The principal concern for this project was to develop a functioning sketch demonstrator of the synchronous coupling between representation and artefact that defines the *Persistent Model*, together with a synergetic material and tectonic language. The explorations into hydroforming provide a conceptually congruent field of material operation, with results driven away from initialising representations and confounding accurate prediction through currently employed methods of simulation. The process provides a very proximate world of perturbation.

Persistent Model #1 introduced another level of material organisation in the form of the macro-scale aggregate (Figure 6). The aim was to develop a method of part connection that would promote rather than restrain the dynamic spatial transform resulting from individual component inflations, providing another scale of behaviour resulting from those of the component, the crystalline structure and the atomic lattice. Individual components were arranged as a layered horizontal stacking to emphasise their flatness and encourage the reading of them as a drawing, which, in this state, they were conceptually closer to (Figure 7). Components were connected at points on the face where high degrees of deformation were expected in order to drive a spatial deployment and unsettle the order of the stacking. In association with *in situ* and sequential inflation, these strategies furnished results of material and spatial transform that could not be predetermined.

The coupling to environment, outlined previously as the prerequisite to considering architectures of transform, actually begins with determining (constructing a model) of the relevant environmental variables. This is conceptually equivalent to designing the environment for the system.[21] For *Persistent Model #1* the environment was not considered beyond the scope of the assembly, and no responsive logic was determined. Rather the concern was to examine how the sequential inflation of discrete components constructs sites of dependency on subsequent inflations – constraint contexts. The critical environmental variable monitored to re-inform the model was the internal pressure during inflation.

Following the opening of the exhibition[22] of which it was a part, *Persistent Model #1* was inflated by hand over the course of four days specifically with the aim of 'demonstrating the relationship between different features on a single scale and between units and aggregates on different scales',[23] and continually error-regulating the dynamic disparity between the artefact as-existing and the idealised representation (see Figure 8).

---

opposite top: Fig 6 The material and spatial potential of *Persistent Model #1* is laid out as a net conforming strictly to the assembly documentation. From microstructure to macrostructure; atomic lattice, grain, component and assembly define its steerable levels of material organisation and dynamic capacity. © Phil Ayres CITA.

opposite bottom: Fig 7 *Persistent Model #1* fully assembled and prior to inflation. The starting configuration was conceived as a layered stacking of 2D planes or 'drawings' awaiting deployment. Even at this stage there is already a measured deviation between the originating idealised representation and the informed representation (bottom right). © Phil Ayres CITA.

Development Paths and the Poetry of a Steered Proclivity

While one is wary not to overinflate the potentials of this work at such an early stage of development, there is nevertheless a compelling sense of cleaving open new territories of expressive and tectonic potential for a material that has such a familiar, established and largely determined morphology. The design space that opens up might permit greater material efficiencies, but it certainly implicates active dynamic transform and progressive performance capacities through an exploitation of material behaviours across hierarchical levels of material organisation. The conceptual framework which has been outlined in the form of the *Persistent Model* presents a means for managing these resources in relation to design intent and, crucially, in a manner that does not prescribe, but steers towards architectural aims in synergy with its material fabric.

There is certainly a great deal of effort ahead before this work reaches any semblance of maturity, but the principal avenues of immediate and necessary enquiry are clear: rigorous testing of material and component performance capacities; research into techniques of simulation for both the forming process and material performance; establishing architecturally relevant scenarios and logics of transform; continued development of the material and tectonic language; extending the palette of materials beyond the mono-material (exhibiting exclusively irreversible transforms) with a view to investigating a suite of architectural conditions. This list is far from exhaustive.

Pérez-Gómez writes: 'History offers ample evidence for an architecture resulting from a poetic translation of its representations, rather than as a prosaic transcription of an objectified image.'[24]

The notion of a representation's poetic translation resonates with the aspirations of the inflation work presented and the broader research scope outlined. But rather than a unidirectional poetic translation of representation, this work argues for the establishment of a poetic matrix in which linkages are bidirectional, sensitively dependent and fundamentally reliant upon establishing a synergy between the digital and the physical.

For this work, the poetic is understood in the sense of steering yet being open to the proclivities established by a complex matrix of variables that sensitively interweave material behaviour and synthetic intent across magnitudes of scale, to the contingent dynamics of the physical world.

Fig 8 The unanticipated artefact. *In situ* sequential inflation constructs sensitive constraint contexts for the inflation of subsequent components. This macro-scale constraint echoes the slip mechanisms at work within the microstructure. The representation as 'complete determination in advance' has been re-informed by the artefact as-existing and performing, capturing its dynamic and unpredictable complexity and providing the ground for further iteration and transform. Photograph: Anders Ingvartsen. © Phil Ayres CITA.

Notes

1   CS Smith, *A Search for Structure*, MIT Press (Cambridge, MA), 1982, p 54.
2   M Boyle, *Journey to the Surface of the Earth: Mark Boyle's Atlas and Manual*, exhibition catalogue, Gemeentemuseum (The Hague), 1970, p 13.
3   Simon Stevin, an early Dutch physicist, published his derivation of the law in *The Elements of the Art of Weighing* in 1586.
4   HA Simon, *The Sciences of the Artificial*, MIT Press (Cambridge, MA), third edition, 1996, pp 1–2.
5   L Hovestadt, *Beyond the Grid – Architecture and Information Technology*, Birkhäuser (Basel), 2010, pp 176–83.
6   Hovestadt suggests that the difficulty of guaranteeing predictable and reproducible three-dimensional results is a principal reason for mechanical engineers yet to exhibit interest in the freeform inflation method (ibid, pp 176–8).
7   Rather cantankerously, Hooke first published his findings in the cryptic form of a Latin anagram. *Ut tensio, sic vis* (as the extension, so the force) appeared as *ceiiinossssttuv* in his *Lectiones Cutlerianæ*, or *A Collection of Lectures: Physical, Mechanical, Geographical, & Astronomical*, together with a similar anagram for his findings on the true mechanical and mathematical form of arches.
8   JE Gordon, *Structures*, Penguin (London) 1991, pp 33–44.
9   EP DeGarmo, JT Black and RA Kohser, *Materials and Processes in Manufacturing*, John Wiley & Sons (New York), ninth edition, 2003, pp 52–64.
10 Ibid, pp 58–61.
11 The use of the term *native* should be qualified as referring to physical and mechanical attributes that are carefully composed by design and nurtured through processes of manufacture. They are native to a material that is synthesised and therefore artificial.
12 Both mild steel (St37) and stainless steel (AISI 304) have been used to make cushion components comprising similar metals and dissimilar metals. In all three cases 22-gauge has been used (this is approximately 0.8 millimetres thick), but some very early tests examined the potential of material biasing through the use of dissimilar sheet thicknesses. These experiments will be revisited in the future.
13 R Evans, *Translations from Drawing to Building and Other Essays*, AA Publications (London), 1997, p 156.
14 L Hovestadt, *Beyond the Grid,* p 183.
15 It must be stressed that at present the material economy argument is conjectural, based on the limited tests by the author and the reports of the footbridge prototype from ETH. The author is unaware of any comparative studies against commercially available stock sections suggesting that such a study would be valuable to conduct. Collaborations are currently being established in order to pursue this line of inquiry.
16 The notion of the Persistent Model was first articulated in P Ayres, 'The Origin of Modelling', in R Glanville (ed), *Kybernetes*, no 9/10, Emerald Group Publishing (Bingley), 2007, pp 1225–37. The notion has also been opened to interpretation and examination by a number of leading architectural practitioners, researchers and academics in the recently published Phil Ayres (ed) *Persistent Modelling: extending the role of architectural representation*, Routledge, (London), 2012.
17 This ambition of generalisation is explicit in the title of Norbert Wiener's seminal book *Cybernetics, or Control and Communication in the Animal and the Machine*, John Wiley & Sons (New York), first published in 1948.
18 F Heylighen and C Joslyn, 'Cybernetics and Second-Order Cybernetics' in RA Meyers (ed), *Encyclopedia of Physical Science & Technology*, vol 4, Academic Press (New York), third edition, 2001, pp 155–70.
19 A Forty, *Words and Buildings*, Thames & Hudson (London), 2000, p 143.
20 J Hill, *Actions of Architecture*, Routledge (London), 2003, p 25.
21 WR Ashby, *Introduction to Cybernetics*, Chapman and Hall (London), second edition, 1957, p 35.
22 The exhibition entitled *digital.material* showcased four recent works by CITA. The exhibition ran from 23 April to 23 May 2010 at the ROM Gallery, Oslo.
23 See note 1 for reference.
24 A Pérez-Gómez, 'Questions of Representation: The Poetic Origin of Architecture', *arq*, vol 9, no 3/4, Cambridge University Press (Cambridge), 2005, p 218.

References

- Ashby, WR, *Introduction to Cybernetics*, Chapman and Hall (London), second edition, 1957
- Ayres, P, 'The Origin of Modelling' in R Glanville (ed), *Kybernetes*, no 9/10, Emerald Group Publishing Limited (Bingley), 2007, pp 1225–1237
- DeGarmo, EP, JT Black and RA Kohser, *Materials and Processes in Manufacturing*, John Wiley & Sons (New York), ninth edition, 2003
- Evans, R, *Translations from Drawing to Building and Other Essays* (AA Documents 2), AA Publications (London), 1997
- Forty, A, *Words and Buildings*, Thames & Hudson (London), 2000
- Gordon, JE, *Structures*, Penguin (London), 1991
- Groák, S, *The Idea of Building*, E & FN Spon (London), 1992
- Heylighen, F and C Joslyn, 'Cybernetics and Second-Order Cybernetics' in RA Meyers (ed), *Encyclopedia of Physical Science & Technology*, vol 4, Academic Press (New York), third edition, 2001, pp 155–170
- Hill, J, *Actions of Architecture*, Routledge (London), 2003
- Hovestadt, L, *Beyond the Grid – Architecture and Information Technology*, Birkhäuser (Basel), 2010
- Pérez-Gómez, A, 'Questions of Representation: the poetic origin of architecture', *arq*, vol 9, no 3/4, Cambridge University Press (Cambridge), 2005, pp 217–25.
- Simon, HA, *The Sciences of the Artificial*, MIT Press (Cambridge, MA), third edition, 1996
- Smith, CS, *A Search for Structure*, MIT Press (Cambridge, MA), 1982
- Wiener, N, *Cybernetics: or Control and Communication in the Animal and the Machine*, MIT Press (Cambridge, MA) and John Wiley & Sons (New York, London), second edition, 1961

Special thanks are due to:
Sarat Babu, UCL Bartlett School of Graduate Studies and Jonathan Warwick, Imperial College London for their diligent preparation, and microscopy, of the inflation samples.
Anders Holden Deleuran (research assistant, CITA) for his persistent and skilled attempts at modelling the metal inflation process using Autodesk Maya.
My colleagues at the Center for Information Technology and Architecture (CITA) and Institute 4, Kunstakademiets Arkitektskole, for their continued encouragement and support of this work.

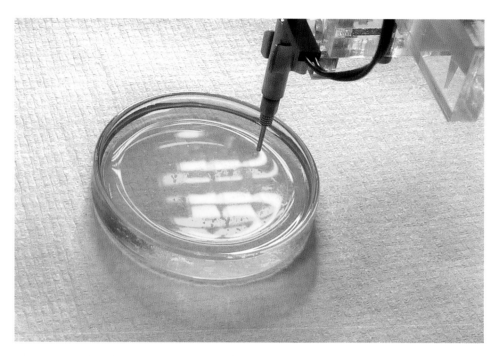

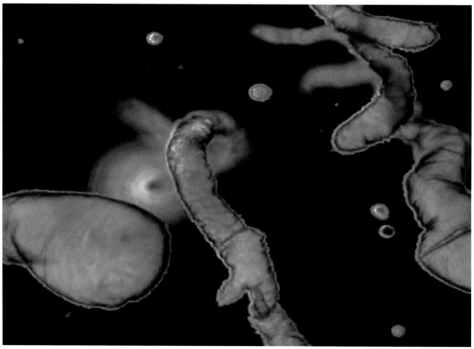

Print to Protocell

Rachel Armstrong

Can we grow building materials, and can we cure decaying or dilapidated structures with materials that behave as though they were living? Qualified medical doctor, science fiction author, arts collaborator, and now also architectural researcher, Rachel Armstrong is exploring the dual possibilities of advanced architectural design and their mythologies in association with new technology, from within a laboratory. Operating at a cellular level, her work, developed in collaboration with a growing network of international architects and scientists, imagines buildings that will transfer from inert to living matter and become part of the biosphere.

The evolutions of biotechnology and computing are closely linked, sharing many common principles and models of organisation where the organism is imagined to operate as a 'machine' that is composed of individual parts connected in a hierarchical order, organised by a centrally driven code embodied in the DNA in a top-down manner. Yet in the new scientific practice of synthetic biology, an important shift in experimental practice engages with a complex model of living organisms and takes a 'rational engineering' approach to the modification of living systems. It takes an interdisciplinary perspective that serves to make the engineering of biology easier, more predictable and actively engaged with the design process during its development and manufacture, by incorporating a bottom-up perspective in the assembly of materials. Digital manufacturing processes are following suit with this more complex, materially based perspective of the organism. Self-assembling materials and valuable approaches for the design of complex chemical systems can be designed so that the manufacturing process incorporates both top-down and bottom-up forms of assembly that would, theoretically, energetically optimise the design process and may form the basis for the development of new materials, and new construction techniques in architectural design practice.

Material Complexity
The natural world has influenced architectural practice throughout the ages. This may partly be due to its innate complexity and dynamic capacity for emergent organisation. The continually surprising and varied manifestations of nature are associated with nonlinear behaviours and continue to inspire architects to strive to create new kinds of building experience.

top: Bütschli protocells, a dynamic, self-organising oil/water droplet system created by the mixing of oil and alkali, is being performed by a Fab@Home 3D printer using Rhino modelling software to create a prescribed distribution of the reagents. © Rachel Armstrong.

above: Bütschli protocells (magnification x10) building spiral microstructures whose morphology is informed by the chemical microenvironment to which the protocells are exquisitely sensitive. © Rachel Armstrong.

Detail of Hylozoic Ground, 2010 Venice Biennale for Architecture. The Bütschli protocell populations are designed with the same metabolism. However, since they are sensitive to environmental conditions, they respond locally to the presence of metal ions in the flasks to produce a colourful landscape of crystals at the oil/water interface that gradually became petrified over the duration of the exhibition. © Bob Sheil.

Biological Complexity

Until recently, the only genuinely complex materials available were biological substrates, and the investigation of complexity in an architectural context has been possible through computer software, mechanical engineering, artificial intelligence and cybernetic theories. While these research areas have led to a greater understanding of and engagement with complexity, the production of genuinely complex architectures based on these investigations has still not been possible. Architecture shares the scientific notion that became popular in the second half of the 20th century where 'information', as biological and computational codes, is the organising force of complex design and has enabled the development and exploration of a conceptual framework through which complex materials, namely biological systems, could be manipulated. The isolation of DNA, the chemical information-processing system that biological systems use, which is conceived of as the chemical 'code of life', gave rise to the new science of biotechnology, which engages with the engineering of living organisms. Through its design connotations it has subsequently become an interesting methodology for architects. This is despite ongoing controversies within the scientific community about the validity of the role of the gene in evolution, a debate that became characterised by the ongoing public exchanges between Richard Dawkins, who favoured a genes-only approach, and Stephen Jay Gould, who argued for a multifactorial mechanism (taking place in the context of an environment) whose complex outcomes occur at the level of the organism. The gene-centric view was more popularly widespread among the scientific community partly because of the elegant simplicity of Neo-Darwinist theory and partly because an analogy was drawn between the genetic code and the principles of computing.[1] Concepts in molecular biology were commonly explained as having analogous information-processing systems to digital computers, an approach that was endorsed by Dawkins. This served to give further weight to the reductionist, Cartesian perspective of genetic systems, as well as giving the impression that genes were obedient to instruction and could be reliably controlled.

Developments in computing, which has increasingly underpinned the modelling of a broad field of interests within architectural design practice, have adopted the language of biology and reinforced its 'code-centric' notions of organisation. Today terms such as, virus, code, sequence and evolution all have biological and digital equivalents that imply identical underlying processes are at work. For the last 50 years this code-centred view of the world has been reinforced by the growing 'homologies' between computers and DNA and is an architecturally testable proposition. Yet the expense of working with highly purified DNA sequences and the degree of training necessary for engineering the system has prevented most architects[2] from working with genetic materials.[3] Despite an increasing understanding that the organisational principles of living systems are based in complexity, the actual design practices used to manipulate living systems continue to employ a Cartesian perspective of the organism, which is likened to a machine in that it is considered as composed of individual parts that are connected in a hierarchical order.

Owing to advances in biology, genetics and genome sequencing in the last few decades, there has been a confluence of a number of factors that have moved research interest from computational modelling of biological systems to engineering practice. Although the cloning of DNA has been available for a few decades, new perspectives have been developed that are contingent on the vast increase in the speed and storage of computers and the internet. Researchers have been able to use a top-down led approach to investigate the organising processes of living organisms in much more detail both at the level of the individual molecules as well as at the systems level. A new approach to biological systems has been adopted which relies on a 'rational engineering' approach to biological design called synthetic biology. Rather than considering the organism as a Cartesian system, synthetic biologists apply systems theory to their biological design practice using models of organisation described in the new scientific field of systems biology. This practice of synthetic biology differs from its predecessor of biotechnology in its approach to the engineering of organisms in terms of its precision. While genetic technologies have relied on random insertion and cultivation procedures that depend more on chance than on intent, synthetic biology engages more strategically to manipulate very precise parts of the cell machinery. This is an important shift in experimental practice since not only are organisms assumed to be ordered differently but also the actual engineering practice is different, benefiting from a collaborative practice that engages engineers, biologists, chemists, physicists, computer scientists, architectural designers and the humanities. It is expected that the scaling up of synthetic-biology-based techniques to a level that is useful to industry will require further cross-disciplinary engagement as the research practice matures. This interdisciplinary approach serves to make the engineering of biology easier, more predictable and actively engaged with the design process during its development and manufacture.

Cartesian Tools and Materials for Complex Systems?

While the intelligence in these converging systems may be genuinely complex, the effectors through which the behaviour of very sophisticated paradigms is observed and implemented are not. Computer-generated algorithms generate outputs to mechanical devices that continue to operate within Cartesian paradigms and no matter how complex the underlying algorithmic data may be, the outputs themselves are compromised by the translational instruments and the materials through which they operate. This paradigm of reduced complexity from design to production is at the heart of digital fabrication. Although rapid-prototyping tools use flexible, varied and complex spatial algorithms, they are limited to the production of intricate, rather than complex objects, which are inert at the time of their final production. The catastrophic data loss that occurs during the information flow from computer algorithm, via machine and to the final material results in models which embody only a notional fragment of the complexity from which they were conceived. In systems biology, this data is lost as structures, which have been described as bio bricks[4] when they are inserted into a complex 'host' organism called a chassis, from which they did not originate. This highlights one of the most important current challenges in bioscience, which is the need to integrate biological information from different physical scales, while simultaneously considering living processes as interconnected systems and networks. While the information loss in the current synthetic-biology-based approach is

Detail of Hylozoic Ground, 2010 Venice Biennale for Architecture. The Bütschli protocells are contained in a flask open to a rich environmental landscape being connected to the responsive neural net of the Hylozoic Ground installation, the chemistry of the carbon-dioxide-rich gallery air and sunlight streaming in through a glass panel in the roof of the pavilion. The protocells respond to this complex landscape by producing a range of brightly coloured crystals at the oil/water interface. © Bob Sheil.

nowhere near as catastrophic as that which occurs during digital fabrication, the principle of data loss remains problematic to both practices during the design process.

Complex Systems and Complex Materials

One approach is to select complex materials in which data is not only preserved but may even be increased. The minimal requirements for a material to embody these properties are those concerning living systems and are being explored in a number of scientific research practices which examine the transition from nonliving to living matter, such as astrobiology, the origins of life sciences and exobiology. Life itself can be thought of as a mechanism that, like digital fabrication, orchestrates the organisation of spatio-temporally resolved information within a system. Uniquely though with living systems, the embodying materials are able to bring about further complexity resulting in characteristic evolutionary and metabolic dynamics.[5] One particular characteristic of living materials that enables this increase in complexity with time is that they are dissipative structures, which exist far from thermodynamic equilibrium and are able to efficiently dissipate the heat generated to sustain them. Complex characteristics associated with living systems can be found in complex chemistry where significant developments in the last five years have produced models that can be thought of as 'living technology', which exhibit some of the properties of living systems but are not considered 'alive'.[6] Taking a bottom-up approach to the practice of synthetic biology, these model chemical systems do not start with the presupposition of an existing (biological) tool 'kit' but start from the basic molecules of 'life'. The two model systems being explored in this context and whose architectural relevance is being explored are 'protocells' and 'chells'. Protocells, are programmable, dynamic, chemical agents that are based on the chemistry of oil and water that exhibit some of the properties of living systems in that they are able to sense an environment, move around it, modify it and even undergo complex behavioural changes, some of which are architectural such as, the shedding of material deposits.[7] 'Chells', or chemical cells, are much simpler agents consisting of a self-organising inorganic membrane that surrounds a vesicle (fluid-filled space) into which new chemistries can be inserted.[8]

Making Artificial Biology

Both of these chemical agents exhibit some of the properties of living systems without the need for DNA. This bottom-up approach has advantages from a materials perspective as it embraces all possible combinations of self-assembling chemical systems, offering a greater solution space than that of synthetic biology, which is limited by the functionality of DNA as an information-processing and assembly system and may be thought of as 'artificial biology'. Currently self-assembling materials exist only in a research context, and for them to become usable substrates for architectural design practice an effective manufacturing platform is necessary. Rapid prototyping already exists in a form where it notionally does the work of DNA, in other words, it is able to spatially and temporally position materials. Using a 3D fabrication unit to spatially position chemical information provides a valuable mechanism through which complex chemical systems can start to be designed. Using a combination of software, hardware and dynamic chemical systems, it may be possible to perform the necessary orchestration of self-assembling chemistry (oils, metallic oxides) using a range of fluidic assemblages in which to manipulate them (microarrays, microfluidic devices, magnetic chips/circuitry, light-operated systems, mazes) and offering an integrated platform and micro architecture for dynamic chemical systems. This system, coordinated using digital fabrication techniques, effectively becomes the platform for the discovery of 'reaction architectures'. The outcome of this rapid-prototyping approach to creating the organisational machinery for artificial biology could give rise to dynamic materials, which are potentially more complex, robust and multifunctional than native biological systems and also give rise to richer and richer communication languages that can connect artificial and natural systems. In this sense the spatial and temporal positioning of self-assembling chemistry can provide versatile, heterogeneous, problem-solving materials that can adapt to variations in a local environment, complete material calculations down to a molecular degree or give rise to useful, new and unexpected properties. Additionally, a new understanding of how cellular chemical structures might imitate and engage with living systems has more than theoretical relevance for the practice of architecture but also, perhaps more importantly, may have a profound practical impact. Protocells and chells may be able to do useful work of a conventional chemical nature (for example, the conversion of CO_2 to more environmentally benign substances), mimic simple functions of natural cells (for example, simple metabolic processes to produce useful secondary metabolites), or carry out novel computation within regimes that are currently beyond our technology (for example, medical nanonics such as nano robots or any other nanomolecular process/system, or chemically based systems for modelling cellular processes). From an architectural perspective, these artificial biologies provide an opportunity to conceive of and design 'wet' interfaces enabling the creation of dynamic surfaces and materials for use in the built environment whose resultant materials and their associated developmental design processes would have a broad applicability across a range of industries. Artificial biologies would effectively give rise to new aesthetic and environmental experiences that architects throughout the ages have sought from their natural biological predecessors and whose new qualities will be similarly desired.

Notes

1   R Armstrong, C-theory, http://www.ctheory.net/articles.aspx?id=621
2   But has not deterred bio artists, for example, Steve Kurtz, Adam Zaretsky: link to 'Amateurity and Biotechnology' http://www.locusplus.org.uk/NJ01.pdf
3   A very recent architectural exception is Terreform, founded by Mitchell Joachim, Toronto: link to http://www.terreform.org/
4   A standard biological part, http://bbf.openwetware.org/
5   L Cronin et al, 'The Imitation Game – A Computational Chemical Approach to Recognizing Life', *Nature Biotechnology*, vol 24, no 10, 2006, p 1204.
6   M Bedau, 'Living Technology Today and Tomorrow', *Technoetic Arts*, vol 7, no 2, *Intellect Journals*, 2009, pp 199–206.
7   MM Hanczyc, T Toyota, T Ikegami, N Packard, T Sugawara, 'Fatty Acid Chemistry at the Oil-Water Interface: Self-Propelled Oil Droplets', *J Am Chem Soc*, 129(30), 2007, pp 9386–91.
8   The 'Chell': A Bottom-Up Approach to In Vitro and In Silico Minimal Life-Like Constructs, http://gow.epsrc.ac.uk/ViewGrant.aspx?GrantRef=EP/G026130/1

Large-Scale Additive Fabrication
Freeform Construction

Xavier De Kestelier and Richard Buswell

Echoing Mark Burry's critique of falsehood within the simplified and inaccurate term 'file to factory', research into large-scale deposition manufacturing is unravelling new layers of scope for design manipulation and tailoring. Resolution, a term once associated with the pixellated image, is becoming a core characteristic of physical components in building construction. Here, Xavier De Kestelier of Foster + Partners and Richard Buswell of Loughborough University share their insight into the evolution of deposition technologies in design methods and strategies over the past two decades, and finish on the primary role that toolpaths play in shaping and forming large concrete elements without formwork. Their investigations remind us of the similarity and difference that continue to exist between architectural information and physical manufacture.

We were uncertain how you might feel about new buildings. You mean the nano tech buildings? ... Yes some people find them disturbing. He knew their sheer brutality of scale from constructs, but virtually had failed to convey the peculiarity of their apparent texture, a streamlined organicism. They are like Giger's paintings of New York, Yamazaki had said but the reference had been lost on Laney. Now he sat on the edge of his bed staring blankly out at these miracles of the new technology, ... the world's largest inhabited structure.

W Gibson, 1996[1]

The Dutch magazine *Kijk* is mainly focused on making innovations in science digestible for teenage minds. In 1987, one of the issues introduced a new machine that could build complex physical objects directly from a 3D computer model. For avid readers this appeared at the time to be a proposition within the realms of science fiction rather than reality. Almost two decades later, we finally came into contact with the process known as stereo lithography (SL or SLA, stereo lithography apparatus) whereby thin layers of ultraviolet (UV) light-sensitive liquid polymer are solidified using a laser. We realised what had been shown in *Kijk* was one of the first digitally controlled polymer deposition machines (the SLA 1 by 3D Systems). Deposition or subtractive manufacturing processes may be explained in simple terms through architectural analogy, where for example the pyramids of Giza, built by stacking layer after layer of stone may be seen as the former and the Deir monastery, carved out of solid rock in Petra, may be seen as the latter.

During printing, every single printed part can be different and customised. © Foster + Partners.

From Rapid Prototyping to Manufacturing

In addition to SLA, a range of additive fabrication technologies followed, including fused deposition modelling (FDM), selective laser sintering (SLS) and layered object manufacturing (LOM). Each commonly produces physical objects directly from a digital CAD model by solidifying a powder or liquid, layer by layer. Material was added incrementally and therefore these processes are called additive or deposition fabrication processes. Each of these technologies uses its own methodology on how the sequential layers of material are deposited and how these layers are then selectively bonded, but the basic concept stays the same. These early technologies and machines were only able to produce models that were limited in resolution and size, and although complex geometrical objects could be made fast and efficiently directly from 3D digital data, the subsequent results in low-grade resins and sintered nylons were often quite poor in finish. Hence, the first applications for this technology were used largely for purposes of visual prototyping, not functional prototypes.[2]

Within the last decade, deposition technologies have evolved considerably to incorporate materials such as ABS, carbon-reinforced polyamide, polycarbonate, titanium and stainless steel at high resolution.[3] Results can now be used as finished products and a shift from rapid prototyping to rapid manufacturing has occurred and been adopted by a broad range of advanced engineering fields such as aerospace, automotive (F1), medical tooling, implants and dentistry. These industries often use rapid manufacturing for small production series with a high geometrical complexity. A growing number of consumer goods companies have also started to use rapid manufacturing to produce unique high-end designer goods. Examples of these are Freedom of Creation and .MGX by Materialise who produce anything from phone covers to lighting. It was only in 2010 that the design museum in Barcelona (Dhub) held an entire exhibition that introduced for the first time additive fabrication to a wider public. The focus of the exhibition was on consumers' products such as highly customised chairs and sports glasses.

Additive Manufacturing for Architecture

It was within academic institutions such as the Bartlett, the Royal College of Art and the Architectural Association, that experimentation with rapid prototyping and rapid manufacturing technologies first began to appear in architecture. Foster + Partners[4] were one of the first practices to fully integrate rapid prototyping within its design process, where the technology was initially seen as a tool for making sketch models, particularly for projects with complicated geometries. It surpassed this purpose within a year and it is now seen as an essential design tool for almost every project running in the office. Morphosis[5] may also be counted among the first architectural practices internationally to adopt the technology as a design tool and it is only in the last few years that physical model making through rapid prototyping has become mainstream. It was, for example, only in 2007 that Wohlers Associates started to mention 'Architecture and GIS' as a separate industry in their yearly industry report on additive fabrication.[6]

left: One of the material researchers at Loughborough University tests the structural properties of a 3D printed sample. © Foster + Partners.

below: To fully demonstrate the capabilities of the concrete printing technology, a 1.5-metre (5-foot) wall component was constructed. © Foster + Partners.

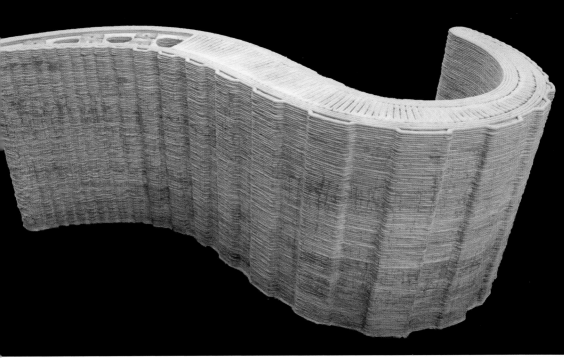

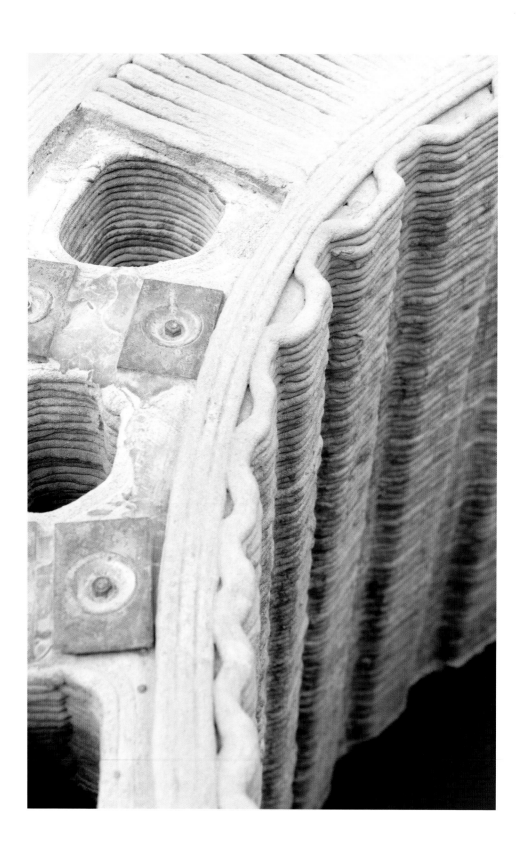

The future of rapid manufacturing technology has clear potential beyond the scale of models or parts, yet the most available additive manufacturing machines are too small or too expensive to be used at an architectural scale.[7] To successfully expand these processes to the scale of building construction, strategies for new machines and technologies need to be developed.[8] Three processes are currently actively pursued: contour crafting,[9] D-shape,[10] and concrete printing.[11] Contour crafting has been developed at the University of Southern California by Dr Behrokh Khoshnevis. The technique produces fixed-width walls by extruding an internal and external trowelled skin with the cavity between filled with a bulk material.[12] The main objective for contour crafting is to produce concrete structures fast, efficiently and at low cost. The path of the wall can continuously vary but resolution is low. D-shape, developed by Enrico Dini in Italy, is a large-scale fabrication technology similar to 3D printing technology from Z Corp. It deposits a thin layer of sand over the full bed-size of the printer (4 x 4 millimetres/0.15 x 0.15 inches). This sand has been premixed with a catalyst that chemically hardens when it comes into contact with an inorganic binder. This binder is jetted on to the sand through a series of jets. Just as with Z Corp's 3D printing technology, the sand is used as its own support structure.

Freeform Construction Project at Loughborough University

Freeform construction is the subject of a research project initiated by the Loughborough University Innovative Manufacturing and Construction Research Centre (IMCRC) and funded by the UK Engineering and Physical Sciences Research Council (EPSRC). The project also comprises a range of industrial partners such as Foster + Partners and Buro Happold. Here an additive manufacturing machine has been developed that is capable of producing large and complex parts out of concrete without formwork. The process compares to FDM (fused deposition modelling), with the difference here that concrete is extruded at a larger scale instead of plastic. A fine concrete mix is pumped through a precision nozzle at a constant speed while supported on a three-axis steel gantry array. Without the use of any formwork, the process allows for an unprecedented freedom in geometrical complexity. As the parts are printed, every single printed part can be different and customised. To demonstrate these functionalities of additive manufacturing, a wall component, illustrated here, was designed and constructed. This component seeks to address new geometrical freedoms that can be associated with additive fabrication. The design for the wall has a varying thickness that can be optimised to local loads. There are also cavities in the component that can incorporate services and locally optimised insulation and reinforcement. Due to the geometrical freedom, local optimisations can be achieved through differentiating geometry.

By developing this prototype it became apparent that current standard CAD tools were not sufficient. The freeform construction process extrudes concrete in beads with a typical diameter of 9 millimetres (0.35 inches). This is about 100 times larger than current commercially

Due to geometrical freedom, local optimisations can be achieved through differentiating geometry. © Foster + Partners.

available rapid manufacturing processes. With this process the actual extrusion parts become visible and can even be seen as part of the aesthetics of the part. It is therefore crucial that these paths are taken into account when designing for this manufacturing process. As part of a graduation thesis at the Architecture and Urban Design Department of the University of Ghent,[13] various experimental extrusion paths were explored. These path designs were not developed to optimise the manufacturing process, but to explore possible design expressions. In most additive fabrication techniques material is added through horizontal layers. This means that toolpaths are in fact only in two dimensions. These studies highlight the scope to explore more complex three-dimensional toolpaths.

Taking into account the lessons learned at the University of Ghent, a parametric model was set up in generative components to produce the wall component at Loughborough University. It became apparent that a traditional method of surface or solid modelling was not going to be sufficient. The design not only defined the external volume of the wall but also the toolpaths themselves, thereby making the toolpath an integral consideration in the design.[14] The toolpath model became the parametric design driver as the manufacturing constraints were programmed within the toolpath. Slight changes in width of the extruded concrete could, for example, be easily adapted into the parametric model. Creating the toolpaths in a parametric model was not sufficient, as it did not visually represent the design. Therefore each of the toolpaths had to be converted into extrusions. This model was then also 3D printed through with a Z Corp printer.

The workflows for most additive fabrication technologies are quite similar. Typically, a design gets modelled up in a 3D package, preferably with a solids modelling engine. This 3D model is then converted to an STL file. This file format is the standard file format for most additive fabrication processes. An STL file is a very simple low-level file format that stores geometry as a simple set of triangles. Depending on the technology, the STL file is sliced horizontally. Each of these 2D contour slices then has to be constructed and filled up by the additive fabrication machine. Each additive fabrication technology will have its own way of generating a set of machine codes to construct and fill these contour slices.

For the wall component no STL file was generated. The generative components model was constructed with toolpaths in mind, although a set of lines is still not enough information to generate G-code for the concrete printer. This G-code is a numerically controlled programming language that is widely used to the standard format that is employed to drive CNC machines. To generate this G-code for the concrete printer, a separate script was written to convert the line geometry that was generated in generative components into a set of machine instructions that is the G-code. No intermediate step was needed to go from the 3D model to a set of fabrication instructions. The fabrication technology was embedded within the 3D model and into the design process. This approach is, of course, only possible when the designer understands the fabrication technology in detail and when there is a constant interaction between the designer, engineer, programmer and fabricator.

It was through such a close collaboration that, on the one hand, the mechanical engineer suddenly understood perfectly how the architect wanted to use such technology.

On the other hand, the architect understood what the limitations and possibilities were of the specific technology and could enhance and adapt the design to these parameters.

The freeform construction project at Loughborough University differentiates itself because it was a collaboration between the mechanical engineer, the material scientist, the structural engineer, the computer programmer, software developer and architect. This is a unique situation: a total new fabrication technology being developed with a multidisciplinary team of professionals and academics.

Notes

1 W Gibson, *Idoru*, GP Putnam's Sons (New York), 1996.
2 T Wohlers, *Wohlers* Report 2007, Wohlers Associates (Colorado), 2007.
3 T Wohlers, *Rapid Prototyping, Tooling and Manufacturing: State of the Industry*, Wohlers Associates (Colorado), 2010.
4 X De Kestelier and B Peters, *Rapid Prototyping and Rapid Manufacturing at Foster + Partners*, proceedings of ACADIA 08, *Silicon + Skin*, conference, Minneapolis, 17 October 2008.
5 Marty Doscher, 'Modelling in a Digital Dimension', Design Build Network, accessed 1 December, 2010, http://www.designbuild-network.com/features/feature75564/
6 T Wohlers, *Wohlers* Report 2007, Wohlers Associates (Colorado), 2007.
7 Branko Kolarevic, *Architecture in the Digital Age: Design and Manufacturing*, Spon Press (New York), 2003.
8 J Gardiner, 'Sustainability and Construction-Scale Rapid Manufacturing: Opportunities for Architecture and the Construction Industry', proceedings of RAPID 2009 conference, 17 June 2009.
9 B Khoshnevis, D Hwang, KT Yao and Z Yeh, 'Mega-scale Fabrication by Contour Crafting', *International Journal of Industrial and Systems Engineering*, 1, 2006, pp 301–20.
10 E Dini, R Nannini and M Chiarugi, 'Method and Device for Building Automatically Conglomerate Structures', WO Patent WO/2006/100,556, 2006.
11 X De Kestelier and RA Buswell, *A Digital Design Environment for Large Scale Additive Fabrication*, proceedings of ACADIA 09, reForm(), conference, Chicago, 22 October 2009.
12 B Khoshnevis, et al, 'Mega-scale Fabrication by Contour Crafting' pp 301–20.
13 S Bernaerdt, K Van Hauwaert and X De Kestelier, 'Large Scale Rapid Manufacturing for the Construction Industry: the Architecture of a New Design Environment', unpublished dissertation at the Department of Architecture and Urban Design, Ghent University, 2009.
14 Ibid.

Material Computation

Neri Oxman

Neri Oxman is from an entirely new breed of architectural researcher, and is a rare individual looking at the profound implications of a wide spectrum of advanced process and material technologies. Her work investigates some of the most pioneering and far-reaching questions on what new openings technological evolution presents the designer. Her work is becoming extensively read and followed worldwide and in her words from elsewhere, 'It's been a long awaited dream of mine to see fabrication enter the very first stages of the design process. Fabrication is slowly shifting from a state of being simply a production protocol, a service station for the designer to gather knowledge, and moving to a point where it can have generative significance.'[1]

This essay proposes a new approach in design where processes of form generation are directly informed by the combination of material properties and environmental constraints. Inspired by nature's strategies where form generation is driven by maximal performance with minimal resources through local material property variation, this approach, entitled *material computation* is introduced as a set of computational strategies supporting the integration of form, material and structure by incorporating physical form-finding strategies with digital analysis and fabrication. In this approach, material precedes shape, and it is the structuring of material properties as a function of structural and environmental performance that generates design form. In proposing a unique approach to computationally enabled form-finding procedures, the essay investigates how such processes contribute to novel ways of creating, distributing and depositing material forms. Experimental designs employing theoretical and technical frameworks are presented, discussed and demonstrated. They support product customisation (architecture and furniture design), rapid augmentation (medical device design) and variable-property fabrication (FAB design). Developed as approximations of natural formation processes, these design experiments demonstrate the contribution and the potential future of a new design and research field.

Nature as Model

Natural structures possess high levels of seamless integration and precision with which they serve their functions. A key distinguishing trait of nature's designs is the capability in the biological world to generate complex structures of organic, or inorganic, multifunctional composites such as shells, pearls, corals, teeth, wood, silk, horn, collagen and muscle fibres.[2] Combined with extracellular matrices, these structural biomaterials form microstructures engineered to adapt to prearranged external constraints introduced to them during growth and throughout their life span.[3] Such constraints generally include combinations of structural, environmental and corporeal performance criteria. The *shape of matter* is

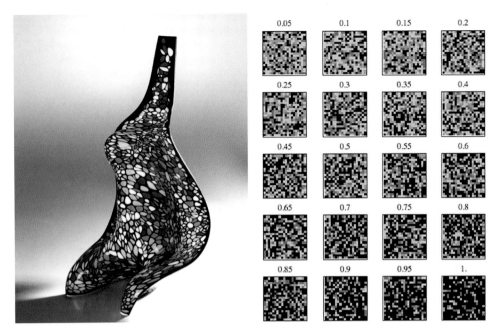

Weighted material selection: a stochastic computational process assigns a stiffness ratio corresponding to structural performance. © Neri Oxman.

therefore directly linked to the influences of force acting upon it.[4] Material is concentrated in regions of high strength and dispersed in areas where stiffness is not required.

The implications of nature's structural heterogeneity, achieved through the informed distribution of composites, holds significant implications from a design perspective. The control of material structure and orientation allows for an almost unlimited design space in terms of geometrical and topological variation. It promotes high levels of functional integration through the assignment of graduated properties; it supports the matching between material property distribution and continuous load paths; and, finally, it allows the designer to consider the possibility of adaptive response, and even real growth.

The Problem with CAD

The dominance of *geometrical* representations of design content has for centuries, prior to the use of computers, contributed to a *geometry-centric* approach in the design of products, buildings and cities. Accordingly, form must first be conceived in order to be constructed. Naturally, it is unfeasible (theoretically or technically) for processes of conception and construction to occur concurrently. Predictably, design has been driven by its many forms of expression defined and conveyed in geometrical terms. Material is consistently secondary in this milieu; and it is due to the priority of geometrical representation over physical material considerations, a phenomenon that has led to streamlining the design process: form first, material later. By methodological extension,

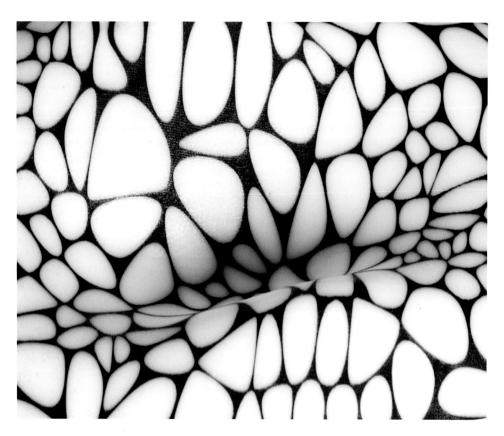

The distribution of shear-stress lines and surface pressure is embodied in the allocation and relative thickness of the stiff vein-like elements built into the skin (black) and the soft (white) cellular components between them. © Neri Oxman.

design conception is to be followed by analysis, simulation and fabrication. Indeed, how can the fabrication of form be manifest without form's conception?

We have seen that nature's way is uniquely different. In nature, forms are the result of the matching between material parameters and their corresponding environmental constraints. Shape is then merely a by-product, a derivative of natural behavioural formation. It emerges as an effect exclusive to its particular environmental template. In nature, we have established, form's geometry is predominantly determined by the interaction between material and environment.

Compared with natural processes of shape formation, digital fabrication strategies assume the design and fabrication of building parts with homogeneous material properties. Since the industrial age, the building industry has been dependent on discrete solutions for distinct functions.[5] Building skins are a great example of such claims. Steel and glass possess significantly different structural and environmental properties that relate to a uniquely different set of performance requirements. Diversity is achieved by sizing, rather than by substance variation, and it is typically mass-produced, rather than mass-customised. As far as material structuring is considered, in the artificial world, especially in the design of building components, one property fits all. This is partly due to the fact that current modelling and fabrication tools within the disciplines of architectural design and construction are rather limited in their ability to represent constructions of complicated heterogeneous composition, which guarantee desired material continuities in all the interfaces.[6]

In cultivating design processes inspired by nature *material computation* seeks to employ alternative computational processes supporting the generation of form based on the interaction between material and environment. This entails a shift from computationally assistive processes to processes of a generative and performative nature that allow the designer to incorporate material properties and behaviour protocols into CAD.

Material Computation

Material computation supports the design of multifunctional products and building elements. It is in the multifunctional condition that variations of material properties and composition correspond directly to specific structural and environmental constraints. This approach to design, supporting multifunctionality over discrete utility through the promotion of heterogeneity over homogeneity, seeks to advance and embrace strategies of material distribution over strategies of material assembly, inspired by nature.

This design approach is proposed as the set of processes enabling the distribution of materials and their properties in the design of a product or a building component. These processes are informed by functional, structural and environmental constraints. *Material computation* is therefore a design approach, a methodology and a technical framework, by which to model, simulate and fabricate functional material organisations with varying properties designed to correspond to multiple and continuously varying functional constraints. Such framework includes processes of modelling, analysis and fabrication. Within each process, certain methods have been identified which carry the potential to rethink design not as form-driven, but rather as a behavioural-driven paradigm.

Following are three explorations into product design (adaptive customisation), medical-device design (rapid augmentation) and fabrication (variable-property fabrication) design, demonstrating some of the methods and principles behind *material computation*.

Material Computation: Adaptive Customisation

Beast – a prototype for a chaise longue – combines structural, environmental and corporeal performance by adapting its thickness, pattern density, stiffness, flexibility and translucency to load, curvature and skin-pressured areas respectively. A single continuous surface acting both as structure and as skin is locally modulated to cater for structural support on the one hand, and corporeal performance on the other. Multiple algorithms were generated that correspond to these variables such that stability is mediated with corporeal and structural integrity.

The traditional chaise is transformed here to promote lounging of a different kind. The cellular pattern applied to its entirety is designed to increase the ratio of surface area to volume in occupied areas where the body potentially rests. A pressure map study was conducted that matches the softness and hardness of the cells to cushion and support sensitive and high-pressured areas. By analysing anatomical structures that cause concentrated pressures, *Beast* becomes softer and flexible where pressure needs to be relieved. The relative volume of each cellular cushion is locally informed by pressure data averaged with values representing structural support and flexibility. Its density is informed by global and local mean curvature values such that denser, smaller cells are organised in areas of steeper curvature whereas larger cells are found in areas of shallow curvature. *Beast*'s natural relation of structural and sense datum is propagated in variable polymer composites offering a wide range of physical properties. Through these algorithms force conditions naturally propagate functionality. Stiffer materials are positioned in surface areas under compression and softer, more flexible materials are placed in surface areas under tension. State of the art technologies are applied here for the first time to cater for a large range of physical properties and behaviours. The surface patches are 3D printed using a new multijet matrix technology that simultaneously deposits materials of different properties corresponding to structural and skin-pressure mappings.

During the initial stages of the design, the texture inherits the geometrical features of the design as defined by the user. Such geometrical features are, in the case of Beast, costumed to fit body curvature criteria. The initial distribution of cells corresponds to the type and degree of curvature: smaller and denser cells are located in regions of higher curvature, and larger, sparser cells are located in regions of smoother curvature. Material properties correspond to both structural requirements (self stability with no additional enforcement members) and environmental requirements (assigned to the body-pressure mappings). For the structural performance, a stochastic computational process was developed in which stiffer materials are assigned to vertical regions, which work for buckling, and softer materials are assigned to horizontal regions that work for bending. The probability of a material being stiffer or smoother depends on the angle defining the level of horizontality in the chaise.

Material Computation: Rapid Augmentation

Nature's engineering expertise matches material properties to environmental pressures, be it the formation of stiff materials for load-bearing functions, or insulating materials as protection from extreme temperature gradients. The human skin is designed in the same fashion and acts simultaneously as a structural and an environmental filter and barrier. In the very same way that load or temperature can be mapped in order to design structures that are highly optimised for their function, physical pain can also be mapped in the design and production of medical assistive devices such as pain-reducing splints.

Since the experience of pain is a very personal one, it is different for each individual. Pain is very difficult to define, and it is one of those conditions that are poorly understood by the Western medical sciences. *Carpal Skin* is a prototype for a protective glove against carpal tunnel syndrome. The syndrome is a condition in which the median nerve is compressed at the wrist, leading to numbness, muscle atrophy and weakness in the hand. Night-time wrist splinting is the recommended treatment for most patients before going into carpal-tunnel-release surgery.

Beast. Prototype for a Chaise Longue, Boston Museum of Science, 2010. The chaise combines structural, environmental and corporeal performance by adapting its thickness, pattern density, stiffness, flexibility and translucency to load, curvature and skin-pressured areas respectively. It is patterned with five different materials colour-coded by elastic moduli. Stiff (darker coloured) and soft (lighter coloured) materials are distributed according to the user's structural load distribution; soft silicone 'bumps' are located in regions of higher pressure. © Neri Oxman.

Carpal Skin. Prototype for a carpel tunnel syndrome splint,
Boston Museum of Science, 2010. © Neri Oxman.

The main problem behind immobilised braces is that as they are mass-produced they are often too big, too small or too constricting in terms of mobilisation. In this case, as is the case with most muscular and nerve-related syndromes, product mass customisation – as opposed to mass production – is crucial.

Carpal Skin is a process by which to map the pain-profile of a particular patient – its intensity and duration – and distribute hard and soft materials to fit his or her anatomical and physiological requirements limiting movement in a customised fashion. The formation process involves case-by-case pain registration and material property assignment. The 3D scan of the patient's hand, including its pain registration, is mapped to a 2D representation on which the distribution of stiff and soft materials is applied. This pain-map is then folded back to its 3D form and 3D printed using photopolymer composites.

The mapping of required material properties and their assignment to the surface area of the wrist-splint is guided by a texture synthesis based on the simulation of local nonlinear interaction, called reaction-diffusion, which has been generally proposed as a model of biological pattern formation.[7] In this context, the reaction-diffusion algorithm dictates the desired distribution of material properties. In this design context, the traditional reaction-diffusion system has been extended to allow anisotropic and spatially nonuniform diffusion of material properties as a function of anticipated pressure on the surface area of the wrist.[8]

In this particular prototype, stiff materials constrain the lateral bending motion at the wrist, and can be identified by the oblique trajectory of dark and stiff materials. Soft materials allow for ergonomic wrist support and comfort through movement. The thickness changes correspond to strategic areas across the surface area of the wrist in cushioning and protecting the wrist from hard surfaces as well as allowing for a comfortable grip. These thickened bumps also increase flexibility and enhance circulation and relieve pressure on the median nerve as the glove acts as a soft-tissue-reshaping mechanism. The custom-fit property distribution built into the glove allows for passive but consistent pulling and stretching simultaneously.

Material Computation: Variable Property Fabrication

Current digital fabrication technologies designed for and applied in the building industry, specifically additive manufacturing platforms, are limited in their capacity to represent graduated material properties.[9] Their basic strategy is typically to assign a material property to preshaped building components such as steel beam profiles or glass panels.[10] Within the design process, this translates into assigning a material property to a predefined solid or closed surface polygon. Neither computer-aided design (CAD) tools nor industrial fabrication processes are thus set up to represent graduation and variation of properties within solids, such as varied density in steel or varied translucency in glass. As a result, the design process is constrained to the assignment of discrete and homogeneous material properties to a given shape.

Historically, the assumption that discrete solids are made from single homogeneous materials is deeply embedded in Modernist design thinking and generally unquestioned.[11] It is also enforced by the logic underlying the dynamics of industrial supply chains; at their lowest levels, supply chains support component manufacturing processes performed by highly specialised machines that operate on particular materials to produce prefabricated building modules. These low-level subassemblies are then put together to form higher-level hierarchical assemblies made of a range of properties corresponding to their respective range of required functions. It is safe to claim that this logic of component-based design fabrication has since the industrial revolution penetrated all stages of the design process from conception to fabrication, particularly in the building industry.[12]

This phenomenon is clearly affecting the way designed goods are being prototyped and fabricated.[13] [14] Additive manufacturing platforms, such as 3D printers, speed product design by facilitating visualisation, physical production and testing of prototypes.[15] However, such technologies are generally limited to using only one material at a time; even high-end 3D printers, which accommodate the deposition of multiple materials, operate discretely; or if they are able to deposit mixtures, these are often premixed.[16] Moreover, varied mechanical properties are currently achieved mostly by injection moulding – a very costly process that presents time and size constraints.[17]

Variable Property Fabrication (VPF) is a new methodological technological platform by which to model, simulate and fabricate material assemblies with gradient properties designed to correspond with multiple and continuously varied functional constraints. Within the VPF environment, the program must translate desired model properties to material properties. The VPF environment gives the value of any property at any point (high or low conductivity/stiff or soft) in order to structure the correct material composition and emulate both its structural and electrical performance. Currently, transition functions that compute gradient property distribution across one or multiple dimensions do not exist in CAD. The VPF environment is developed in order to cater for such requirements and present physical data and material composition by treating voxels as tensors (geometrical entities containing multiple physical parameters), or by computing transitions between multiple compositional phases as extrapolation functions.

Conclusion: The Material Shift

The Modernist tradition typically promoted the division of functions implicit in the architectural elements: their pre-assigned forms, structures and materials (ie, the separation between structure and facade and the assignment of steel columns and glass walls respectively to each function). Coupled with automation in construction, this logic gave birth to an architecture that is easily mass-produced, assembled and built of replicated modules. Despite its obvious advantages, the application of the modular logic of building holds some fundamental limitations in considering requirements driven by site-specific functionality and customisation.

Alternatively, design based upon material properties and environmental conditions promotes customisation through formal, structural and material heterogeneity. Our ability to quantify a building's structural and environmental performance allows the designer to account for site-specific differences of use and behaviour.

Given such ability to predict and respond to performance criteria and desired effects, this research holds implications for shifting design practice from *homogeneous modular design* driven by the *logic of material assembly* to *heterogeneous differentiated design* driven by *material distribution*. In this approach, matter is distributed where needed responding to its structural, environmental or, indeed, social performance. In fostering material integration of architectural elements across various scales, architectural elements such as structure and facade are no longer divorced in function and/or behaviour, but rather negotiated through the informed distribution of matter. Perhaps the most significant consequence of design that is informed by matter is the incorporation of difference: gradients of structural and material effects emerge modulating their thickness, transparency, porosity and thermal absorption according to their assigned function or desired condition of stability (structure) and comfort (environmental conditions). Here is to a new design revolution.

Notes

1   Neri Oxman interviewed by Sean Hanna, R Glynn and B Sheil (eds), *Fabricate: Making Digital Architecture*, Riverside Architectural Press (Waterloo, Ontario), pp 144–51.
2   JM Benyus, *Biomimicry: Innovation Inspired by Nature*, Quill (New York), 1997.
3   JFV Vincent, *Structural Biomaterials*, Macmillan (London), 1982.
4   S Vogel, *Comparative Biomechanics: Life's Physical World*, Princeton University Press (Princeton, NJ), 2003.
5   N Oxman, 'Oublier Domino: On the Evolution of Architectural Theory from Spatial to Performance-Based Programming', Proceedings of *Critical Digital Conference: What Matters?* Harvard Graduate School of Design, Harvard University (Cambridge, MA), 2008, pp 393–403.

6   K Shin and D Dutta, 'Constructive Representation of Heterogeneous Objects', *Journal of Computing and Information Science in Engineering 1*, 2001, p 205.

7   A Witkin and M Kass, 'Reaction-Diffusion Textures', *ACM SIGGRAPH Computer Graphics 25(4)*, 1991, pp 299–308.

8   N Oxman, 'Material-Based Design Computation', doctoral thesis, Massachusetts Institute of Technology, 2010.

9   N Oxman, 'Structuring Materiality: Design Fabrication of Heterogeneous Materials', *AD The New Structuralism: Design, Engineering and Architectural Technologies*, vol 80, no 4, 2010, pp 78–85.

10 N Oxman, 'Oublier Domino' pp 393–403.

11 Ibid.

12 N Oxman, 'Material-Based Design Computation'.

13 Ibid.

14 N Oxman, 'Variable Property Rapid Prototyping (VPRP)', United States Patent Pending US 61/248,555, 2009.

15 E Sachs, M Cima et al, 'Three-Dimensional Printing: The Physics and Implications of Additive Manufacturing', *CIRP Annals – Manufacturing Technology*, 42(1), 1993, pp 257–60.

16 C Chang, 'Rapid Prototyping Fabricated by UV Resin Spray Nozzles', *Rapid Prototyping Journal* 10(2), 2004, pp 136–45.

17 R German, 'Powder Injection Molding', *ASM Handbook 7*, 1998, pp 355–64.

The work reported upon in this paper was partly supported by the Holcim Foundation Award for Sustainable Construction and the Earth Award for Future Crucial Design. The overall descriptions of the design experiments and further investigations into VPF have been included in my doctoral dissertation entitled 'Material-based Design Computation'. I would like to thank Professor William J Mitchell for his continuous encouragement and support throughout my doctoral studies at MIT. I would also like to thank Professor Craig Carter for providing some of the mathematical foundations at the basis of this work, specifically the design experiments. Special gratitude goes to Professor Lorna Gibson and Professor Woodie Flowers from MIT for their comments and insight into the VPF approach and its implications for design. Finally, I would like to thank two of my undergraduate assistants, Rachel Fong and Mindy Eng from the Department of Mechanical Engineering at MIT, for executing the mission to assemble the first VPRP prototype.

Models of Risk
Craft Past and Present in Prototyping for Human Space Flight

Constance Adams

'In long-duration space flight, the astronaut's interplanetary vessel may be equipped with a solar array manufactured by nanodeposition, but all they have to fix it with is tape, wire and dental floss.' The constraints put upon spacecraft architect and prototype designer, Constance Adams, make those of the earthbound architect seem easy. Many of the materials we assume she might deploy, such as plastics, are deadly in closed loop environments. Designing for the most extreme and uncertain of scenarios is considerably more than a technical task; by necessity it is a forecast on core human relationships with issues of survival, ability, skill and adaptation.

What is a prototype? A moulding of the *typos* – a sneak preview of the fundamental form; an estimate; a guess; a beta test; an assay; a proof of concept. The history of this form before the form, the predawn of the idea, this constructed *déjà vu* – is bound to the complex relationship between craft, invention and manufacturing. Before the industrial revolution, a prototype was an early production model; afterwards, it was the die from which the entire run would be cast. Somewhere in between first glimmer and final product, the prototype embodies the questions its production seeks to answer. In this 'what if?' manifestation, the prototype thus permanently enshrines the poignant, fleeting moment of inspiration: the holy grail of its tool-making creators, the human species.

Here, on the first laps of our journey to the stars, moments of inspiration are relatively few in comparison with the enormous technical, material, mechanical and physical challenges posed by every problem we tackle. Whereas, for the architect, a scale model is sufficient to convey the spatial and structural properties of a project, an engineering prototype is a deadly serious thing. Material properties, after all, exist only in a one to one relationship; one cannot scale down the molecules of aluminium to make a 1:20 model with appropriate material properties, and unless a prototype actually represents the mechanism under design, it cannot fulfil its purpose. Risk mitigation must come first as a goal of every phase of design when experimental technologies are concerned, particularly technologies that intend to support human life in hostile, high-energy environments.

One essential strategy of aerospace engineering is to stack up as much knowledge as one can possibly amass against the unknown quantities of environment, experience and unintended consequence that inevitably stack up against the project at hand. When materials are selected, not only are the stated material properties calculated, but also the specific properties of each batch, each source point, each supplier, each mechanic. In designing a spacecraft, the known risk ratios for all materials are joined to the risks of failure known to arise in their interaction, and so on until an objectively reproducible overall risk level can be assigned to every component, every assembly, every system, and

Built to transport International Space Station modules and mock-ups from site to site, the Boeing 'Super Guppy' aircraft resembles a flying whale when airborne. © NASA.

each and every vehicle. Thus, in the course of designing components and vehicles for human space flight, one has the opportunity to develop, test, assess and interact with numerous prototypes of varying scales, functions and degrees of fidelity.

There are mock-ups, to impress the taxpayers and elicit reactions from the crew; there are aeronautical models, material samples and test assemblies; there are engineering test units of every conceivable type from ballistic testing to flammability, stress, thermal and vacuum testing; there are qualification units; there are flight units; there are first flights and hangar queens. There are 'iron birds'. These last, usually high-fidelity prototypes or even first-run units, have for one reason or another remained grounded while their successors are put into service, and over time may function as trainers, troubleshooting facilities and eventually, a source of spare parts. But all are made, painstakingly, by hand.

This is one aspect in which the aerospace prototype still resembles the functional model: despite the finely balanced equipment and machinery used to ensure absolute precision in manufacture of spacecraft components, there is still an enormous amount of precision handwork involved. An entire culture of craftsmen engineers functions in the environs of the NASA design and test centres, individuals and family concerns often accustomed to seeing only sporadic employment as project funding rises and falls but nonetheless committed to offering the highest quality of craftsmanship over an unpredictable array of media as their contribution to the human conquest of space.

For examples of these products, let us take a look at some of the prototypes developed by NASA and NASA contractors for long-duration human space missions.

STRUCTURES

TransHab Pressure Shell

- *MISSIONS*: Mars Design Reference Mission (DRM);[1] Low Earth Orbit (ISS)
- *PROJECT*: TransHab[2] – habitation module for long-duration human space flight, either Mars transit and return, or crew quarters module for International Space Station (ISS). With an inflatable outer shell attached to hard core structures, TransHab was the first of a new generation of hybrid spacecraft developed for human habitation requirements in extreme, nonterrestrial environments.[3]
- *SUBTASK*: development of a flexible structural shell capable of withstanding up to four times Earth atmosphere pressure differential
- *WHAT*: full-scale shell structure prototypes
- *MATERIALS*: woven Kevlar straps, aluminium clevises, steel test gurney
- *PURPOSE/APPLICATION*: strain testing, design, design development/inflation testing while submerged in a 6,000,000 gallon (27,276,000-litre) research pool
- *RISK ADDRESSED*: ability to maintain habitable pressure in vacuum conditions, with four factors of safety
- *RESULT*: several weave designs were developed and tested; the successful weave went on to be developed in full scale for thermal-vacuum testing and space flight certification; variations in development for various applications
- DESIGNERS: TransHab structures team: Schneider, de la Fuente, Johnson, Raboin, Spexarth, Valle

TransHab Shell Assembly: membranes, structural layer, MMOD[4]

- *MISSIONS*: Mars DRM; Low Earth Orbit (ISS)
- *PROJECT*: TransHab – habitation module for long-duration human space flight
- *SUBTASK*: total outer shell system (membranes, structural layer, MMOD shield, MLI)
- *WHAT*: full-scale prototype, 8 metres (26.24 feet) long x up to 8.3 metres (27.23 feet) diameter
- *MATERIALS*: Combitherm membranes, Kevlar woven straps, Nextel, open cell foam, Beta cloth
- *PURPOSE/APPLICATION*: develop and demonstrate design able to fold compactly for launch and berthing and deploy to full-inflated configuration without human extravehicular intervention/deployment testing in hard vacuum conditions at Thermal/Vacuum Chamber Facility, NASA-Johnson Space Center
- *RISK ADDRESSED*: ability of inflatable module system successfully to launch and deploy as designed; loss of mission
- *RESULT*: successful proof of concept; variations of this system test-flown in space by Bigelow Aerospace
- DESIGNERS: TransHab project team (Schneider, de la Fuente, Fender, Raboin, Johnson, Spexarth, Kennedy, Adams et al)

top: The first TransHab shell test article, undergoing
relative-pressure testing inside a giant pool of water. © NASA.

above: Full shell assembly packed for launch configuration in vacuum chamber. © NASA.

ERGONOMICS

TransHab Level One Mock-Ups
- *MISSIONS*: Mars DRM 4.0; Low Earth Orbit (ISS)
- *PROJECT*: TransHab – habitation module for long-duration human space flight
- *SUBTASK*: spacecraft operations and utilisation: vehicle interior volumes
- *WHAT*: low-fidelity, full-scale mock-up of two configurations for the crew common and primary function areas, showing detail of galley, conferencing and stowage areas
- *MATERIALS*: steel structural members, veneer foam core, blackout curtains
- *PURPOSE/APPLICATION*: assessment, trade study; outreach/crew and management review of the configuration selected; public demonstration of potential Mars mission spacecraft design[5]
- *RISK ADDRESSED*: ability of configuration to accommodate equipment and tasks associated with the relevant missions; public and Congressional support for programme
- *RESULT*: one configuration overwhelmingly demonstrated to meet or exceed operational requirements
- DESIGNERS: TransHab project architects: Constance Adams, Kriss Kennedy

SYSTEMS

Lunar-Mars Life Support Test Project: water recycling (Advanced Life Support Systems) 1994–7, NASA – Johnson Space Center
The Skylab training structure in a test building at JSC was retrofitted to support a crew of engineers for a few weeks at a time as they sought to validate an array of physicochemical and biologically based systems for life support. Several tests were run, of increasing duration and crew size. The last was a 90-day mission for four.
- *MISSIONS*: Mars DRMs
- *PROJECT*: Lunar-Mars Life Support Test Project (LMLSTP)
- *SUBTASK*: Water Recovery System (WRS) – biological, sustainable water recycling for long-duration human exploration on surface of Moon or Mars
- *MATERIALS*: steel, Lexan, tubing, bacterial substrate
- *WHAT*: full-scale prototypes
- *PURPOSE/APPLICATION*: development and testing of biologically based advanced life support system/integrated in closed-loop chamber for crew-in-the-loop testing during LMLSTP test runs
- *RISK ADDRESSED*: robust, reliable life support systems for long-duration missions that are independent of consumables and resupply needs
- *RESULT*: final test closed water loop in excess of 95 per cent; versions of this system now deployed at Concordia Station, Antarctica, and on board the International Space Station[6]

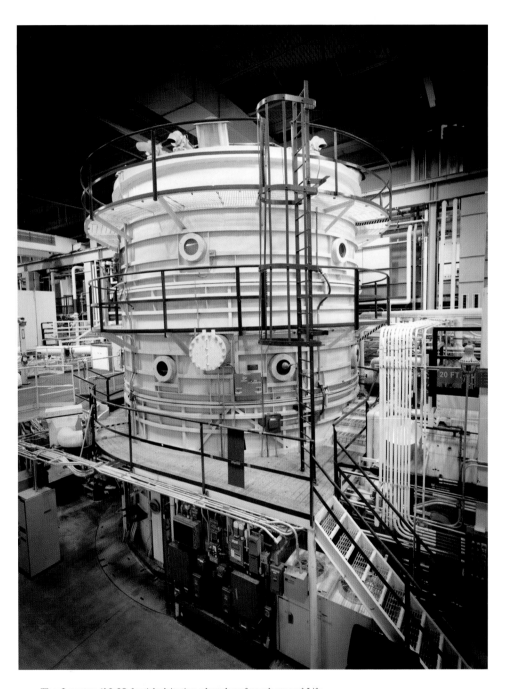

The 6-metre (19.68-foot) habitation chamber for advanced Life
Support Water Reclamation System and bacteria filters. © NASA.

BIO-Plex Chamber build-up (Human Systems) 1997–2004, NASA – Johnson Space Center

Developed as a facility for testing more mature systems for long-duration space missions, BIO-Plex was to supplant the LMLSTP with larger, more integrated life support tests. Even weathering several funding challenges as the political winds shifted against support for its mission, the facility was slowly built up over the course of a few years while the Advanced Life Support engineers waited for full funding to start their activities.

It was never used.

- *PROJECT*: Bioregenerative Life Support Systems Test Complex (BIO-Plex), NASA – Johnson Space Center
- *TASK/SUBTASK*: full-scale, medium-fidelity mock-up of multichamber facility for development and testing of integrated advanced life support systems able to sustain a human crew for periods up to 500 days in a closed-loop environment /multiple chambers, including habitation module, lab module, workstation/command centre and life support modules
- *WHAT*: full-scale, functional prototype
- *MATERIALS*: steel, aluminium, flight certified foams and fabrics
- *PURPOSE/APPLICATION*: develop and test integrated life support systems with crew in the loop/facilities and furnishings that optimise architecture around social interactions and crew performance of known tasks using an iterative design/assessment process similar to pre-/post-occupancy reviews; designed for crew of four to six to live and work during enclosed test runs of between 120 and 500 days in duration
- *RISK ADDRESSED*: socioergonomic and operations risks associated with intensive, long-duration use of closed-loop facility by a crew of four to six; environmental design stressors
- *RESULT*: 90 per cent completed; never used for full-scale testing
- DESIGNERS: BIO-Plex project team: Henninger, Tri, Fortson, Smith, Barta et al; habitation module architect: Constance Adams

Comprised like the International Space Station mockup (shown here) of metal modules based on the Space Shuttle's dimensions, the BIO-Plex facility was intended for continuous, extended occupation to test the life support systems needed for a mission to Mars. © NASA.

CONCLUSION

Prototyping is an essential part of the design process for vehicles, systems and components intended to support our exploration of space. At all stages of design and development, full-scale prototypes of varying degrees of fidelity are made for a broad range of purposes, from failure testing and proof-of-concept assessment to user interface assessment and outreach to the public. Not one of these functions is less integral to the space programme than any others. Whether a particular assembly of materials at a given dimension will demonstrate the desired physical properties under catastrophic conditions is, of course, a fundamental area of enquiry for any programme seeking to bring human researchers into environments alien to Earth life. At the same time, capturing the hearts and imaginations of a group of schoolchildren on a field trip and encouraging them to wonder what it would be like to travel to the stars is surely the most powerful way to ensure a future fuelled by enquiry and wonder.

What is the form of our future? How is the *typos* of anything that is part of our world different from that of another? It is one thing to speculate on such a question philosophically; yet a very different thing altogether to invest whatever skills one has at hand in assaying an answer. Whether we create the future we want by imagining it, or whether larger and more inevitable conditions drive our imaginations instead, the history of those attempted answers – those PROTO *typoi* – is rich in its combination of ancient craft and extraordinary imagining. Through their role in supporting the test and development of tomorrow's spacecraft, our prototypes wordlessly inject the conditions of our planet, the craft and methods we earthlings developed over millennia for our uses here, into our journeys to other worlds. The basket-weaving of the TransHab structural layer meets the arcaded structures of the BIO-Plex in echoes of Stone Age civilisation; yet both are likely to influence future designs intended for human habitation on the Moon or Mars.

And perhaps these prototypes represent better than anything else the inherent nature of the human purpose – the role this tool-making animal plays in the overall biosphere. The more we learn about the cosmos, the less common are any exceptions to the rules. If our craft has enabled us to differentiate so markedly from our fellow life forms, surely this serves some evolutionary purpose; it would be almost impossibly arrogant for us to assume otherwise. Imagine we are looking at the Earth in a time-compressed film, from a position 10,000 miles (16,093 kilometres) beyond the Moon. Over time, the colours change, lights appear at night ... and then, tiny specks are seen jumping off the world, a minute seething at the outer limits of the atmosphere. Moments pass, then: the occasional pea shoots off on a trajectory to rendezvous with another body. Another follows it. And 10 more.

Our tools – the product of our minds as informed, through prototyping, by the skills of our hands – are enabling us to leave our home world ... and sow the seeds of life on others.

Perhaps there truly is nothing new under the sun.

Notes

1   Mars DRM 5.0: http://ntrs.nasa.gov/archive/nasa/casi.ntrs.nasa.gov/20090012109_2009010520.pdf
2   http://spaceflight.nasa.gov/history/station/transhab/
3   NASA Tech Brief: Design Concepts for the ISS TransHab Module, Johnson Space Center, 1 April 2002. http://www.greenproductdesignanddevelopment.org/component/content/article/3084. http://www.highbeam.com/doc/1G2-3408800430.html
4   Dan Schrimpsher, 'Interview: TransHab Developer William Schneider', *TheSpaceReview.com*, 21 August 2006. http://www.thespacereview.com/article/686/1 (retrieved 6 October 2007).
5   Kriss Kennedy, 'Lessons from TransHab: An Architect's Experience', AIAA Space Architecture Symposium, Houston, Texas, AIAA 2002–6105, 10–11 October 2002.
6   Lunar-Mars Life Support Test Project http://adsabs.harvard.edu/abs/2006cosp...36.2562B

Index